H.S.

COMRADE J

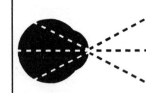 This Large Print Book carries the
Seal of Approval of N.A.V.H.

COMRADE J

THE UNTOLD SECRETS OF RUSSIA'S MASTER SPY IN AMERICA AFTER THE END OF THE COLD WAR

PETE EARLEY

THORNDIKE PRESS

A part of Gale, Cengage Learning

GALE
CENGAGE Learning·

Detroit • New York • San Francisco • New Haven, Conn • Waterville, Maine • London

GALE
CENGAGE Learning™

LIBRARY OF CONGRESS CATALOGING-IN-PUBLICATION DATA

Earley, Pete.
  Comrade J : the untold secrets of Russia's master spy in America after the end of the Cold War / by Pete Earley. — Large print ed.
     p. cm.
  Includes bibliographical references.
  ISBN-13: 978-1-4104-0800-6 (hardcover : alk. paper)
  ISBN-10: 1-4104-0800-0 (hardcover : alk. paper)
  1. Tretyakov, Sergei O., 1956– 2. Spies — Russia (Federation) — Biography. 3. Intelligence service — Russia (Federation) — Biography. 4. Soviet Union. Komitet gosudarstvennoi bezopasnosti — Officials and employees — Biography. 5. Sluzhba vneshnei razvedki Rossiiskoi Federatsii — Officials and employees — Biography. 6. Defectors — United States — Biography. I. Title.
  JN6529.I6E17 2008
  327.1247073092—dc22
  [B]   2008010950

Published in 2008 by arrangement with G. P. Putnam's Sons, a member of Penguin Group (USA) Inc.

Dedicated to my son,
Evan William LeRue Luzi

Everyone wants to be James Bond, but I am the real James Bond and we don't operate like in the movies. I will tell you how Russian intelligence operatives actually work. I will tell you how we steal America's secrets.

Sergei O. Tretyakov,
KGB code name Comrade Jean

CONTENTS

CONTENTS

PREFACE

This is a book I almost didn't write.

It began with a telephone call from a lawyer who said he represented a Russian defector — a former intelligence officer — who wanted to tell his story.

"What's his name?" I asked.

"I'd rather not say on the phone."

I'd been approached before by former Soviets. Most ex–KGB officers believed their life stories would make compelling reading. But few, if any, really did.

"I'm sorry," I replied after a few more moments of evasive chatter. "I'm not interested."

Two months later, an FBI agent called. We'd first met when I was writing about Aldrich Ames, the CIA traitor responsible in the mid-1980s for the execution of at least ten U.S. spies and the arrest of a dozen more.

"You should talk to this defector," he

explained. "He's read your book about Ames and really wants to meet you. Trust me, he's the real deal."

I agreed — reluctantly. My FBI contact said he'd call me on a Thursday with details for a meeting. When Thursday arrived, he told me to drive to the Ritz-Carlton Hotel in Tysons Corner, Virginia, not far from CIA headquarters. Two FBI agents were in the lobby. They escorted me to a suite where snacks, soft drinks, and two CIA officers, who told me only their first names, were waiting. Seconds later, a tall, balding Russian dressed in a well-tailored suit entered from an adjoining room and extended his hand.

"I'm Sergei Tretyakov," he announced.

I suddenly understood why he merited a four-person, joint FBI and CIA escort, and a Ritz-Carlton rendezvous. He was not a Cold War leftover from the old KGB. His story was ripped from the front pages, the Boris Yeltsin and Vladimir Putin presidencies.

Tretyakov had been a colonel in the SVR (Sluzhba Vnezhney Razvedki) — the Russian foreign intelligence service that replaced the KGB's overseas arm — before he disappeared with his wife, Helen, and their daughter, Ksenia, from the Russian residential compound in New York City. Although he vanished in October 2000, neither the U.S. nor the Russian government revealed his disappearance for nearly four months.

In late January 2001, an unnamed State Department official told the Associated Press news service that a Russian diplomat named Tretyakov had been granted "asylum" in the U.S. That tiny disclosure ignited a firestorm in Russia. Yevgeny Voronin, a deputy director in the Russian Ministry of Foreign Affairs, lambasted the State Department for telling the media about Tretyakov before it officially informed the Kremlin. Voronin said his government had been trying through diplomatic channels to learn about Tretyakov's whereabouts since October, but the U.S. had refused to even acknowledge that it knew the missing diplomat. Voronin demanded the U.S. arrange a face-to-face meeting between a Russian delegation and Tretyakov to ensure that "neither he nor his family were coerced in any fashion and that they are okay." Without public comment, the State Department refused.

A week later, *The New York Times* revealed that Tretyakov's diplomatic title — First Secretary in Press Relations at the Permanent Mission of the Russian Federation to the United States — had been a cover. The newspaper quoted unnamed U.S. sources saying Tretyakov was actually a top Russian intelligence officer.

Because the U.S. and Russia were no longer considered formal adversaries, the Bush administration's decision to grant Tretyakov asylum suggested he was an extremely valuable catch for U.S. intelligence, the newspaper noted. Otherwise, the White House would not have risked irritating the Kremlin. The newspaper explained that the CIA had become selective about accepting defectors in its resettlement program because of the expense involved in relocating, protecting, and financially supporting them. But Tretyakov and his family had breezed through the process — another tip-off that he was important.

Three weeks after the *Times* outed Tretyakov, the FBI arrested one of its own agents: Robert Philip Hanssen. The twenty-seven-year FBI veteran was caught hiding stolen U.S. secrets in a suburban park near his home for the SVR to pick up later. *The Washington Post* and other newspapers speculated that Tretyakov had told the FBI about Hanssen. But when then FBI director Louis J. Freeh was asked at a press conference about Tretyakov, the director refused to answer any questions about the mysterious defector.

From that moment forward, Tretyakov went off the grid. Neither the FBI nor the CIA would answer questions about him or discuss his whereabouts. In Washington, a city infamous for leaks, there were no disclosures in shadowy parking garages by Deep Throat sources. Tretyakov remained hidden, and the motive behind his defection and what he had done to merit asylum remained a top secret.

Now Tretyakov and I were shaking hands in a glitzy hotel suite. Even more bizarre, our meeting had been arranged by the FBI and CIA, the two bureaucracies that had been carefully protecting his privacy for more than four years.

During the next several hours, Tretyakov and I discussed his career and it quickly became clear why I'd been told that he was "the real deal."

From April 1995 until October 2000, Tretyakov was the SVR's deputy *rezident* in New York City — a second-in-command job that put him in charge of running *all* SVR intelligence day-to-day operations. *Every* SVR intelligence officer stationed in Manhattan reported directly to him — all sixty of them. He oversaw the handling of *every* foreign source working for Russian intelligence in Manhattan — more than 150 of them. And Tretyakov had personally directed *every* covert operation that the SVR had launched against the U.S. in the city. Put simply, he had been the SVR's "go-to guy," the keeper of the Russian foreign intelligence service's most cherished secrets. He knew the names of foreign diplomats spying for Russia inside the United Nations and the identity of a Russian immigrant living in the U.S. who was delivering millions of dollars' worth of stolen medical research to the SVR.

During the coming months, I would discover an even more dramatic disclosure about Tretyakov that further explained why he was such a prized catch. Not only had he been a senior SVR intelligence officer, Tretyakov had worked for U.S. intelligence as a spy inside the Russian Mission for at least *three years* before he defected — a fact that is being revealed only now in this book. He had stolen thousands of SVR top-secret diplomatic cables and hundreds of classified Russian intelligence reports.

"Sergei Tretyakov is the highest-ranking Russian intelligence officer ever to defect while stationed in the United States," a

16

senior FBI agent involved in the case explained. "This man literally held the keys to a Russian intelligence gold mine. What makes his story even more incredible is that he used those keys to unlock its doors and go into the mine every day to bring us nuggets."

This book is an exposé.

It reveals many of the Russian secrets that Tretyakov has disclosed to U.S. intelligence. In these pages, Tretyakov identifies UN diplomats who he claims spied for Russia during his stint as deputy *rezident.* One of his more dramatic accusations is that Eldar Kouliev, a popular and well-known permanent representative to the UN from Azerbaijan in the 1990s, was secretly a deepcover SVR intelligence officer. The president of Azerbaijan had no idea that his nation's ambassador was an undercover SVR officer and neither did former U.S. secretary of state Madeleine K. Albright, who frequently met with Kouliev. At the time, the Clinton administration was wooing Azerbaijan because of its rich oil reserves and its militarily strategic location. As a trusted confidante, Kouliev participated in sensitive meetings with Albright without the White House or his own government knowing he was reporting every conversation back to

Moscow.

In addition to accusing Ambassador Kou-liev, Tretyakov identifies two other UN representatives as SVR spies. One still represents his government at the UN. The other currently serves as an ambassador to China.

Tretyakov also claims that several UN diplomats who work for countries that are U.S. allies and members of NATO are secretly Russian spies. He identifies them in these pages.

But perhaps the most shocking disclosure that Tretyakov makes in this book is that the Russian foreign intelligence service successfully embedded one of its "deep cover" officers inside the $64 billion Oil-for-Food Program administered by the UN before Iraqi President Saddam Hussein was toppled. This Russian operative, working under the guise of being a diplomat, became a pivotal player in the UN humanitarian aid program and was able to use that position to help Russia steal millions of dollars that were supposed to be spent to help starving Iraqi women and children. Investigations by the UN and by U.S. congressional committees already have revealed that nearly half a billion dollars was diverted from the corrupt UN program into Russia. But Tretyakov's revelations, for the first time, provide a "smoking gun" that ties the SVR and the Kremlin directly to the UN thefts. He explains how Russian intelligence circumvented the UN's checks-and-balances system, and he reveals that when Russian president Vladimir Putin was told about the looting, rather than stopping it he rewarded the deep-cover SVR officer for his larceny by giving him one of Russia's highest medals.

In yet another troubling disclosure, Tretyakov claims Russian intelligence targeted President Clinton's deputy secretary of state, Strobe Talbott, and ran a carefully calculated campaign designed to manipulate him. Talbott was the architect of U.S. policy toward Russia and its former republics during a crucial seven-year period after the Soviet Union breakup. According to Tretyakov, the SVR used Russia's then deputy minister of foreign affairs Georgiy Mamedov to deceive and manipulate Talbott, in part by massaging his ego. Unbeknownst to Talbott, his Russian contact was a longtime "co-optee," which meant Mamedov often did the bidding of Russian intelligence, Tretyakov said. In return, it helped promote Mamedov's diplomatic career. There was no reason for Talbott to suspect that Mamedov was acting as an SVR conduit.

According to Tretyakov, the SVR prepared specific questions for Mamedov to ask Talbott during their private, one-on-one conversations, including times when the two diplomats were socializing. Talbott considered Mamedov a friend and respected colleague. According to Tretyakov, the Russian diplomat used their personal relationship to glean information from Talbott that the SVR considered helpful to Russia.

Talbott was shown a copy of Tretyakov's accusations before this book went to press. In a written response, Talbott called Tretyakov's "interpretation of events erroneous and/or misleading." He wrote that he knew that Mamedov was relaying all of their conversations, including their private ones, back to Moscow. Talbott challenged Tretyakov to provide "specifics and corroboration" that showed he had been manipulated by Mamedov. "There can be none," Talbott concluded, "since what went on in my channel with Mamedov, in fact, advanced U.S. policy goals."

Just the same, the FBI took the accusations about Talbott seriously when Tretyakov raised them after he began secretly helping the U.S. In 1999, FBI officials asked Secretary Albright not to share information with Talbott about an ongoing espionage investigation at the State Department because its agents were afraid he might inadvertently tip off the SVR through Mamedov, according to private and published sources.

Tretyakov said the SVR considered Mamedov's handling of Talbott so clever that Russian intelligence identified the senior American diplomat in correspondence and classified internal reports as a SPECIAL UNOFFICIAL CONTACT — a specific term that the SVR used to identify its most secret, highly placed intelligence sources.

Of course, when Tretyakov and I first met in the Ritz-Carlton Hotel, I did not know about any of these revelations or that he had spied for the U.S. At the time, I was cautious about speaking to him. Why, after four years of keeping Tretyakov hidden, were the FBI and CIA suddenly willing to let him talk openly? When I raised this question, my FBI contact said: "Our only purpose here today is to introduce you. We are not encouraging him to tell his story, nor are we discouraging him. He wanted to meet you and we agreed to facilitate it. We will have no part in your talks."

Even so, I remained skeptical. Sources always have a motive when they speak to reporters. Few do it purely out of goodness. But I decided to put aside my concerns about the FBI and CIA and concentrate on Tretyakov. I asked him that afternoon if he expected to be paid for telling his story, because cash traditionally is what most former KGB spies are after.

"I don't care about money," he replied. "No publisher alive has enough money to pay me for what I know. I am worth millions because I *am* Russian intelligence." (I later learned the U.S. government had already set him up financially for the rest of his life.)

Moving down my checklist, I asked if he was seeking fame.

"Of course, I want people to know what I have done. However, most Americans can't pronounce Tretyakov, nor will they remember the name longer than a few seconds — so this, too, doesn't concern me."

I told him there was a difference between paying a ghostwriter to write his story and being interviewed by a reporter. A journalist would try, as best he could, to investigate all his accusations.

Tretyakov smiled. "I do not want to be the author. It will be your book to write, not mine."

If Sergei wasn't interested in money,

didn't care about fame, and was eager to waive any editorial rights to a book, then what was he after?

"I want to warn Americans. As a people, you are very naive about Russia and its intentions. You believe because the Soviet Union no longer exists, Russia now is your friend. It isn't, and I can show you how the SVR is trying to destroy the U.S. even today and even more than the KGB did during the Cold War."

Continuing, he said, "My wife, Helen, and I are from families who were extreme patriots. We were taught to be proud of our homeland. We were members of the Soviet Party elite. We were *apparatchiki* [*people who were part of the Communist Party apparatus*]. In Moscow, we had a luxury apartment worth more than a million dollars. We had two summer houses. I was feared and respected by the officers under my command. I was going to be promoted to the rank of general after I returned from Manhattan to Moscow. But Helen and I decided to leave everything behind us — all of that. We brought nothing really with us when we defected, only what we could carry in two tiny suitcases. This was intentional on our parts. My wife and I know our friends and former colleagues in Moscow are asking:

'Why? Why did Sergei and Helen do this? How could they turn away from their motherland?' They want to know why we would walk away and leave all of this wealth and property and privilege behind. I want to explain my decision, our decision."

Every man who is born in one country and who later turns away from his native land and actively works to help its enemies seems compelled to explain his actions. I had witnessed this twice before. My first book was about John Walker Jr. and his family of spies. A former naval officer, Walker became a KGB spy in 1968 during the height of the Cold War and recruited his best friend, his brother, and his own son to join him as traitors. During our jailhouse talks, Walker spent hours justifying his actions. Because the U.S. and Soviet Union were not at war, he claimed, his treason had not damaged U.S. interests. If anything, his willingness to sell U.S. military secrets to the KGB had helped the Kremlin realize that its military forces were inferior and how pointless it was to continue spending billions to challenge an overwhelming U.S. military.

The CIA traitor Aldrich Ames wrote me long, detailed letters filled with rationalizations for his treason when I was writing about him. Much like Walker, he insisted nothing that he had compromised had harmed U.S. interests. While regrettable, the KGB's decision to execute ten FBI and CIA sources was part of the Spy-versus-Spy game. Each executed spy had known he was putting himself in harm's way — just as Ames had recognized that his decision to betray the U.S. had placed him in jeopardy. The dead men's blood was on their own hands, not his.

It was not surprising, then, that Tretyakov wanted to explain himself.

Our initial meeting that Thursday afternoon led to more and longer sessions that eventually stretched out well over a year. These tape-recorded interviews were done at Tretyakov's home without the FBI or CIA being present. And Tretyakov kept his word. He never interfered with my research or tried to take control of the writing of this book.

Although Tretyakov defected in October 2000, many of his disclosures are incredibly fresh in the intelligence world. The SVR still has not had time to change many of the technical devices and procedures that it uses in New York City and elsewhere, according to FBI sources familiar with Tretyakov's case. Several of the SVR officers and their spies — whom Tretyakov describes in these pages — are still working in New York. Several Russian officials identified in this book can be spotted on nightly news broadcasts from the Kremlin. Tretyakov's career spanned both the old KGB system and the post-Soviet era, giving him a unique vantage point and the ability to compare and judge if the reforms brought on by the end of the old Soviet system have made a difference in Russian intelligence gathering today.

The more time I spent with Tretyakov, the more I realized he was telling me two stories. He was revealing top secrets about how Russian intelligence operates in Manhattan, and he was telling me a personal story. Tretyakov had been groomed to become a KGB officer. He'd received the best possible education the Soviet system offered its intelligence agents. He'd been an enthusiastic Communist Party member and a willing participant in the *nomenklatura* (the Communist system of rewarding people in political favor). Although he attempted to distance himself in interviews from the cruelty inflicted by the KGB — explaining that he spent his entire career inside the First Chief Directorate (foreign intelligence) and never in the directorate that persecuted dissidents — Tretyakov was still part of a bureaucracy that brutalized its own people. The KGB exploited anyone who might be useful: husbands spied on their wives, children on their parents, neighbors on neighbors. Tretyakov was a cog in that oppressive regime regardless of where he hung his hat at work. He had closed his eyes to the blood being spilled around him like so many Russians had.

And like them, Tretyakov came to support the changes of *glasnost* (public discussion of issues) and *perestroika* (President Mikhail Gorbachev's campaign to revitalize the nation). In December 1991, when the Soviet Union ceased to exist, Tretyakov celebrated its demise and looked forward to the construction of a more democratic country. But he soon became bitter about what he witnessed and he ultimately became so disillusioned that he silently rejected Russia's leaders, decided to betray his native land, and ultimately defected to a nation that was its most hated rival.

This book exposes secrets told by a top Russian intelligence officer who had access to information denied his countrymen. This book also describes an odyssey, a personal story about the disillusionment of a former Soviet patriot and the reasons he put his life and that of his family at risk by becoming a spy for the United States.

■ ■ ■ ■

PART ONE:
BORN A COMMUNIST

■ ■ ■ ■

Give us the child for eight years and it will
be a Bolshevik forever.
Vladimir Ulyanov Lenin (1870–1924),
founder, Russian Communist Party

ONE

April 1995

Sergei and Helen didn't look back when the Aeroflot jet lifted off from Sheremetyevo Airport en route to New York City. Neither was sad to be leaving Moscow. Only Sergei's mother still tied them to Russia. Now in her seventies, Revmira continued to live by herself in the family's spacious apartment on Frunzenskaya Street across from the Moscow River near Gorky Park.

Even though Sergei had never lived in the U.S., his years of working in the North American Department of the old KGB and months of pre-departure briefings at SVR headquarters — known simply as "the Center" — made him feel as if he were going home.

In Manhattan, the Russian government operated from three buildings. The most ornate was the Russian Consulate at 9 East Ninety-first Street. The most out-of-the-way

31

was the Russian living compound at 355 West 255th Street in the Bronx. The most important was the Russian Permanent Mission to the United Nations at 136 East Sixty-seventh Street. The Russians also owned two estates on Long Island — a forty-nine-room house in Glen Cove and a second mansion in Oyster Bay. The Glen Cove residence was used only by the ambassador and his top deputies. The Oyster Bay mansion could be used by others, including the SVR *rezident,* who had a suite with a private balcony in one of its wings. The *rezident* often entertained visiting SVR generals there.

The Russian Consulate was within walking distance of Central Park and easy to spot. A Russian flag dangled from a pole above its entrance, and there was usually a line of applicants on the sidewalk waiting to apply for visas. Helen had been offered a job at the consulate working as a "clean" secretary, which meant her job would have nothing to do with the SVR or GRU (Glavnoe Razvedyvatel'noe Upravlenie), which was Russian military intelligence. Eventually, the couple's only daughter, Ksenia, also would work there. Whenever possible, the Russian government hired spouses and children of its diplomats to fill posts overseas, rather than flying employees in from Russia.

The consulate had a handful of SVR intelligence officers working inside it under diplomatic cover. Most were from Line N (*illegals*). They copied or simply stole U.S. documents from persons applying for travel visas and other Russian travel papers. The U.S. documents — passports, birth certificates, etc. — were sent to the Center, where they were either duplicated or altered slightly before being issued to illegals — SVR intelligence officers who entered the U.S. surreptitiously, often posing as Eastern European immigrants. Illegals needed the counterfeit identification papers to buttress fake backgrounds — *legends* in spy parlance — and hide their true identities. The officers were part of the SVR's underground "invisible" network. They tried to become U.S. citizens, marry Americans, and find jobs working for the U.S. government or some other political or military organization that could prove useful to the SVR. Clerks at the consulate were trained to tell U.S. citizens who complained about their identification papers disappearing that they had been misplaced or lost.

The Russian residential compound was in the Bronx, which extends from the Hudson

River to Long Island Sound and is the northernmost of New York City's five boroughs. The complex was edged by a chain-link security fence that encircled some smaller buildings and a twenty-story apartment house. It jutted up awkwardly from a neighborhood of modest, two-story older brick homes in a neighborhood called Riverdale, where Mark Twain and Theodore Roosevelt had once lived. Constructed in the early 1970s, the facade was devoid of decoration and had been built as cheaply as possible by Soviet laborers from Moscow. Not long after it was completed, one of its sides had started to break free from the rest of the structure. Engineers pulled it back in place by bolting thick steel cables to the failing wall and anchoring them to the center of the building. Holes for the cables had been punched through walls without any thought about tenants. Some rooms on the upper floors had steel lines shooting through them at eye level, forcing tenants to duck whenever they walked through the rooms.

In a shortsighted move, U.S. officials approved the sale of the Riverdale land to the Soviet Union without realizing how strategic its location was for spying. The high-rise was built on a steep hill that was one of the tallest points in the city. Concealed under wooden boxes on the building's flat roof were dozens of antennas designed to snatch signals and conversations from New York City's airwaves. Similar antennas could be found on the roof of the Russian Permanent Mission in Manhattan. These two listening posts were part of a sophisticated surveillance system called "Post Impulse" that was operated by Line VKR (*foreign counterintelligence*). The SVR used the rooftop stations to survey a swath of forty miles, intercepting police broadcasts, cell phone calls, and other communications throughout Manhattan and much of Long Island and New Jersey. Over time, the SVR and GRU had been able to identify and lock onto signals from every law enforcement operation in the area. They used the signals to keep track of the location of FBI agents and other officers. If the Russians saw that several FBI agents were in the same vicinity as one of their SVR officers, they knew he was being followed.

The computers and other devices used by Post Impulse were housed on the building's nineteenth floor, which was off-limits to everyone except SVR officers and their sources. It served as the SVR's "second *rezidency*," with its primary headquarters being housed in the Sixty-seventh Street mission.

The tenants referred to the living compound simply as Riverdale. Sergei was required to live there so he could be close to the second *rezidency.* The hallway ceilings were covered with asbestos. The walls were dingy and needed painting. Sergei had been assigned a two-room apartment on the tenth floor. As deputy *rezident,* he could have demanded one of the three-room units that were being used by larger families. But he didn't like to take advantage of his rank. The main room of Sergei's apartment would serve as a combination living and dining area with a kitchenette. Because of the long hours he would be working, often late at night, Sergei would sleep on a pullout couch in the front room, leaving Helen and Ksenia to share the bedroom. It was barely large enough for a double bed. A tiny bathroom was in a corner. There was one closet.

The walls of the apartments were hollow and the odors from different kitchens frequently permeated the hallways. Neighbors could hear whatever was being said next door and it was not uncommon to walk down a hallway at night and hear a squabble or sounds of lovemaking.

Riverdale's ground floor had a reception

area and a concert room used for diplomatic functions. A small bar, where liquor and hot sandwiches were served, and a grocery store, where prices were kept artificially low, were on the second floor. Cigarettes that sold for $30 per carton in New York could be bought for $10. Booze was one-tenth the Manhattan price. It was illegal for Russians to resell items from the store outside the living compound. The third and fourth floors were taken up by a school and a medical clinic. Teachers and doctors from Russia were flown in after undergoing extensive background investigations. Hiring preferences were given to Russians who had relatives at home because those family ties reduced the risk of defections. Riverdale had an underground parking garage and a swimming pool. Sergei had been issued a midsize Mercury sedan to drive. His rank-and-file SVR officers drove Ford Taurus models. The lowest employees stationed in the U.S. got the keys to a Ford Focus.

Even though Riverdale had a permanent ant and cockroach infestation that exterminators couldn't seem to eliminate and the apartments were in shabby condition, few Russians asked for permission to live elsewhere. Cost was the main reason. Sergei's rent was $100 per month.

Russia's permanent representative to the United Nations, who held the same rank as an ambassador serving in an embassy overseas, was not expected to live in Riverdale. In April 1995, the representative was Sergei Lavrov, a seasoned diplomat who would later become the Russian minister of foreign affairs under President Putin.

"Ambassador Lavrov was constantly changing apartments in Manhattan, paying as much as $30,000 per month in rent, and moving from one part of the city to another," Sergei would later recall. "He was required to alert the SVR each time he moved so our technical experts could make certain his apartment was free of FBI listening devices. But Lavrov was moving without telling us and I suspect he was more afraid and concerned about SVR bugs than he was about anything the Americans might hide in his apartment."

In addition to Ambassador Lavrov, Russians who worked for the United Nations Secretariat were also expected to live away from Riverdale because they were UN employees and supposed to be impartial and keep an arm's-length relationship with their native country. Just the same, most of these Russians socialized at the Riverdale bar and bought commodities at its store.

The SVR's headquarters, called the *rezidentura*, was located inside the Permanent Mission of the Russian Federation to the United Nations at East Sixty-seventh Street between Lexington and Third avenues. Located across the street from a synagogue and a fire station, there was nothing about the mission's twelve-story office building that made it stand out. The only sign that identified it was a plaque near the main entrance. A guard was posted there, but none of the security officers inside the mission were armed and, surprisingly, no firearms were kept there, according to Sergei. Instead, the building was protected by a series of electronically dead-bolted doors and video cameras. If a guard at the entrance needed help with an unruly protestor or came under attack, the mission staff called 911.

"Clean" diplomats and other office personnel employed by the Russian Ministry of Foreign Affairs used the mission's lower five floors. The ninth through the twelfth floors contained several large residential apartments. Ambassadors from former Soviet republics, such as the Ukraine and Georgia, had occupied these units before the breakup of the USSR. Now that those republics had their own independent missions elsewhere in New York, the apartments had been rented to Ambassador Lavrov's top deputies, with one exception. The representative from Tajikistan still lived there. The SVR *rezident* — Sergei's direct boss — also had an apartment in the building so he could be close to the *rezidentura* and its communications center.

There was one other group of Russians who were required to reside inside the mission, but their units were much different from the spacious apartments that housed the diplomats and the SVR station chief. Code clerks — the foreign intelligence employees responsible for encrypting and deciphering secret cables — were crowded into a tiny area near the communications center. During the Cold War, the clerks had been held much like prisoners in the mission because the KGB did not want to risk having one of them defect or be recruited to spy. In those days, KGB security officers met the clerks and their families at the airport, drove them to the building, and literally kept them locked inside it until they were scheduled to return to Russia. They were then driven to the airport under guard and put on an airplane. The SVR had lifted many of the KGB's tight security restrictions placed on code clerks, but their living conditions in New York remained grim. "There were four families with children sharing one tiny bathroom and one small kitchen in the mission," Sergei said. "I remember one of the wives coming to me and saying, 'My dream is to one day have a stove where I can use more than one burner.' "

The sixth, seventh, and eighth floors of the mission were heavily protected and classified as top-secret. The sixth was where the permanent representative and Russia's senior diplomatic corps worked. The seventh was used by code clerks. And the eighth housed the SVR and GRU *rezidentura*s. It was nicknamed the "submarine" because of the extraordinary security precautions that had been taken when it was built.

A special technical team had flown into Manhattan from Moscow to customize the entire floor. The team attached hundreds of heavy springs to the bare concrete, covering the floor, walls, and ceiling. An entirely new and separate structure had then been built on top of the springs so that none of the interior surfaces touched the concrete building. This new interior "floated" inside the original.

The walls of the submarine were several inches thick and had a core made of sheet metal. Its joints had been welded and checked with an X-ray machine for microscopic cracks. To further shield the submarine, KGB technicians had combed its walls with a spider net of wires that constantly vibrated, emitting a "white noise" that reminded Sergei of the buzzing that comes from a cheap electric transformer attached to a toy railroad set. Sergei once asked an SVR doctor if the constant noise could harm a man's hearing. The doctors had said no, but Sergei hadn't believed him and would later claim that he often could still hear the noise buzzing in his head. The extra-thick walls caused the interior ceilings to be a foot shorter than others inside the mission.

There were no windows in the submarine, no phone lines connecting it to the outside world, and the computers inside it did not have access to the Internet. Even the floor's electricity and ventilation system were self-contained to prevent tampering by outsiders.

The lion's share of the submarine was used by the SVR with the remainder going to the GRU, but the two *rezidenturas* were completely independent and neither had access to the other's. The ambassador was the only "clean" diplomat in the mission with access to the submarine.

After an SVR officer passed through various checkpoints in the mission's lower floors, he would take an elevator or stairs to an eighth-floor lobby that had two steel doors. Neither had any identifying signs. One was used by the SVR, the other by the GRU. The SVR's door had a brass plate and knob, but there was no keyhole. To open the door, the head of the screw in the lower right corner of the brass plate had to be touched with a metal object, such as a wedding ring or a coin. The metal would connect the screw to the brass plate, completing an electrical circuit that would snap open the door's bolt lock and sometimes shock the person holding the coin.

The door opened into a small cloakroom. No jackets or suit coats were allowed inside the *rezidentura* because they could be used to conceal documents and hide miniature cameras. SVR officers left their coats, cell phones, portable computers, and all other electronic devices in lockers. A camera videotaped everyone who entered the cloakroom. It was added after several officers discovered someone had stolen money from wallets left in jackets. Another solid steel door with a numeric lock that required a four-digit code to open led from the cloakroom into the *rezidentura.*

A male secretary sat near the door and kept track of who entered, exited, and at what times. A hallway to the left led to the main corridor, which was ninety feet long and had offices along either side. Because the New York *rezidentura* was one of the largest and most important in the SVR, it contained all of the SVR's Lines (departments). They were Line OT (*technical operations*), Line N (*illegals*), Line ER (*economic intelligence*), Line RP (*radio interception*), Line X (*science and technology*), Line VKR (*foreign counterintelligence*), and Line PR (*political intelligence*), which was the biggest and the most important. *Rezidents* were always from Line PR. The *rezidentura* also contained a file room (called System Contact) with 1.5 million microfiche cards. Most of the information on the cards was about Americans. There was a "photo room" on the floor, too. The SVR did not send written reports by its officers to the Center in diplomatic pouches. Instead, it photographed each report and sent the film to the Center to be developed and printed. Unless a document had some apparent, future value, it was destroyed after it was photographed.

8th floor of the Russian Mission

136 E 67th St., New York, NY.

67th Street (across the street - police precinct, fire station and synagogue.)

corridor ≈ 90 feet long

Line PR | typists | System Contact

Line RP | Line ER | Mens Room | Photo Room

Line OT | Ladies Room | accountant

Line N

Head of line PR/deputy resident (Serge?) | Post Impulse | Spare Room used mainly by line PR | Resident | Head of line X | Line X | Information (report) officer | VKR Line | Head of VKR line

secretary | cloak-room

SVR Rezidentura

GRU rezidentura

elevator | stairs

SVR code clerks' apartments

45

A limousine driver from the mission was waiting at JFK Airport when Sergei, Helen, and Ksenia landed from their Moscow flight. As soon as the two women were settled at Riverdale, Sergei left for the mission. Because of the seriousness of his job, he was stone-faced and all business. But he felt as excited as a boy attending his first day of school. At age thirty-eight, Sergei was the youngest deputy *rezident* ever sent to New York. Yet he was completely confident. He had spent his entire professional career preparing for this assignment, and he was eager to begin matching wits with the FBI and CIA.

As a child, Sergei had gone to bed dreaming of a day when he could become a KGB officer battling against the motherland's *glavny protivnik* (main adversary) — the United States. He had come a long way since those youthful fantasies when he was tucked safely in his bed on Frunzenskaya Street, and his career had taken several unexpected twists and turns. But his moment had finally arrived.

When he touched a coin on the door that led into the mission's "submarine" and heard the dead bolt slide open, Sergei did not hesitate.

Two

October 1956

From birth, the KGB seemed to flow through Sergei Tretyakov's veins. His maternal grandmother, Lyubov Ionina, was the source. During World War II, she supervised a secretarial pool in the People's Commissariat for Internal Affairs (NKVD), the forerunner of the KGB. Lyubov and twenty-five typists worked exclusively for Lavrenty Pavlovich Beria, the infamous director of the secret police who oversaw the final stages of the Great Purge of the 1930s. Some 1.7 million Russians were arrested during Joseph Stalin's campaign of terror. Seven hundred thousand were executed.

Lyubov worked within the Kremlin's walls in a secret bunker, and she would describe an incident there to her family that said much about Beria and the times. The story would be repeated in hushed sentences. According to Grandmother Lyubov, Beria appeared one morning in the bunker and announced that he needed help.

"Girls," he said, "yesterday I gave a typed report to Comrade Stalin. I have forgotten what it said. Who typed this report and can you tell me please what it was about?"

No one stirred, and then a young typist rose from her chair and said, "Oh, Comrade Beria, it was me. I typed it, and I can recall every word for you."

The next day the girl disappeared.

Lyubov and the others got the message. Their job was to type documents, but not read them or dare remember what they contained. Lyubov always finished her story with the same warning: "It's best in our country to never ask questions and to have a very poor memory."

Lyubov knew Stalin personally, and even though she never held a top military rank, she rose higher in the secret police than most other women at the time. Flamboyant and independent, Lyubov married four times, but bore only one child, a daughter, whom she named Revmira, which is an abbreviation for "World Revolution." She treated her child as a contemporary. As soon as Revmira was old enough, she went to work in the financial office of the KGB. At night, mother and daughter would stop for drinks in a private KGB club next door to Lubyanka, the Soviet secret security headquarters in downtown Moscow.

Revmira met Oleg Tretyakov, the man whom she would later marry, at a nightclub. His background was much different from hers. Prior to the 1917 revolution, the Tretyakov family had been aristocrats. Tsar Nicholas II had declared Oleg's father an "Honored Citizen of Russia." But the Bolsheviks stripped the family of its titles and wealth, and by the time that Oleg was born in 1921, the family was destitute. On the first day of World War II, Oleg joined the Soviet Army, and when Germany invaded Russia in 1941, he was sent to the front. Oleg was twice wounded before he was transferred to Russia's eastern border. Stalin believed a Japanese attack was imminent, but it never happened. Meanwhile, Oleg's comrades in the west were slaughtered by German troops.

Russia suffered more military and civilian casualties during the war than any country, some 20 million. The Russian soldiers who survived were declared heroes and awarded privileges. Oleg was told he could enroll in any Moscow university. He selected a mining institute because it gave students uniforms and he didn't have enough money to buy a change of clothes. After graduation, he was sent to work in the Soviet Union's secret atomic weapons program.

It was during this period that Oleg and Revmira met and married. In 1956, their only child, Sergei Tretyakov, was born.

At work, Oleg handled uranium, and he received a lethal dose one day. Incredibly, he survived, cheating death for a second time. But his days at the lab were over. He was sent to the Soviet Ministry of Foreign Trade and, within a year, dispatched to Iran as a trade representative. Like all Soviets who were allowed to live overseas, he was required to report to the KGB.

"My father never loved the KGB," Sergei would later recall. "He called it a nest of morons and idiots. But he was practical and accepted being part of it because, in return, he was able to travel and live overseas."

In the 1960s, Iran was run by Mohammad Reza Pahlavi — the shah of Iran — and was the world's second-largest oil producer. Its capital, Tehran, was a modern city, and the Tretyakov family took advantage of their pro-Western surroundings.

"My father was passionate about jazz. In the Soviet Union, jazz was considered poisonous and was banned," Sergei said, "but in Iran, my father introduced me to all of the great jazz. He was a huge fan of Hollywood movies, too, and we saw every new movie and had access to American culture. My mother constantly criticized my father because she said I was supposed to live in the Soviet world, not the Western one, but my father didn't care. 'Our son must be raised on the absolute best standards,' he would reply, 'not on the bullshit that is called Soviet music and Soviet movies.' Of course, this became a paradox for me because my father was a passionate patriot. He loved his country and was an active member in the Communist Party. Yet I knew growing up that he never believed that Communism was a superior idea. We lived abroad and all of us could see with our own eyes how people lived better lives outside Russia than our comrades back home."

When Sergei turned nine, his father sent him back to Russia to complete his schooling and become "Soviet-ized." He was placed under the care of "Aunt Shura," a nanny who treated him, in his own words, "as if I were a little prince." One day, Revmira arrived unannounced at the family's Moscow apartment just as her son was about to eat. Sergei didn't see her, but he did notice that he didn't have a napkin so he snapped his fingers and declared: "Napkin, please!" Aunt Shura was scrambling to fetch one for him when Revmira slapped her son on the back of his head and told him to get a napkin for himself.

"My mother was the ultimate general in our household, and outside it, too. She wasn't afraid of anyone, even the KGB. She knew important people and she knew how to use the system. She was brilliant, and I listened to her every word. To me, she became everything."

Sergei had trouble at school. Other Moscow students were envious of his family's status and affluence. The best and most important jobs in the Soviet Union were held exclusively by party members. Out of a population of 300 million, only 18 million were allowed in the party. A youngster had to study for several years and pass a background check to be inducted. Because of his family's KGB connections, Sergei was on track. At age seven, he'd become a Son of October, which was the first step. At age ten, he became a Young Pioneer. Four years later, he would be eligible to join the Komsomol, which was the Young Communist League. He would then be well prepared to apply for party membership by his mid-twenties.

In elementary school, other students bullied him. They took whatever rubles he had. He didn't tell anyone, but his mother noticed during one of her visits from Iran that Sergei's face was bruised. She got him to tell her what was happening and then she became angry — at him. She arranged for her son to take boxing lessons.

"Don't be an idiot!" she lectured. "You're a big boy, fight back. Hit them as hard as you can in their heads with anything you can. If you don't, you will get a second beating when you come home."

The next time Sergei was preyed on, he fought. Almost overnight, he went from being a victim to becoming a bully. Teenage thugs in his neighborhood eventually gave him a nickname — "Small" — out of respect because he was big for his size and had become one of them. The police called him in for questioning about several fistfights.

As soon as Revmira learned what was happening, she jerked Sergei out of his tough neighborhood school and put him in a more prestigious one. He stayed there five years, but a month before graduation, the principal threatened to expel him because Sergei had started bullying other students again. This time Revmira used her connections to enroll Sergei in what was arguably the city's most elite academy.

"I discovered that a person could do whatever he wished in Moscow — without fear of consequences — if he had the right connections. My mother had those connections and she enrolled me in an academy that was filled with total idiots. The education was less than zero, but it didn't matter because my classmates were the children of the most powerful Communist Party members, the *nomenklatura.* This meant they could get by without doing anything. No work at all. Fortunately, I had already received an excellent education in my previous school. I had read all of the classic Russian, English, American, German, and French literature as a teenager. Without those fundamentals, I would have been a complete imbecile because I was much more interested in chasing girls and getting into trouble with friends, than my studies."

Sergei was accepted into the Moscow Institute of Foreign Languages, the second-best university in the Soviet Union. Only years later would he learn that the Department of Interpreters, which was the group that accepted him, was financed entirely by the KGB. It used the department to identify promising recruits.

Sergei's willingness to bully his classmates

and his parents' strong KGB and Communist Party connections had made him someone the KGB wanted to watch.

THREE

"You know, our children get along quite well, what would you think about them getting married?"

Revmira was speaking about Sergei. She and Oleg had returned to Moscow but were scheduled to leave for another tour in Iran, and she was worried about leaving her immature son behind. Now nineteen, Sergei was barely passing his university classes. Revmira knew it was because he was socializing rather than studying. Her solution was to find him a wife. She telephoned Valentina Nikolayevna Strunkina, whose granddaughter, Yelena (Helen) Mikhaylovna, had caught Sergei's eye.

Sergei had gone out with lots of girls and Revmira had disliked all of them except for Helen. She was a year older than Sergei and was an excellent student at the Soviet Union's most prestigious university, the Moscow State Institute of International

Relations. She lived with her grandmother because her parents were divorced and both had remarried and started new lives.

A friend introduced them, and Helen had been instantly enamored. Sergei hadn't asked for her telephone number, however, and she assumed that he wasn't interested. A few days after they met, she spotted him walking his Scottish terrier outside her apartment building. He didn't live nearby and she noticed he was circling the block, so she stepped onto her balcony and asked him what he was doing. He acted surprised, pretended that he was in her neighborhood by chance, and invited her to join him on his walk. After that, they became serious.

The phone call to Helen's grandmother came three months later. "If you agree with my idea," Revmira told the older woman, "I will send Sergei over to propose to Helen this afternoon."

"I like Sergei very much," Grandmother Valentina Nikolayevna replied, "and Helen's father likes him, too, and so does Helen, so we have nothing against a marriage."

A few hours later, Sergei obediently knocked on Helen's door. "Helen," he said, "I don't know how to propose this, but my mother wants us to get married."

"Well," she replied, "your mother is a very

smart woman, so if she wants us to get married, then let's get married."

They got a license and had a civil ceremony. Because the families weren't certain if the marriage would last, Sergei and Helen promised not to have children for several years. A photograph of the newlyweds shows an attractive couple. He is fit, tall, with blue eyes, a mop of blond hair, a confident smile, and a round Russian face. She is petite with shoulder-length dark blond hair, porcelain skin, and a shy glint in her eyes.

Like Sergei's father, Helen's had fought and been wounded during World War II, even though he was technically too young to join the army. Mikhail Pavlovich Tulisov had lied about his age. During fighting on the western front, he was wounded and half buried in mud after a cannon round exploded near him. His commanding officer sent word to Mikhail's parents in Moscow, telling them that their son was dead. But when another soldier began tugging off the seventeen-year-old's boots the next morning, Mikhail's toes twitched and his comrades dug him out of the muck. After the war, Mikhail studied diplomacy in Moscow, which is where he met Helen's mother, Kira Dmitrievna Strunkina, a stunningly beautiful but vain woman who was being pursued by several suitors. Mikhail impressed her by tossing one of her boyfriends off a bridge into the Moscow River during a jealous confrontation. Mikhail and Kira married and lived in Poland, where he worked as a cultural attaché at the embassy. Helen grew up there. But her parents divorced as soon as they returned to Moscow, leaving their teenage daughter to live with her grandmother.

Sergei's parents felt comfortable leaving their son behind as soon as he married Helen. With her help, Sergei's grades improved. Helen, meanwhile, graduated at the top of her class and went to work as a senior economist at the Ministry of Foreign Trade. Not long after that, Helen and Sergei were admitted into the Communist Party.

Without warning, a KGB officer telephoned their apartment one afternoon and asked Sergei to meet him at the Hotel Tsentralnaya, one of the city's best-known hotels. Sergei was told to arrive at the entrance at exactly 11 a.m. and wait for a man carrying a newspaper.

Sergei did as instructed, and a stranger holding a paper led him upstairs into one of the rooms. After flashing his KGB credentials, the man announced that the KGB had been watching Sergei. "We know everything," he declared. "We know your family background, how you were a bully and poor student. We know about your marriage, and based on what we have observed, we are considering you as a possible candidate for our service."

"Why me?" Sergei asked.

"The KGB doesn't explain anything," the man snapped. "Just do as you are told and understand that if this door opens for you, it is a great honor, and if you walk through it and it closes behind you, then there is no way out. You belong to our organization forever."

The man said the KGB had an assignment for him. It wanted him to go on a student exchange to France that was being planned by one of his teachers. The KGB asked him to spy on his fellow students and any French college professors the group would meet. It was 1978 and the Cold War was hot.

"But my teacher already said I would not be allowed to go on the trip," Sergei replied. "She doesn't like me and she said the only way for me to travel would be 'over her dead body.'"

"Just do what you are told," the man lectured. "We will take care of the teacher."

When Sergei arrived at class the next day, his teacher rushed up and in a scared voice said: "You are on the top of the list to go to France."

Sergei was thrilled. He'd wanted to join the KGB since childhood, had read countless spy books and watched every James Bond movie. Helen was happy, too, because she felt the KGB would be a good career choice for her new husband. Because Sergei's mother had worked for the KGB, she approved. Even his father, who had a low opinion of KGB officers, thought it was a good idea. "It's better to drink blood than eat rabbit food," Oleg advised his son, explaining that in a repressive society, "being an oppressor is superior to being a victim."

Twenty-six students left for France on the university exchange trip. Sergei suspected that he wasn't the only one who'd been asked to spy. The KGB had told him that Stanislav Rudin, an older participant on the trip, was its official contact. Not long after they arrived in France, Rudin took Sergei aside and suggested that he write daily reports about his spying on toilet paper. Twenty-four hours later, Rudin hustled Sergei into a public toilet and asked for his report. They stood next to each other, and after Rudin read each sheet of toilet paper, he dropped it into a urinal and peed on it so the ink would become unreadable.

Sergei later recalled his reaction. "I thought, 'What kind of stupid organization is this?' But I decided it was this man who was a total moron, not the entire KGB."

Sergei knew his actions were being watched. "The KGB wanted to see how willing I was to inform on my fellow students. If you were too enthusiastic, it wasn't good because it showed you had no character. But if you didn't report anything, that meant you were lazy. The KGB never wanted the best or the brightest students, nor did it want the dumb or lazy ones. It wanted well-balanced prospects. There was a KGB saying: 'A heart must be in the center of the body.' And the men the KGB recruited had to be in the center."

Midway through the French tour, a student named Vladimir Kozlov was caught stealing a women's bra in a store. The teacher in charge of the students claimed that Kozlov was the victim of a "provocation" — a trap set by the Gendarmerie, the French military police, to embarrass the Soviet Union. But none of the students believed her. Kozlov had taken the bra because he wanted to be arrested. Once he was in French custody, he could defect. Although Kozlov was detained at the clothing store by a clerk, the French police did not arrest him. He was released to the tour group, and the KGB began looking for a quiet way to get Kozlov back home before he tried another stunt. Sergei was ordered to befriend Kozlov and persuade him to go on a train for a six-hour ride to a remote station. Once there, the KGB would grab Kozlov and fly him back to Moscow. The KGB asked Sergei to betray Kozlov because it didn't want to send in officers from its Paris KGB station, as French intelligence would then know who they were.

Although Sergei had not received any training, he was able to trick Kozlov. "I got him very drunk and put him on the train with me. He didn't know what was happening until it was too late. My actions impressed the KGB."

After the group returned to Moscow, Sergei reported to the Hotel Tsentralnaya for a follow-up session. He gave his KGB handler a hundred-page report written on ordinary paper about what he had observed in France.

"If we decide we want you, we will call," the officer said. "If not, have a good life."

Sergei would later discover that the KGB had been performing an exhaustive background check during this time period. "It was routine for at least four generations of your family members to be investigated. You were required to tell the KGB where all of your relatives were physically buried because they went to the actual cemeteries to verify the information." The KGB wanted to make certain none of its recruits were foreign agents hiding behind "legends" — false backgrounds. The KGB was also choosy about what sort of recruit it accepted. According to Sergei, Jews were nearly always barred and women were never recruited to work as KGB officers, only as secretaries or as prostitutes. Candidates whose relatives had been captured during World War II and had spent time in a prisoner-of-war camp were automatically rejected because the KGB questioned their loyalty. If a recruit's parents worked in a service job — driving a taxi or working as a waiter — they were disqualified, too, because those professions involved tips and the KGB didn't want candidates who could be bribed. Anyone whose family members received mail from outside the Soviet Union also came under suspicion. At one point, Sergei was grilled about a letter that a woman in Poland had mailed to Helen's mother — fifteen years earlier. The two had become friends while Helen's parents were living in Warsaw.

Sergei had no idea who the Polish woman was.

A few days before Sergei was scheduled to graduate, a dean called him into his office and announced that he had passed the KGB's scrutiny. "They are ready to offer you a job."

"What kind of job?" Sergei asked.

"Let me give you some advice," the dean answered. "If you want to be successful in this organization, never ask questions. Just do what you are told, work with whatever materials are given to you, and keep your mouth shut, because no one cares what you think. Asking questions will only get you into trouble."

It was the same advice that his grand-mother had given his mother when she started working for the KGB, and the same advice that she had already shared with him.

The dean scribbled an address on a slip of paper and handed it to Sergei. It was a building on Flotskaya Street. A sign near its doorway identified the office as the All-Union Scientific Research Institute of Systems Analysis. That nonsensical title was meant to confuse passersby. The building actually housed the Scientific Research Institute of Intelligence Problems of the First Chief Directorate of the KGB, better known by the abbreviation NIIRP. Some two thousand employees there sifted through hundreds of newspapers and magazines each day from all over the world, looking for information that might prove helpful to the intelligence service. Sergei was disappointed. Working there would be nothing like the James Bond adventures that he had watched.

FOUR

Sometimes Hollywood reflects life and sometimes life imitates Hollywood — even in Moscow.

NIIRP was a relatively new venture when Sergei reported to work. Several KGB generals at the Center had seen the 1975 film *Three Days of the Condor,* which starred Robert Redford as a bookish CIA analyst who returns from a coffee break one day to find all of his coworkers murdered because they had stumbled upon a secret government plot. The film convinced the KGB generals that the CIA was spending more money and putting more effort into analytic work than the KGB was. It had been part of the reason the Center had decided to create NIIRP, Sergei was told. There was only one problem. The KGB instructors at NIIRP didn't appear to Sergei to have a clue about how to dig out useful information. New recruits were not taught any secret Soviet analytical techniques for gleaning information from copies of Western publications, such as *The New York Times, Le Monde* in Paris, and even *Playboy* magazine. Instead, NIIRP told them about tricks that CIA analysts had used. "Our instruction was all about the CIA and what it was doing. We were told its analysts looked for scraps of information — maybe a new railroad station opening in Siberia or a new movie theater under construction that could seat eight hundred people. Because there was nothing else in these desolate Siberian areas except polar bears and wolves, they'd know they'd found the location of a Soviet military base. Why else would you need a rail station or movie theater there?"

Sergei was assigned to monitor the North Atlantic Treaty Organization (NATO). A stack of fifty newspapers and other publications from U.S. and European cities would be waiting for him when he reported each morning. He was fluent in Russian, French, and English and was responsible for analyzing the publications. When he wasn't reading, he answered questions that came from "the Center," the nickname for the KGB's First Chief Directorate's headquarters. Some could be answered in minutes. Oth-

ers could take up to three months of research.

Sergei learned that NIIRP often moved at
glacial speed when it was required to submit
an important study to the Center or to the
Central Committee of the Communist
Party. After information was collected,
reports were drafted, rewritten, corrected,
criticized, rewritten, and often criticized
again based not on facts but on the party's
political agenda.

Sergei hated working at NIIRP. He wanted
to be an operative in the field, not a "paper
worm." The pace of work was exhausting
because it required him to read thousands
of often boring publications in the hope of
extracting a few lines of data that had to be
made politically correct.

One of his first assignments was to search
for differences that could be exploited
concerning weapons being used by NATO
troops. He looked for faults in NATO's efforts to standardize its weaponry and then
was required to explain in his reports why
Soviet weapons were superior even if they
weren't.

Despite his best efforts, Sergei failed to
uncover any useful secrets in his research.
Then finally, one day, he spotted something.
Sergei read that the Library of Congress

published a monthly index of reports prepared by U.S. congressional committees. One of them was an investigation of living conditions at U.S. military bases. Sergei ordered a copy and discovered it identified the location of every U.S. military installation inside the U.S. and throughout the world. The report also contained details about each military base's housing capacity. Sergei pored over the report and was able to extrapolate from it how many U.S. soldiers were stationed at each U.S. post. The report also listed the length of airfields at U.S. facilities, and Sergei used those figures to deduce what sort of U.S. and NATO aircraft could safely land at each installation. He used that information to determine how far U.S. and NATO fighter aircraft would reach when they left each base and how long it would take planes to fly to remote areas in the Soviet Union and elsewhere.

When Sergei proudly delivered his conclusions to Colonel Vladlen Gorkovski, the head of NIIRP's American department, the KGB officer was so impressed that he removed Sergei's name from the research and claimed he'd done it.

"One day, if you are lucky, you will get rewarded for information that you never produced," Gorkovski told him. A short while later, Sergei was required to attend a ceremony at NIIRP where Gorkovski was given a medal for *his* research about U.S. bases.

A more experienced analyst at NIIRP took pity on Sergei. He taught him how to move quickly through documents and pick out useful information. He showed him how to write reports for the Center. Sergei began to respect his job even though he still disliked doing it.

"You will never become a good KGB officer in the field unless you first become an excellent analyst," he said later. "You have to immediately recognize what is useful and what is not, and then you have to know how to communicate this to the Center."

Sergei spent fourteen hours at work each day. He was recognized as NIIRP's expert on NATO and its members. In 1981, the Center ordered NIIRP to prepare a report about newly elected French president François Mitterrand. It was typical of top-level Center requests. Sergei was responsible for uncovering "compromising material" about Mitterrand's sex life and any "political scandals or corruption" in his past. Using French and European publications that dated back to World War II, Sergei began collecting skeletons. He reported that Mitterrand had been given an award by the pro-Nazi, French collaborator government during the war. He learned that France's premier political leader, Charles de Gaulle, despised Mitterrand, and that Mitterrand had a history of changing his political views based on whatever was popular. Although Mitterrand was married, he was known to have fathered at least one illegitimate daughter and to have engaged in numerous sexual affairs. All Sergei's information was pulled from public records, but when he compiled it, his conclusions were declared top-secret by the Center. Among other things, his report identified what sort of woman would most likely be able to seduce Mitterrand and become his mistress based on her hair color, height, weight, bust size, and personality.

Most recruits spent three years at NIIRP before continuing with their KGB careers. But Sergei's NIIRP tour was extended. Once again, he became discouraged. He wanted to quit, but Helen and Revmira urged him to stick with it. In 1982, he went from being a civilian employee at NIIRP to becoming a KGB lieutenant. Despite the promotion, he would stay stuck at NIIRP for another two years before his application to attend the Red Banner Institute was approved. The institute was the Soviet Union's training facility for intelligence officers. Before Sergei could enter it, however, he had to pass several psychological and physical tests.

Sergei was worried about one of them. He had inherited high blood pressure from his mother — a defect that should have barred him from the KGB. But his mother had managed to keep his condition hidden because of her KGB connections. Revmira had bribed a nurse who worked at the KGB Central Military Medical Commission located in a hundred-year-old building on Kiselniy Lane, not far from Lubyanka. She'd plied the nurse with Western goods, including expensive perfumes, Marlboro cigarettes, and denim jeans, that ordinary Russians couldn't buy but that Revmira and Oleg could purchase because of his job as a foreign trade representative. In return, the nurse had forged all of Sergei's medical records.

When Sergei told Revmira about the new round of medical tests, she visited the nurse, armed with Western goods, and a deal was quickly struck. Sergei was reported to be in excellent health.

But a few days later, Sergei was told that

his application for the institute had been denied because of medical reasons. It wasn't his health. It was Helen's. The KGB required that both its officers and their spouses be in excellent physical condition. Otherwise, they might be vulnerable to recruitment by a foreign government because many Western countries had better medical facilities. A KGB doctor had declared Helen unfit because he'd found a cyst.

Sergei hustled Helen before a different doctor, who signed a report stating that Helen was in excellent health. Armed with the new evaluation, Sergei contacted the nurse whom his mother had bribed, but she didn't have enough authority to overrule the first doctor's diagnosis. She told Sergei that he would have to appeal directly to the head of the KGB medical commission. The nurse volunteered that the commission's director was a woman with a huge ego.

Sergei rushed to the commissioner's private office and burst inside, ignoring the protests of her secretary. He interrupted the director while she was conducting a meeting with doctors. Falling on his knees in front of the surprised assembly, he begged the director for mercy. "I knew my actions would appeal to her huge ego and make her look good and important before her colleagues." Sergei explained that his entire career was about to be ruined because of an incorrect diagnosis and that only she could rescue him. Within the hour, the first report about Helen's cyst had been removed from her medical records.

Sergei next went to see the deputy director at NIIRP, Colonel Vladimir Grigoryevich Mityaev, who had told him that his application for the Red Banner Institute had been rejected. Sergei confessed everything: how Revmira had bribed a KGB nurse for years to conceal his high blood pressure and how he had just come from begging the medical director to change Helen's diagnosis. Sergei would later recall what happened next.

"This is an example of how differently U.S. bureaucrats and their KGB counterparts think. In the U.S., my actions would have caused a reprimand and scandal. I had just admitted bribing a nurse to falsify medical records. I had just gotten a medical director to destroy Helen's initial report. But Mityaev stood up from his desk, shook my hand, and said, 'Sergei Olegovich, I will green-light your application to the Red Banner Institute because I have never seen results like this in my entire career. You will make a good spy.' I had impressed him because I had found a way to overcome all obstacles to get what I needed."

FIVE

In 1984, the Red Banner Institute, the KGB's training school for intelligence officers, had four campuses, located on the outskirts of Moscow. The facilities were top-secret and the disclosure of their addresses was considered treason. Each campus was in a forested area and rimmed by wire fences with signs posted that warned: ABSOLUTELY NO TRESPASSING. Anyone caught by the guards who patrolled the grounds was detained, questioned, and his name was added to a "black list" kept by local police. The institute's administrative offices were housed at the biggest campus near the northern suburb of Chelobit'yevo.

Only three hundred new candidates were admitted each year for training. They came from KGB departments across the USSR. Competition was fierce because the school was the gateway to overseas assignments. From the start, Sergei noticed that many of his classmates were the sons of top KGB and party officials, and the institute would later come under fire when it was discovered that one of the generals running it had accepted bribes for approving admissions.

The institute's training programs lasted from one to three years, depending on each entrant's linguistic skills and background. Because Sergei was already fluent in French and English and had spent five years at NIIRP as an analyst, he was enrolled in a one-year program. As soon as a student was admitted, he was issued a false identity and a legend. The KGB found there were fewer mistakes if a student retained his actual first name, so Sergei Tretyakov became Sergei Turanov. The false names and backgrounds were not intended to protect a student's true identity. Their purpose was to help students get used to working undercover.

During his first month as a student, Sergei was sent to the city of Pskov, where a Soviet Army paratrooper division was headquartered. He was taught how to parachute, fight hand to hand, fire weapons, survive in the wilderness, and other rudimentary military skills. Sergei would later describe it as a waste of time. "Intelligence is a game of wits, much like chess. Spying is done in secret and silence, not by firing machine guns and using kung fu on your opponents like they do in movies."

When he returned to the main campus at Chelobit'yevo, he began attending forty-four hours of classes held six days a week. Students were not permitted to leave the grounds except between the hours of 3 p.m. on Saturdays and 9 a.m. on Mondays. Because the KGB had traditionally claimed that women were not "emotionally stable" enough to work in intelligence, Sergei was surprised to learn that four female students had been admitted to the institute. All of them were married to intelligence officers but none would do well, in part because of sexual harassment and pressure from students to quit.

At Chelobit'yevo, the instructors lived in the same dormitory as students. There was no privacy and no chance to avoid the teachers' constant supervision. Prior to Sergei's arrival, students had been allowed to drink alcohol at night and play cards, but both practices had been banned because Soviet officials wanted to reinforce discipline in the school. Being caught doing either was cause for expulsion.

New students were divided into two groups. Those with university degrees in the liberal arts entered the institute's political intelligence section. Those with technical backgrounds, such as engineers, mathematicians, and physicists, were sent to the scientific and technological school. During the year, students in the political section were further divided. Those who did well learning languages would continue studying to become foreign intelligence officers in the political affairs section. But those who did poorly or who were less socially polished were diverted into foreign counterintelligence work. Their job overseas would be to spy on their colleagues.

Students being trained to recruit spies were told there were three reasons people betrayed their native countries and helped the KGB. They were motivated by (1) political or ideological beliefs, (2) psychological factors, or (3) financial compensation. Before a KGB officer could successfully recruit a spy, he needed to identify which motive, or which combination of them, he was facing.

The instructors said the easiest spies to recruit were fellow Communists. An example was the famed British spy Harold Adrian Russell Philby, better known as Kim, and the so-called Cambridge Five — Britons who decided to work for the KGB after they became infatuated with Communism while they were still university students.

Deciphering psychological motives was trickier, the instructors warned. Homosexuality was considered a psychological motivation because a target could be coerced into spying through blackmail. Flattery was another, especially if a target believed his government did not recognize his brilliance and had not regularly promoted him.

When it came to recruiting U.S. targets, Sergei's teachers preached the same sermon. American traitors were only interested in money. "Their spying can be bought," he was told.

At the institute, the KGB had turned intelligence work into a science with its own specific set of laws, axioms, and vocabulary. Students were expected to learn and become familiar with specific terms so other KGB officers would know exactly what they were saying. For instance, KGB "sources" were split into four types.

The most common was the "neutral contact." These were not spies; they were simply people whom KGB officers befriended while working overseas. They could be hotel doormen, cleaning ladies, or clerks in a store. Although "neutral contacts" did not provide an officer with any useful information, they could be helpful during covert operations. A KGB officer, for instance, might speak to a dozen persons while taking his dog on a walk. One of them would be a source. But the others would be "neutral contacts" whom he was using to camouflage the identify of his source. If the FBI or CIA was watching, they wouldn't know which person was the spy.

The next category of sources was the "information contact," and once again, these were not spies. They could be diplomats, journalists, businessmen, politicians — any expert who had access to helpful information. If a KGB officer needed to learn how many tons of steel was manufactured in Germany during a given year, he could ask a government bureaucrat. In his cable to the KGB Center, he would explain that he'd gotten the statistic from an "information contact." Often "information contacts" would not know they were dealing with the KGB because its officers would be posing as Soviet journalists, trade representatives, or diplomats.

"Neutral contracts" and "information contacts" were known inside the KGB as "auxiliary sources." They could help an officer do his job, but they didn't provide "concrete results." That term was used specifically by the KGB as a euphemism for "recruitment." It didn't want its officers to write in a cable that a target had been recruited, because the cable might be intercepted. Instead, an officer would report that he had been able to achieve "concrete results" with a target.

Spies for the KGB were divided into two groups: *agents* and *trusted contacts.* The word *spy* often has been misused. A KGB intelligence officer was *not* a spy. A spy was someone who was spying *for* a KGB, CIA, or FBI officer. Spies betrayed their countries. Because the CIA and FBI called their own employees agents, that word also was frequently applied incorrectly in the West to Soviet intelligence. The KGB never referred to its own employees as agents. They were officers or operatives. An *agent* in KGB terminology was a spy whose relationship with the KGB was not known to a rival foreign counterintelligence service. A *trusted contact* was a KGB spy whose meetings with Soviet intelligence were often carried out in public and were known to a foreign counterintelligence service, but whose covert relationship with the KGB was concealed.

An example of an *agent* would be a spy who contacted the KGB secretly without anyone knowing except Soviet intelligence. A *trusted contact* would be a United Nations diplomat who met openly with Soviet officials on a routine basis as part of his job, but whose spying for the KGB was kept secret from his own country.

As part of his studies, Sergei was taught the steps that the KGB used to recruit a spy. It was a painfully slow process that could last up to twelve months or more. His instructors emphasized that while a KGB officer in the field did the actual legwork, the KGB Center made all the decisions about when and how someone would be pitched. The teachers drilled into their students' heads that no KGB officer could work independent of the Center. The KGB was not a place for cowboys.

The first step in the process was selecting a target who was worth the effort. He had to have access to information that the KGB wanted. If he did, the Center would authorize one of its KGB officers to invite the target to have coffee or to eat lunch together. During this initial get-together, the KGB operative would be under specific orders *not* to talk about spying or make any attempt to recruit the target. His only assignment was to become friendly with the target and discreetly obtain some basic information. The KGB used a one-page sheet called "Form 21A" to pass this personal data to the Center. Form 21A had a place on it for the target's name, age, race, occupation, educational background, and profession. The KGB operative also had to explain in detail on the form how he had first met the target, noting specifically who initiated contact. This was important because the KGB was always worried about "dangles" — rival intelligence officers who were pretending to be disgruntled and seemed eager to spy. Students were taught that U.S. intelligence frequently sent military officers into Soviet embassies posing as "walk-ins" (volunteers). These "dangles" would be interviewed by the KGB and then would return to their CIA and FBI bosses and tell them whom they met with inside the Soviet embassy. It was a simple way to identify which Soviets were KGB officers pretending to be diplomats.

The Center would compare the information on Form 21A with its records. The archives contained the names of several million persons. Sometimes, the Center would recognize a CIA dangle because the U.S. had used him before on a different continent and had thought his identity was still secret.

If a target passed the Center's records check, the KGB operative would be told to schedule another lunch or dinner. But he would again be instructed *not* to mention spying. His goal this time would be to ferret out more personal information and observe the target's demeanor. Did he seem nervous, act stable, was he sociable? What were his political views, especially about the Soviet Union? If a target mentioned spying or hinted that he was willing to work for the KGB, it was viewed suspiciously by the Center as a tip-off that he probably was a dangle. If a target tried to rush the recruitment process, he was seen as a probable dangle. Students were taught to be wary of anyone who seemed too good to be true. For example, if a KGB operative was having dinner with an expert on trade negotiations and the conversation turned to biological warfare, the KGB officer needed to be suspicious if the trade expert suddenly offered to see what he could learn at his job about chemical weapons. "Why would a trade expert have access to this information?" the instructors explained.

After their second meeting, the KGB officer was required to send the Center another detailed report. No fact was considered frivolous. Where was the lunch held? Who paid the bill? If the target offered to pay a bill at an expensive restaurant, he was probably a dangle. Why? Because he was likely spending someone else's money and that's why he could afford to be so generous. These subtle signs were the "tells" that the teachers taught their students to look for. If a diplomat openly complained about an ambassador, he was probably a dangle. "Only other intelligence officers — posing as diplomats — are bold enough to criticize their ambassadors," the instructors warned.

The Center liked to have a KGB officer meet with a target a minimum of seven times before moving to the next step, which was known as the "DPI," an acronym in Russian for "first stage of operative development." It was during this stage that the Center issued the target a code name followed by a six-digit number. The first digit was a two, which indicated that the target had not yet been recruited.

The Center, however, was still not ready for its officer to make a "pitch." It demanded more background information, including the names of the target's parents, his family history, and a detailed personality profile that pinpointed known weaknesses and vulnerabilities. Did the target drink too much? Did he have a drug problem? Cheat on his wife? Was he in debt? The DPI stage could require as many as fifteen more social interactions before the Center felt comfortable enough to move forward.

The final step was "DOR," an abbreviation for "dossier of recruitment." The target kept his original code name, but a different six-digit number was assigned to his file. It began with a 1 and it was his permanent KGB identifier — for the rest of his life.

It was during DOR that a KGB operative would finally pitch the target and get him to steal a document. Sometimes, an operative's first request would *not* be for a classified document. This was a way to draw a recruit gradually into the process. It helped the target see how easy it was to take documents without being caught. As soon as a target delivered a secret document, even if he hadn't expected or asked for anything, he was paid. Expensive gifts and cash were essential, the teachers said. After the target accepted payment, all pretenses ended. The relationship shifted from being a delicate dance to becoming a business agreement. The Center now felt free to push its new spy for material.

The lessons taught inside the institute's classrooms were supplemented with practical exercises, most done on Moscow streets. Students practiced how to make "brush contacts" (passing items to a source in a crowd without being noticed), perform dead-drop exchanges, and elude and conduct surveillance.

Gorky Park was a favorite spot for practicing dead-drop exchanges. A typical exercise would begin with a KGB officer and a spy arriving at the park at the same time but at different locations. They would walk clockwise through the grounds. This circular route prevented them from accidentally bumping into each other. At some point, both would discreetly make a signal. The KGB officer might pause at one of the park's streetlamps to light a cigarette, striking a specially made match against the post's metal, leaving behind a small white scratch. His contact would leave a different signal — a crushed pack of cigarettes at the base of a specific tree near the boating pond area. Both would continue their strolls. Because they were walking in a circle, they would eventually reach the other's mark. The KGB officer would spot the crushed cigarette pack and the spy would see the scratched lamppost. Both would continue walking, but they now would know that they were both in the park and ready to make an exchange.

Their clockwise course would cause them to return to their original signal spots. Each would leave a packet there. The KGB officer would place a concealment device — which looked like a small rock but actually held tightly rolled rubles inside it — near the lamppost. The spy would leave a cache of microfilm in a different concealment device at the boating pond. They would continue walking.

When the KGB officer reached the boating pond, he would retrieve the microfilm and leave yet another signal, indicating that he had gotten the delivery. Meanwhile, across the park, the spy would be collecting his rubles near the lamppost and would leave his signal there. This was the most dangerous part of the exchange, because neither wanted to be caught holding microfilm or rubles. They would walk the route a final time. When they passed their drop sites, they would spot the other's sign and know their exchange had been successful. They could then exit the park. A dead drop allowed an officer and his source to exchange packages without ever seeing or speaking to each other.

Students also learned how to use basic KGB technical devices, such as micro tape recorders, hidden microphones, and miniature cameras. Their teachers taught them how to write cables, too. Each had to be about a single subject. "One cable, one topic" was an ironclad rule. If the cable was intercepted and somehow deciphered, it meant that only one secret had been compromised.

Some students were required to attend classes about Western society. In the mid-1980s, the Soviet Union was still isolated and many students, especially those who had never traveled abroad, were unfamiliar with banking, credit cards, mortgages, and taxes. The institute ran a driving school as well, not because it wanted its officers to know how to perform evasive stunts, but because many of its students didn't know how to drive because they couldn't afford cars. Others weren't prepared for traffic in foreign capitals.

As part of their homework, students were required to analyze KGB case histories. Each was a real case, but the facts had been edited to hide the identities of the participants. A case that happened in France was moved to Spain. The students wrote papers about what had been done correctly and what hadn't. These were Sergei's favorite assignments. He devoured case histories, checking out as many files as he could each night to study.

Not long after he arrived at the institute, Sergei befriended a mentor, Vladimir

Ivanovich Belchenko, an instructor in the school of political intelligence. In the 1970s, Belchenko had been assigned to Tel Aviv, where his main target had been Golda Meir, the Israeli prime minister. He showed Sergei several photographs of the two of them socializing, but was elusive whenever he was asked whether or not Meir had been a KGB source.

Sergei turned to Belchenko for help when the faculty announced that every student would have to compete in a footrace. Sergei wasn't worried about competing in the race. He was afraid of what would happen after he crossed the finish line. A doctor would be stationed there to examine each student and take his blood pressure.

The night before the run, Sergei confided in Belchenko.

"My wife, Helen, has pills from the West [blood pressure medicine was not yet common in Moscow] that can keep my blood pressure low enough to pass any exam," he explained. But Sergei had no way to get the pills into the institute because he couldn't leave the compound during the week. Sergei asked Belchenko if he would meet Helen at a subway station the next morning and bring him the medicine before the race.

Belchenko agreed. He delivered the pills

and Sergei easily passed the blood pressure check. "Belchenko could have turned me in," Sergei said later, "but by this point, we had spent enough time together that I understood how he thought, and I knew he believed intelligence officers couldn't be successful if they only operated by the book. Instead of being upset, he saw my request as a confirmation that I had learned what he had been teaching me."

It didn't take long for Sergei to realize that instructors at the institute overloaded their students. There was not enough time to do all their assignments. This was intentional. They wanted to watch how students used their time and which knew how to prioritize the work.

Overtaxing students was not the only game the teachers played. "You would be ordered to prepare a presentation about one topic and then an instructor would change the subject moments before you were supposed to make your presentation," Sergei recalled. "Would you panic? Would you become depressed? Did you have a sense of humor? If you were too serious, it was not good. If you were too carefree, it was not good. They applied pressure at all possible points and they were always totally critical.

There was never any positive reinforcement. None."

Every assignment could have been performed better. "Every effort was made to belittle you, to tear you down." There were no casual conversations, no moments when a student was not being studied and evaluated. One afternoon, Sergei was verbally berated by an instructor who spotted him walking in a hallway with his hands in his pockets.

"If you want to grab your balls, do it in private!" the teacher snarled. "We are training you to become a future diplomat, and you must look and act like an aristocrat, not a bum. We will send you to Africa if you can't stop playing with your nuts."

Sergei got only three hours of sleep most nights. He was always the last student to leave the institute's library when it closed at 3 a.m. One evening he was waiting in a long line to check out a case file when he was pushed out of the way by an older, heavyset figure.

"Excuse me," Sergei said indignantly. "I was next."

"And who are you?" the man replied.

"Comrade Turanov," Sergei answered. "And who are you to be pushing your way in?"

"I'm the new head of the party committee in the institute," Vladimir Piguzov replied.

Sergei immediately apologized and said: "The party always goes first."

Despite the late hour, Piguzov invited Sergei back to his office, where he grilled him about his background. During their exchange, Sergei mentioned that he had been appointed editor of *Soviet Intelligence Officer,* a magazine published inside the institute for students and faculty.

"I've always had trouble expressing myself," Piguzov said, "but you're a journalist so I want you to do me a favor." He asked Sergei to write a feature story about him and his adventures while he was stationed in Indonesia. Piguzov then recounted how he had met a spy one night in a jungle. After getting a package of stolen documents, Piguzov had made his way to a clearing where he was supposed to be picked up by another KGB officer. But his ride never came and Piguzov spent the night with snakes and wild animals.

Sergei spun Piguzov's yarn into a dramatic and heroic tale, and after it was published, Piguzov was so grateful that he began inviting Sergei to his office several times a week. Sergei used the sessions to learn as much as he could about overseas assignments.

Sergei was told early that he would be sent to an overseas post in Latin America after he graduated. He didn't object, but he really wanted to work for the more prestigious and more exciting First Department, which covered the U.S. and Canada. One of his instructors told him that the only way he could get into the First Department was if he became the best student in his class. Because the U.S. was considered the Soviet Union's main adversary, the head of the First Department had "the right of first refusal," which meant he could claim any student whom he wanted — even if they had already been promised to a different department.

The head of the First Department was General Dmitri Ivanovich Yakushkin, a much-feared and highly respected legend inside the KGB. In the West, however, Yakushkin was not held in such high esteem. In the mid-1970s, Yakushkin had been the KGB *rezident* in Washington, D.C., and he had made a number of blunders. He arrived shortly after President Richard Nixon was forced to resign, but Yakushkin refused to believe Nixon had been ousted because of public outrage over the Watergate scandal. Instead, Yakushkin claimed in cables to the KGB Center that Nixon was the victim of

Zionist plotting and the U.S. military industrial complex. He wrote that both were intent on undermining détente (the thawing of Cold War relations between the U.S. and Soviets). Unashamedly anti-Semitic, Yakushkin peppered his cables with Jewish-riddled conspiracy theories and claimed America's Jewish lobby controlled the U.S. media.

Not only were his cables off-base, Yakushkin also missed a chance to develop a U.S. spy. One morning, Yakushkin received a note from an anonymous source offering to sell CIA secrets. Yakushkin contacted the Center and decided along with its generals that the note was a CIA trick. A second message arrived a few days later asking Yakushkin why he had not answered the first. He ignored it. The note writer then tossed a package over the fence at the Soviet embassy. A guard there delivered it unopened to Vitaly Yurchenko, the station's foreign counterintelligence officer. But rather than looking inside, Yurchenko assumed it was a bomb and turned it over to the D.C. police. The package actually contained stolen CIA documents and a note asking for $3,000 to be left at a specific location. The note writer offered the KGB more documents in exchange for an additional $197,000. The D.C. police turned the packet over to the FBI, and it set up a sting operation. When Edwin G. Moore, Jr., went to retrieve what he thought was $3,000 from the KGB, FBI agents swooped in. Moore, who had retired from the CIA three years earlier, had ten boxes of classified CIA documents stored in his apartment. He was sentenced to fifteen years in prison, but was paroled after serving three.

Despite those foul-ups, Yakushkin had been made head of the First Department in 1982 when he returned to Moscow. He had been promoted thanks to the patronage of Yuri Andropov, the head of the KGB. Andropov was on the verge of becoming the secretary of the Communist Party, and during his tenure he would propel Mikhail Gorbachev from relative obscurity into the Kremlin's top leadership, setting the stage for Gorbachev to eventually take control of the Soviet Union.

Sergei set out to impress General Yakushkin, and when the year-end grades were posted, Sergei had the highest marks in his class. General Yakushkin sent word that he wanted to see him. An excited Sergei reported to a KGB safe house — a historic mansion in the center of Moscow. Yakushkin and a personnel officer were seated in a conference room at a table covered with file folders about students. Sergei waited patiently until Yakushkin acknowledged him.

"I understand you went to France as a student," Yakushkin said. "Tell me, how do you like French women? Are they different from Russian women in bed?"

Sergei didn't know how to react. After an embarrassing long pause, he stammered: "General, I'm married, so I don't know anything about French women."

"Then you are an idiot!" Yakushkin declared.

The general ignored Sergei and talked to his personnel clerk for several moments. Then Yakushkin turned back and asked, "Tell me, what do you think about the decision to end negotiations with the Americans in Geneva? What is your view?" The general was referring to Andropov's announcement that he was breaking off ongoing talks with the Reagan administration about the unratified SALT II Treaty, which restricted production of nuclear weapons.

"It's a very smart decision to cut off talks with the Americans," Sergei quickly replied. "We must show America our teeth."

"Then you really are an idiot," Yakushkin declared. "Why do you want to work for me? You should be working for Gromyko [the Soviet foreign minister, Andrei

Gromyko] at the foreign mission. You don't belong to the KGB. Go work for him."

Once again, the general turned away from Sergei. After being ignored for five minutes, Sergei mustered his courage: "Excuse me, General."

Yakushkin seemed shocked to see him. "Why are you still here?" he asked. "Get out!"

A glum Sergei returned to the institute.

"How did it go with General Yakushkin?" one of his instructors asked.

"I'm done. He will not take me. I made a terrible impression."

"You are a poor psychologist," the instructor replied. "General Yakushkin loved your answers."

The general had been testing him, Sergei was told. If he had bragged about having sex with French women, Yakushkin would have thought that he was disrespectful. Sergei and the general were not drinking buddies exchanging sex stories. He had answered that question correctly and had given the right response about the SALT talks, too. As a KGB officer, he was expected to enthusiastically support every decision made by the Kremlin — just as he had done.

"Do you think he will select me for the First Department?" Sergei asked.

Head of the KGB

First Deputy

Deputies (approximately seven).

Chief Directorates and Directorates of the KGB (16),
which had approximately the same statuses

[1] [2] [3] [5] [6] [7] [8] [9] [12] [15] [16]

1. First Chief Directorate (Intelligence)
2. Second Chief Directorate (Counterintelligence)
3. Third Chief Directorate (Counterintelligence in the
   military - KGB counterintelligence officers in the
   Armed Forces). 5. Fifth directorate (Persecution of dissidents).

7. Seventh Directorate (Surveillance).
8. Eighth Chief Directorate (Cryptography).
9. Ninth Directorate (Secret Service).

12. Twelfth Directorate (Technical Spying on foreigners
    inside the country; monitoring bugs, video devices).

15. Fifteenth Chief Directorate (Secret communications:
    tunnels, bunkers, underground and underwater cables, etc.).

16. Sixteenth Chief Directorate (Interception, decoding of
    intercepted materials).

Among the other Chief Directorates and Directorates -
border troops and some others.

My whole professional career was only within the
First Chief Directorate of the KGB (Intelligence).

Yet, this is the approximate structure
of the KGB.

"Who knows?"

On graduation day, Sergei and his fellow students were called one by one into a conference room and given their assignment. When it was his turn, Sergei stood before the chief of personnel for foreign intelligence, Nikolai Ivanovich Nazarov, and a dozen KGB generals who oversaw various KGB departments, including General Yakushkin.

Nazarov, who had a reputation for cruelly toying with young officers, read Sergei's evaluation aloud.

"Student Turanov, you showed excellent results in your studies and your practical training. You passed all psychological, physical, and morale tests with good results. Therefore, we have decided to send you back to the Scientific Research Institute of Intelligence Problems [NIIRP]. Do you have any questions about this assignment before you are dismissed?"

Sergei was stunned. Not only had General Yakushkin not selected him, but he was not going to Latin America, either. He was being returned to a job that he despised. Still, he hid his disappointment.

"I have no questions," he answered. "Thank you, comrades."

"Then you are free to go," Nazarov replied.

Sergei began walking to the exit, but before he reached the door, General Yakushkin called out: "It was a joke. I'm taking you for the First Department."

Years later, Sergei would recall that event with clarity because it had been such an emotional experience. "This was typical KGB. The generals had unlimited powers and they always wanted to show their authority. They wanted you to understand they could crush you at any time. You were nothing, a nobody."

The student who followed Sergei into the conference room did not react as Sergei had. When Nazarov announced the officer's next assignment, he protested. At that moment, the student had unknowingly sealed his fate. Instead of giving him the assignment that he had wanted, the committee ordered him to report to the post that it had initially intended as a joke. Only later would he learn his mistake in arguing with the generals.

Sergei was finally on his way to becoming a KGB foreign intelligence officer — or so he thought.

Six

Nineteen eighty-five was a heady time to be a young Soviet intelligence officer.

The KGB, the so-called "sword and shield" of the Communist Party, was the largest and the most powerful intelligence service in the world. It was composed of some four hundred thousand officers, most stationed inside the Soviet Union, along with two hundred thousand border troops. It had a massive network of paid informers spread across the Soviet Union. The KGB had almost unlimited funds and unchecked powers. And the crème de la crème of the KGB were its foreign intelligence operatives. The First Chief Directorate had its own separate headquarters away from the ancient KGB administration building in Lubyanka in the center of Moscow.

Each morning, Sergei caught a KGB-owned-and-operated bus a few steps from his apartment near Gorky Park. It was one of 140 unmarked KGB buses that criss-crossed Moscow each day. They ran every half-hour during rush hour and every hour after that, exclusively for KGB employees. It took Sergei forty-five minutes to reach the first security gate at the First Chief Directorate compound near the town of Yasenevo.

Built in a wooden area about a half-mile southwest of Moscow's outer ring road, the Center had opened in 1972 and was also sometimes called "Yasenevo," or simply "the woods." It was guarded more heavily than the Kremlin. Its perimeter was ringed with barbed wire and electronic sensing devices, and it was patrolled by guards with attack dogs. No costs had been spared. Construction materials had been shipped in from Japan and Europe. Furnishings had been purchased in Finland. The Center was designed to impress those who worked there. To remind them that they were the elite.

Sergei's free bus ride was one of dozens of entitlements. There were shops inside the Center with discounted prices. There might be shortages outside its fences, but the shelves of its internal grocery stores were filled with salmon, sausage, cheese, bread, produce, and caviar. Western clothing was sold in its department store. For relaxation, there were two saunas, a swimming pool, gymnasiums, and tennis courts. The Center had its own medical staff, including doctors who made office calls. There was a modern clinic and dental facilities. Masseuses could be summoned by officers for a relaxing rubdown. For a token fee, KGB officers could rent the compound's banquet hall for a wedding reception or a private party. They could hire a KGB bus that would pick up guests at a central Moscow location, whisk them inside the Center, and then return them downtown afterward.

In George Orwell's classic anti-Communism tale *Animal Farm,* the farm animals erect a sign that states "all animals are equal, but some are more equal than others." At the Center, everyone knew who was "more equal" without a placard. About a mile west of the main building and its parking lots, tucked into the picturesque forest, was a separate living compound. These were dachas — twenty summer homes — provided to First Chief Director-ate generals. The houses came furnished with servants to clean the rooms, do laun-dry, cook meals, and tend each house's garden. If a general wished, he could walk along manicured paths through the woods to work each morning, or he could summon his Volga limousine. Each general had two drivers, who took turns so that someone was always on duty.

From the air, the main structure at the Center resembled a giant cross. The northern tip contained a circular assembly hall. A twenty-two-story office building rose from its western end. Its eastern tail was divided into two wings, known simply as the "left wing" and the "right wing," in keeping with the Communists' utilitarian attitude toward identifying buildings. The wings branched away from the corridor much like feathers jutting from an arrow. Underground walkways connected various outbuildings to the headquarters so officers didn't have to venture outside during inclement weather.

Employees entered the main building through the grounds of a park with a man-made pond. A stern-faced granite bust of Lenin stood watch at the door. A private bank of elevators whisked generals to their offices.

The First Chief Directorate was subdivided into smaller directorates and services, each identified by a letter. Directorate K was foreign counterintelligence. Directorate T was foreign science and technology. And so forth. At the Center, none was more important than the political officers who worked in the First Department, the so-called North American department, which was where Sergei had been assigned. He reported to the Canadian section.

"I saw so many highly polished, intelligent human beings I immediately felt inferior," Sergei later said. "But I worked hard, and General Yakushkin, who had a reputation for not paying attention to his subordinates, noticed me. I felt I was in the presence of a god. He was a descendant of Russian aristocracy. One of his relatives had been mentioned in a poem by the great nineteenth-century Russian poet Pushkin. General Yakushkin introduced me to other generals who were living legends."

One of them had recruited spies in Europe, and one day Sergei asked him how he had done it. "Sergei, it is very easy if you have the amount of money that I had," he replied. "I start with a million dollars, and for that, you can buy almost anyone."

In August 1985, Sergei arrived at work one day and found General Yakushkin's office in an uproar. An aide told him: "Vitali Sergeyevich Yurchenko has been kidnapped by the CIA!"

Yurchenko was one of General Yakushkin's favorites. He was the foreign counterintelligence officer who had worked for the general in Washington, D.C., in 1976 when Edwin Moore had tossed a package of stolen CIA documents over the embassy fence. It had been Yurchenko who foolishly turned the packet over to the D.C. police without looking inside.

By nightfall, Sergei had heard the story that was being spread throughout the Center. General Yakushkin had sent Yurchenko to Rome to investigate an illegal gun-trafficking ring that involved a KGB officer. That was the official story, but there were whispers that the gun investigation had been a ruse and Yurchenko had been sent on a much-needed vacation. He had become involved with a married woman in Moscow and became despondent when their ill-fated affair ended. While in Rome, he went on a sightseeing tour and the CIA slipped a knockout drug into his drink and kidnapped him.

When Sergei arrived at work the next morning, he was summoned into the office of Anatoli Lebedev, the chief deputy to General Yakushkin. Lebedev knew that Sergei had been the editor of the *Soviet Intelligence Officer* magazine while he was at the Red Banner Institute and he ordered him to write an article about Yurchenko's disappearance.

"But I don't know anything," Sergei protested.

"You are a KGB officer," Lebedev replied. "This should be enough for you. The CIA drugged him. Make up the rest."

Because Sergei worked in the Canadian department, he had access to Western news reports, and the stories that were being published abroad were much different from what he'd been told. According to overseas reports, Yurchenko had walked into the U.S. embassy in Rome and asked for asylum. Of course, Sergei ignored that and wrote how the CIA had kidnapped Yurchenko. Lebedev approved the story and told him to deliver it to Vyacheslav Gurgenov, the deputy head of information for the First Chief Directorate. Gurgenov read it carefully and said: "You know what I am going to do with your article? I am sending it to the personnel department and I'm going to tell them to keep this bullshit in your dossier for the rest of your professional life. This is nonsense." Gurgenov threw the story away.

Years later, the details of Yurchenko's defection would be published in numerous newspaper accounts and retold in several books. He had not been kidnapped. He had fallen in love with Valentina Yereskovsky, the wife of a Soviet diplomat who had been sent from Moscow to Canada, and Yurchenko had convinced himself that she would divorce her husband and join him in the United States if he defected. Two months after he entered the U.S., the FBI quietly arranged for Yurchenko to meet his lover in Canada, but she rejected his proposal and Yurchenko returned to Washington, D.C., dejected. The CIA tried to brighten his mood by offering him a million dollars, but the cash didn't make him any happier.

On November 2, 1985, a Saturday, some three months after Yurchenko switched sides, he was eating dinner in a swank Washington, D.C., restaurant with a young CIA security officer when he suddenly asked: "What would you do if I got up and walked out of here? Would you shoot me?"

"No, we don't treat defectors that way," the officer replied.

Yurchenko stood up and walked out, leaving the frantic security officer scrambling to pay the check. Yurchenko went directly to the Soviet embassy, where he asked for asylum.

The CIA was badly embarrassed, but it never doubted that Yurchenko had been a legitimate defector, mostly because he had helped U.S. intelligence identify two U.S.

traitors. The first and most damaging was Edward Lee Howard, a bitter ex–CIA employee who had been fired. The second was Ronald W. Pelton, who had worked at the National Security Agency. In addition, Yurchenko told the CIA about "spy dust." It was invisible to the naked eye, but could be seen with special glasses. The KGB was squirting it on U.S. embassy cars in Moscow and then looking for traces of it on the skin and clothing of Russians who were suspected of helping the CIA. If a CIA officer picked up an informant in a car, the passenger would be covered with spy dust.

On November 6, 1985, Yurchenko boarded a Moscow-bound Aeroflot Ilyushin jet surrounded by KGB security officers. About two weeks later, he repeated his kidnapping charge at a Kremlin news conference. The KGB played along. Yurchenko was given a medal for being an "Honored Chekist" — the highest internal KGB award — by Vladimir Kryuchkov, then head of the First Chief Directorate and General Yakushkin's boss. Afterward, Yurchenko was assigned a desk job at NIIRP and shunned by other employees.

General Yakushkin and his deputy, Anatoli Lebedev, meanwhile, were quietly forced to resign. Yakushkin had been Yurchenko's patron. His handling of the affair was one of several blunders. Sergei was invited to the general's send-off. "Yakushkin was not crying, but he was close to tears," Sergei recalled. "He told us, 'These have been the best years of my life. Unfortunately, I trusted people who betrayed me, and so now I need to resign. But I don't do this because of my willingness to do it, but because I am being forced.' "

The fact that Yurchenko had been given a medal and Yakushkin had been forced to resign made an impression on Sergei. "Inside the KGB, there were always at least two versions of every story. Only a very few top officials ever really knew what had actually occurred in any scandal, and even they were not always told the whole truth. I was beginning to learn that it was close to impossible to find out what the truth really was inside the KGB. We lied to each other and we lied to the public all of the time."

At age twenty-nine, Sergei also was surprised at how quickly the general had fallen. "A lot of people had made their careers thanks to Yakushkin. One moment they were devoted servants, but now that he was in deep shit, they turned their backs on him. I realized I was living among wolves. If you were strong and had good teeth, you became a leader. If you became old or weak, they would eat you alive and do it with great pleasure. I decided at that moment that I would be more wolf than any of them."

SEVEN

In the midst of the Yurchenko defection scandal, a KGB major named Sergei Motorin was assigned to work at the desk next to Sergei's. This was unusual because Motorin was not an officer in the Canadian branch. He had been living in Washington, D.C., but had been called home abruptly and reassigned to a desk job at the Center. Even stranger, Motorin was not given any work to perform. He spent the day reading newspapers.

Sergei welcomed Motorin, but before they could become friends, the major vanished. No one at the Center seemed to know what had happened to him. When Sergei asked, he was told that Motorin had been caught rifling through personnel records. As punishment, he had been demoted to a clerical job in another department.

Not long after Motorin disappeared, Sergei was ordered to report to Aleksandr

Anufrievich Pechko, the secretary of the Communist Party's Committee of the Intelligence. Pechko told Sergei that he'd been chosen for a prestigious job. The party wanted Sergei to take charge of the Komsomol of the First Chief Directorate of the KGB. Created in 1918, the Komsomol was the party's youth organization, which had 41.2 million members. Officially, it was known as the All-Union Lenin Communist Youth League and was formed to teach persons between the ages of fourteen and twenty-eight the principles of Marxism and Leninism. As head of the Komsomol of the First Chief Directorate, Sergei would be in charge of crushing political dissent among young Soviet intelligence officers and for maintaining "high Communist morale and Soviet patriotism."

Sergei didn't want the job, because it was a political post. But he understood that he didn't have a choice. "If I said no, I would be considered immature as a party member and would be shirking my responsibilities as a good Communist. The correct answer was exactly what I told Comrade Pechko. I said, 'I am a soldier and will do whatever assignment you have for me.' "

According to the Communist Party's bylaws, Sergei had to be elected by a majority vote, but Pechko told him that the election was a formality, and reminded him of a famous quotation attributed to Joseph Stalin. "The people who cast the votes don't decide an election," Stalin had said. "The people who count the votes do."

Sergei was chosen on the first ballot and was taken before the head of the KGB Communist Party Committee to be congratulated. At the time, a major general named Suplatov held that job. Sergei knew that Suplatov had risen through the ranks because he was an *apparatchik* with important party connections, not because of anything he had accomplished as an intelligence officer. Suplatov told him there was a special task that he personally wanted Sergei to perform. "Our beloved KGB is being sabotaged because of nepotism," the general declared. Favoritism was "undermining the integrity of the First Chief Directorate" and needed to be stopped.

Sergei said he would launch an immediate investigation, but even as he was mouthing those words, he knew that he never would. "General Suplatov had a son who was so obese he couldn't physically pass any of the KGB's physical requirements. Yet his son had been accepted into the First Chief Directorate," Sergei explained later. "I knew

117

better than to mention that or to begin investigating other acts by powerful KGB officers."

As the head of the Komsomol in the First Chief Directorate, Sergei rubbed shoulders with the KGB's elite. He was expected to attend all First Chief Directorate functions and give toasts and speeches when called on. But he knew he was actually nothing more than "a piece of furniture" at these affairs. "I was required to smile, be clever, and know my place." Still, his position gave him a look inside the First Chief Directorate during an especially interesting time. Mikhail Gorbachev had recently been elected head of the Soviet Union, and he was introducing his concepts of *perestroika* and *glasnost.* The KGB generals in charge of the First Chief Directorate, along with those who were running the entire KGB, were suspicious of Gorbachev and his new "democratic" ideas.

Sergei was promoted to the rank of captain, but because of his new Komsomol position, he actually wielded more political power than many KGB officers with higher ranks. For instance, his former instructor at the Red Banner Institute, Vladimir Piguzov, now answered to him about Komsomol activities at the school.

Overnight, doors opened. Sergei began attending parties at the Dzerzhinsky Club — the KGB's exclusive nightclub next door to Lubyanka. One night, he spotted Piguzov there. Sergei had called Piguzov's office several times to discuss Komsomol business but had been told by a secretary that Piguzov was not available. He began walking toward Piguzov, but a huge fellow stepped between them, blocking Sergei. Piguzov rushed out of sight. A few days later, Sergei again noticed Piguzov, this time at a meeting at the Center. But when he tried to approach him, the same bodyguard intervened. Angry, Sergei called Piguzov's superior to complain.

"You should leave Comrade Piguzov alone," Sergei was warned, "and do not be seen with him."

Sergei began making discreet inquiries and learned that Piguzov was under investigation. Not long after that, KGB officers arrested Piguzov while he was being given a physical examination at a KGB clinic. They had wanted Piguzov naked to make certain he was not carrying a suicide capsule.

Sergei did not hear anything more until several months later, when he was invited to a private dinner attended by General Vladimir Kryuchkov, who had become the second in command of the KGB.

"I am happy to report that the traitor Piguzov has been executed," Kryuchkov declared.

Everyone at the dinner rose from their chairs and started to applaud. A stunned Sergei joined them. Continuing, Kryuchkov said that another U.S. spy had been executed. General Dmitri Polyakov was a well-known, retired GRU officer. Once again, the crowd applauded — as did Sergei. But quietly his stomach was churning. Although he had not met Polyakov, Sergei and Helen were close friends with Polyakov's oldest son, Aleksandr, and his wife, Larissa. Helen and Larissa had been students together at the same Moscow university, and the two couples had frequently gotten together in their Moscow apartments. Under Soviet law, children could not be held responsible for their parents' actions. But Sergei knew the KGB would confiscate every possession the retired general and his wife owned. Aleksandr had a younger brother named Petr, and the KGB would penalize both sons. Their apartments would be seized and both of their careers would be over. Sergei told Helen as soon as he got home about Polyakov. Neither she nor Sergei ever spoke to Aleksandr and Larissa again.

General Kryuchkov had explained at the dinner that Piguzov and Polyakov had been captured because of KGB counterintelligence work. But Sergei would later learn the truth. Both men had been arrested because of two KGB spies. The CIA mole Aldrich Hazen Ames had sold the KGB the names of at least twenty U.S. "human assets," including Piguzov and Polyakov. FBI agent Robert Hanssen had also identified Polyakov.

FBI and CIA sources would later acknowledge in interviews that Piguzov had been recruited by the CIA in Indonesia in the 1970s, but the U.S. had not been in contact with him since 1979 when he returned to Moscow and went to work at the Red Banner Institute. Of the two Soviets, Polyakov had been a much more important U.S. asset. He first started working for the FBI in the 1960s and had given the Bureau enough classified Soviet military documents during his two decades of spying to fill twenty-seven file drawers.

A few days after Sergei was told that Piguzov and Polyakov had been executed, he learned that his former officemate Major Sergei Motorin had also been accused of spying. As the head of the Komsomol of the First Chief Directorate, Sergei was expected to make an appearance at Motorin's military trial, which was being held in the USSR Supreme Court building on Vorovsky Street.

Sergei barely recognized Motorin when he was brought into the courtroom. His face was pale and weary. Sergei tried to catch Motorin's eye, but the defendant seemed oblivious, and Sergei suspected Motorin had been sedated. The defense attorney was an elderly World War II combat veteran who was missing an arm. He never objected to any of the evidence that the prosecution presented, and he frequently berated his own client for his obvious acts of treason. The chief prosecutor claimed Motorin had been seduced by an American woman while working in Washington, D.C., and had been blackmailed by the FBI into spying.

That is not the story that U.S. intelligence officials would later tell during interviews. When Motorin arrived in Washington in 1980, he tried to buy a $950 television and stereo system on credit at a suburban Chevy Chase, Maryland, store. But because he was a Soviet diplomat, the store owner refused. He knew diplomats had legal immunity, and if Motorin didn't pay the bill, there would be no way for the store to collect its money. The FBI had been watching Motorin when he went into the store, and after he left, its agents persuaded the owner to telephone Motorin and propose a deal. The owner told Motorin that he would give him the equipment in exchange for several cases of Russian vodka, which Motorin could buy at the Soviet embassy's living compound for about a third of its selling price in the U.S. When Motorin returned to the store with several cases, the FBI videotaped his actions and confronted him. It was against Soviet law for a diplomat to sell or trade discounted liquor overseas. The FBI threatened to tell the KGB what Motorin had done. At that point, he agreed to spy.

It was bitter cold and snowing when Sergei left Motorin's trial, but he didn't pay attention to the weather. "Motorin was a man with nice manners and an appealing personality," Sergei said later. "He had very important relatives in the Soviet bureaucracy who had arranged for him to join the KGB as a good career. But it was really not the life for him. He was naive, easily manipulated, and had a weak character." Rather than catching a bus or riding on the subway, Sergei walked several blocks in the cold to Lubyanka, where he had to attend a meeting. Sergei knew Motorin would soon face *vyshaya mera* (the highest measure of punishment). He would be taken into a room, made to kneel, then shot in the back of the head with a high-caliber handgun so his face would become unrecognizable because of the blast. His body would be dumped in an unmarked grave. His relatives would not be told where.

Sergei was invited to another foreign intelligence KGB dinner a short time later, and Kryuchkov announced at it that Motorin had been executed. Once again, the guests rose and began to clap.

Sergei stood and applauded, too.

"I had a feeling of human pity toward those who were executed, but at the same time, I sincerely thought their punishment was justified. I believed the Soviet system, despite all of its obvious drawbacks, was still the best in the world, and I couldn't understand why a patriotic citizen would turn his back on his motherland. To me, it was unimaginable."

EIGHT

Although Sergei disliked having a bureaucratic Communist Party job, he and Helen enjoyed its many perks, especially weekend Komsomol excursions. Most of these retreats were held in luxurious KGB-operated resorts near Moscow. Usually, the resorts were open only to the KGB's elite. The prices charged were symbolic. It cost less than five dollars for transportation, accommodations, and all meals. KGB Komsomol members and their families would perform in amateur musicals and plays. In the winter, they would have ice-carving contests, creating sculptures ten feet high and thirty feet long. Russian rock stars would be invited to entertain them. During summers, there would be campouts that attracted as many as 450 members. These were the KGB's up-and-coming foreign intelligence officers, and Sergei was their leader. They would socialize around campfires, perform skits, and sing. Just in case, Sergei always took a unit of Vympel soldiers with him for protection.

Vympel were KGB special forces, much like U.S. Navy SEALs. Although Vympel was not officially formed until 1982, its roots could be traced to December 1979, when a specialized KGB-trained unit assassinated Afghanistan president Hafizullah Amin in the Tajbeg Palace in Kabul. A few select commandos snuck into the palace and murdered him while he was being protected by two hundred bodyguards. Only one KGB soldier was killed and he was shot accidentally by one of his own comrades.

Sergei used his Vympel unit twice. Its soldiers knocked out a drunk Russian who was terrorizing the camp on his motorcycle. In another episode, a single Vympel officer tossed two local roughnecks into a river after they verbally abused a woman.

Because Sergei admired Vympel officers, he was surprised when he was told during a KGB Communist Party meeting that *dedovshina* was being practiced at the Vympel training center in the town of Balashikha-2. *Dedovshina* was the Soviet term used to describe bullying done to new soldiers. It was comparable to "hazing" in the U.S., but was much more brutal. When translated, the word literally meant "grandfather's rules of law." Party officials considered *dedovshina* a major morale problem in the Soviet military, and reports that it was commonplace at the elite KGB Vympel facility were especially embarrassing. As the KGB Komsomol leader in the First Chief Directorate, Sergei was ordered to investigate.

Sergei decided to conduct a surprise inspection. He arrived at the training base unannounced one night and entered several barracks. He discovered that Vympel soldiers were not bullying one another. Instead, *dedovshina* was being practiced by the six hundred regular army troops who provided support at the camp. They were responsible for cleaning Vympel military uniforms and equipment, policing the base, cooking, and other routine services. In one barrack, Sergei found a naked man sitting under a sun lamp that was scorching his skin. The conscript was being punished by older soldiers. In another, Sergei discovered a soldier tied to a metal bed frame that had been put onto a steam radiator, making the frame scalding hot. When Sergei entered a third barrack, tears welled in his eyes and he gasped. Older soldiers were harassing twenty new recruits by placing old wooden skis on a heater, filling the room with noxious fumes. "It was like a gas chamber." Sergei was told that soldiers frequently beat conscripts. Some had been struck so violently they were crippled for life.

Sergei promised the recruits that he would make certain the KGB's leadership heard about how they were being terrorized. But when he filed his report, it was Sergei who received a lecture, not the bullies.

"A vice admiral named Khmelyov, who was in charge of the training facility, invited me to have cognac and explained there was a military tradition at stake here. He said new soldiers were picked on for two years and then those who survived became the bullies and made those under them suffer. It helped make the troops tough. And then he said, 'These boys who are being abused, they are simply peasants. They are not sophisticated and they are not really valuable people. They are not humans to worry about.' "

Sergei was warned to stop complaining about *dedovshina*.*

*Apparently little in the Russian military has changed since Sergei's probe twenty years ago. In 2006, investigative journalist Anna Politkovskaya published *Putin's Russia,* a critical examination of life under President Vladimir Putin. Much of the

Sergei was told the KGB's leadership had more pressing problems in 1988 than bullying. The old Soviet system was under attack. In June, Secretary Gorbachev moved to reduce the Communist Party's stranglehold on the government. He pushed through changes that created the Congress of People's Deputies — a move that led to the first real elections ever held in the Soviet Union. By this time, General Kryuchkov had become chairman of the KGB, and while he rarely spoke out against Gorbachev in public, he privately opposed the democratic reforms beginning to take root. As a KGB Komsomol official, Sergei attended endless meetings at the Center and in Lubyanka where Gorbachev and his political reforms

---

book criticized the Russian army's practice of *dedovshina.* Politkovskaya accused the military of operating much like "a prison camp." Young soldiers were routinely brutalized in an "unaccountable system with hundreds of soldiers being wounded and killed each year because of *dedovshina.*" Although Politkovskaya's exposé was released in the West, no Russian publishers printed it. Politkovskaya was shot to death in October 2006 in the elevator of her apartment building by unknown gunmen after she wrote more stories critical of Putin and his government.

were hotly debated. Sergei had mixed feelings about them. As members of the *nomenklatura*, Sergei and Helen benefited from the system that Gorbachev wanted to reform. But they also saw daily how the *nomenklatura* rewarded loyalty and political connections over competence and productivity. In their minds, the KGB was above the party spoils system. Inside the First Chief Directorate, there was a saying: "A KGB officer must have clean hands, an ardent heart, and a cold and clear-minded head." Sergei believed that slogan — or he had before he became a Komsomol leader.

One afternoon he attended a speech that the deputy head of KGB personnel, Lieutenant General Vitali Ponomaryov, was delivering to a new class of recruits. "A KGB officer needs only a small bed to put his head on," Ponomaryov declared. "The joy and happiness that comes from serving in the KGB should be enough reward for your service."

Sergei knew Ponomaryov was a political hack. He also knew the KGB had provided Ponomaryov with a luxurious dacha in Zhukovka, a Moscow suburb popular with KGB generals and other *apparatchiki*. Boris Yeltsin had a summer house there, too.

Sergei and Helen had visited summer

houses in Zhukovka several times. They frequently were guests of Konstantin Mishchenko, whose father was an influential aide to the chairman of the KGB. The Mishchenko family's dacha, which was given to him by the KGB, reminded Sergei of the palaces that he had seen in France. It was a huge, ornate mansion complete with servants. During one weekend visit, Sergei and Helen rose early to go for a walk and as soon as they stepped outside, a groundskeeper raced up and immediately started to apologize. He had not had time to clear the driveway of a handful of leaves that had fallen during the night. The groundskeeper's hands were trembling.

Later, Sergei told Konstantin about the groundskeeper's fear. It was obvious that he was terrified of Konstantin's father, who, as Sergei put it, "could crush him and make both him and his family disappear because of a few fallen leaves."

Konstantin chuckled and said: "Do you ever wonder, Sergei, if these peasants will revolt again?"

That comment, coming after Sergei's investigation of *dedovshina,* left an uncomfortable taste in Sergei's mouth. "In public, these KGB generals and Communist Party officials spoke about the need for modesty and asceticism. They described themselves as 'servants of the people' and expressed compassion for peasants. But in private, the lives of ordinary Russians meant nothing to them."

Sergei and Helen talked about the hypocrisy. "We recognized it for what it was, but all of us in the KGB went along with the charade because we wanted those same rewards, we wanted the power to crush someone. We knew we were part of a corrupt system where the oppressors reaped the rewards. We were intentionally blind because someday we thought we would be the ones in those mansions."

After three years, Sergei's tenure in the Komsomol ended. In 1989, he was told that he and Helen were going to be sent overseas, to Ottawa, Canada. Sergei was finally going to get his chance to work as a KGB intelligence operative in a foreign post.

■ ■ ■ ■

PART TWO:
SPIES, BRIBES, AND
NUCLEAR BOMBS

■ ■ ■ ■

An army without secret agents is exactly like a man without eyes or ears.
— *Chia Lin, quoted by Sun Tzu,*
The Art of War

NINE

Sergei flew to Ottawa in January 1990, eager and excited. But his new post was hardly glamorous or welcoming. The Soviet Union's embassy in Ottawa was housed behind a tall iron fence in a rectangular building with an off-white stone facade on Charlotte Street near the banks of the Rideau River. It reminded Sergei of a dilapidated jail.

The KGB *rezident,* Leonid Ivanovich Ponomarenko, did not greet him warmly. Because Sergei was coming from a Komsomol job, Ponomarenko assumed Sergei was a political hack. He spoke to him briefly but didn't offer the new arrival any help or advice.

Sergei had worked in the Canadian department at the Center, so he already knew the only reason the KGB operated in Ottawa was to conduct operations against the U.S. At the end of the Second World War, the U.S. had been designated the "main adversary" by the Soviet military. Next in line came NATO and China. As a Line PR officer, Sergei's job was to collect political and military intelligence from Canadian sources that could be used to undermine those three enemies. No one cared about stealing Canada's national secrets.

Sergei didn't know anyone in Ottawa. He also didn't have any practical experience. So he decided to put the analytical skills that he had learned at NIIRP to work by delving into the dozens of intelligence reports that flowed endlessly into the *rezidentura* from public and private sources. Sergei was determined to outshine the other thirteen officers stationed in Ottawa. He was the first to arrive at work and the last to leave. During his first six weeks on the job, he set a record for sending intelligence cables to the Center. He averaged twelve per month, and all of them were based on tidbits that he had dug out of documents.

Not surprisingly, his peers didn't appreciate being shown up by a newcomer. Sergei didn't care. He dismissed their grumbling as jealousy. He didn't realize how bitter some of his colleagues were until he got caught in a trap.

One morning, he mentioned to Aleksandr

Fokin, a fellow Line PR officer, that he and Helen wanted to buy a Trinitron television but they had not yet saved enough money.

Fokin had lived in Canada for two years and was working undercover as the executive director of the Soviet-Canadian Friendship Society. That group was supposed to promote goodwill and cultural exchanges, but it actually was a front for the KGB. Sergei and Fokin had first met in Moscow, but they hadn't really liked each other. At the time, Fokin had been assigned to counterintelligence and his job was harassing and blackmailing Soviet scientists into spying on one another. Just the same, when Sergei and Helen first arrived in Ottawa, Fokin greeted them as if they were old friends. He offered to help them get settled and explained that in Canada, he was using the name Foshin, not Fokin, because he thought Fokin sounded too much like "fucking" when it was said in English. Sergei and Helen had laughed later about that.

"Why are you waiting to buy your television?" Fokin asked Sergei when he mentioned it. "I can help you." Fokin offered to loan him $1,400 from the Soviet-Canadian Friendship Society's checking account. "You can pay me back as soon as you save the money."

Sergei wasn't sure it was legal for him to take money from the KGB account, even if he did pay it back. But Fokin assured him that no one would complain. "People here do it all the time. I am like a friendly banker," he said. Sergei agreed, and that night he and Helen bought a television.

A few days later, Sergei received a message from a friend in Moscow who worked at the KGB Center warning him about Fokin and the loan. Fokin had filed a complaint about Sergei, accusing him of using KGB funds for his personal enrichment.

Although he was angry, Sergei decided not to confront Fokin. After all, he'd taken the KGB cash. Instead, he went to see the *rezident*. He told Ponomarenko everything and apologized for his naïvete. Ponomarenko had seen how hard Sergei worked. He also didn't like Fokin. The *rezident* said he would take care of any problems that Sergei might have because of the loan. Then he added, "I'm sure you are not the first Fokin victim." If Fokin had betrayed Sergei, then he probably was reporting on other officers, too.

Ponomarenko had access to all the correspondence that was sent between the Ottawa *rezidentura* and the Center in the diplomatic pouch, including private letters. He told Sergei that he wanted him to begin removing Fokin's letters and reading them before they went to Moscow.

Within a week, Sergei had found what he was after. Fokin had written a letter to the Center about Ponomarenko. The *rezident*'s wife was drawing a salary as a typist, but she didn't really work at the embassy.

Ponomarenko was enraged. "I'll destroy this cockroach, and you, Sergei, will help me!" he snapped. "We will get him."

Sergei began shadowing Fokin whenever he left the embassy. As director of the Friendship Society, Fokin met regularly with his Canadian sources and sent cables to the Center each week filled with information that he claimed to have gleaned from them. But Sergei noticed when he tailed him that Fokin rarely talked to anyone. Instead, he sat at a coffee shop and read newspapers. Sergei read the intelligence cables that Fokin was sending to the Center. As he had suspected, Fokin was writing reports based on what he was reading, not what anyone was telling him. "He didn't have any actual sources."

Sergei tipped off Ponomarenko. The *rezident* called Fokin into his office and handed him a tape recorder. "I want you to begin tape-recording all of your conversations," he said.

Fokin balked. His sources would be afraid to talk if they knew he was recording them. Ponomarenko gave him a miniature microphone so that he could run the tape without their knowing.

A few days later, a sheepish Fokin surrendered the recorder and microcassette. "Fokin could barely speak passable English and the tape showed the Canadians — who he did interview — barely knew who he was," Sergei said. "It was obvious Fokin had been putting into the mouth of these Canadians information that he was reading. Nevertheless, this information had been well received at the Center because it matched what they were also reading in press reports."

Ponomarenko had exposed Fokin, but he didn't tell the Center. As the *rezident,* he had signed off on Fokin's fictitious cables. Instead, Ponomarenko began sending negative performance evaluations about him to the Center. He accused Fokin of being incompetent and lazy. Ponomarenko did not show Fokin these critical reviews. He gave him fake evaluations that were glowing with praise.

"It was a classic KGB maneuver," Sergei recalled. "The Center was told that Fokin was an unscrupulous officer who must be not only recalled from Ottawa but expelled from the entire service, without receiving a pension. Meanwhile Fokin was personally being patted on his back." Not long after that, Fokin was called back to the Center and discharged from the KGB.

Their experiences with Fokin had caused Sergei and Ponomarenko to bond. The veteran *rezident* took him aside. "I will put you on skis," he told Sergei. "You are a good worker, so I will teach you how to produce."

Ponomarenko gave Sergei a list of names, all of them Canadians who worked for either the government or non-government agencies, called NGOs, that supplied information and services to it. None of the dozen people on the list had been successfully recruited as spies, but based on their past encounters with other KGB officers, they were considered promising targets.

"Be careful," Ponomarenko warned. He suspected that some of the Canadians had reported their earlier contacts with the KGB to the Canadian Security Intelligence Service (CSIS), which was responsible for protecting Canada's national security. "Canadian intelligence will be watching you closely, but if you can befriend any of these targets, perhaps you will get lucky and persuade them to help us."

Sergei eyed the list and said: "Comrade Ponomarenko, I will get more than one."

TEN

Sergei could not have chosen a better moment.

The Canadian Security Intelligence Service was only six years old when Sergei arrived in Ottawa. Its officers proved to be no match for the collective experience of the KGB. Canadians' attitudes about Soviets also were changing. The Kremlin's diplomats were being viewed with less suspicion because of Mikhail Gorbachev. On March 15, 1990, he was elected as the first-ever executive president of the Soviet Union, and he continued to push for improved relations with the West. The Berlin Wall had come down. Dramatic changes were sweeping across the old Soviet empire.

"Canadians were fascinated with Gorbachev," Sergei said later. "The Canadian Parliament wanted information about what was happening, and the best way to learn was by talking to Soviet diplomats. It cre-

143

ated opportunities for us."

Canada had a stormy past when it came to Soviet spying. For much of its history, Canadians hadn't believed they needed an intelligence service. But on September 5, 1945, Igor Gouzenko, a cipher clerk at the Soviet embassy in Ottawa, defected, bringing with him 109 top-secret documents. Those cables revealed that the Soviet Union had created an extensive spy ring inside Canada during World War II — a revelation that angered the nation. Russia had fought side by side with the Allies against Germany, and the Soviet Union had been seen as a friend. Gouzenko's cables showed Moscow had actually been conducting a secret campaign to undermine Canada, Britain, and the U.S. at the same time Soviet troops were fighting alongside their soldiers.

Gouzenko was the first important Soviet defector after the war, and historians would later credit his disclosures with helping spark the Cold War. Twenty Canadian spies were arrested. His defection also laid the groundwork for U.S. senator Joe McCarthy's witch hunts a few years later. Gouzenko would periodically appear on Canadian television after he defected, always hiding behind a paper mask shaped like a white KKK hood. He lived outside

Toronto until 1982, when he died at age sixty-three.

Gouzenko's revelations convinced Canadians they needed to be protected from spies. The Royal Canadian Mounted Police were assigned the task. From the start, it was a bad fit. Mounties were expected to investigate burglaries and issue traffic citations one day and shadow KGB operatives the next. The RCMP flubbed it. In the 1970s, its commanders created a separate, specially trained RCMP counterintelligence department to take over the task. Rather than going after foreign operatives, it began performing dirty tricks. The RCMP unit burglarized the headquarters of the prime minister's rivals and peppered it with listening devices. When the illegal bugging was exposed, the Canadian government tried to cover up the RCMP's wrongdoing. That scandal prompted the Canadian Parliament to strip the RCMP of all counterintelligence duties and create the CSIS as an independent agency. To make certain the CSIS didn't overstep its bounds, Canadians did not give its officers any police powers. They had to call in the RCMP to make arrests, just as the CIA has no police powers in the U.S. but must depend on the FBI.

From the moment Sergei was handed the

names of potential recruits, he decided the best way to fool the CSIS and RCMP was by operating in plain sight. He would not lurk in the shadows or pretend to be anything except what he was: a friendly Soviet diplomat who wanted to learn more about Canada.

Sergei contacted every person on the list. He answered their questions about Gorbachev and the changes happening in Moscow. In return, he asked them general questions about Canada. In the weeks that followed, Sergei gradually narrowed his list until he had pared it down to five promising Canadians. He invited them to lunch and to dinner. "I wanted them to become my friends — good friends — and over time, I genuinely came to like each of them personally," he recalled. "I knew Canadian intelligence was watching me, and my goal was to convince the Canadians that they had completely outsmarted me. If anyone was being recruited, it was me — at least that is what I wanted them to believe."

As best he could, Sergei put himself in his target's shoes. "What did they want? I needed to understand their desires so I could find a way to fill them."

Sergei found a common thread among the five. All of them felt patriotic toward

Canada, but none of them was pro-U.S. "It was my entryway. It is much easier to recruit someone if you are not asking them to harm their own nation. Their contempt for the U.S. opened the door."

Sergei got one of his targets to give him a list of commercial products that were going to be made available for sale to the Soviet Union in six months. These Western goods had previously been banned. They were part of an embargo that France, Germany, Great Britain, Italy, Japan, the U.S., and Canada had imposed against the Soviet Union. "This doesn't sound like a sexy secret, but because I was able to get this document in advance, our government had a six-month jump on what goods we would now be able to purchase."

That head start, Sergei later explained, had given the Kremlin a financial advantage. "If you have been forced for years to use only typewriters and you learned that in six months you could buy a computer, then you stop ordering typewriters and begin searching for the best computer deals. This list saved the Soviet Union millions of dollars."

Sergei's next stolen document caused an even bigger stir at the Center. It was about Canada's plans to replace its aging submarine fleet.

"The title of my cable to the Center was 'The Future of the Canadian Submarine Fleet.' It was single-spaced and eleven meters long [more than thirty-three feet] when I finished sending it."

No one in Ottawa had ever sent such a wordy cable to the Center, and one of his colleagues in Moscow warned Sergei a day later that he was in trouble for sending such a costly and frivolous report. "Everyone is laughing at you," he said. "They are questioning your mental stability." What had made Sergei think that the Center cared about Canada's submarine fleet?

For a week, the Center was completely silent about the cable. And then, finally, a diplomatic pouch arrived in Ottawa with a message addressed to the *rezident* about Comrade *Jean,* which was Sergei's KGB code name.

It was from Comrade *Spartac,* the code name for Major General Vyacheslav Trubnikov, a top official in the North American Department of the First Chief Directorate. He was one of the most feared generals in the KGB. Trubnikov had spent most of his career in India, Bangladesh, Nepal, and Pakistan, where he'd proved to be an incredibly productive operative, so much so that even his Western counterparts would later

148

describe him as one of the KGB's best.

"Comrade Jean has written a brilliant cable," Trubnikov declared. The general had recognized what others had missed. Even though the Canadian submarine force was Lilliputian, it played a pivotal role in the Cold War submarine cat-and-mouse games.

According to international law, Canada controlled huge sections of the Arctic region, including the famed Northwest Passage, the route from the Atlantic Ocean to the Pacific Ocean that runs through the Arctic archipelago of Canada. During a war, this underwater passageway would serve as the quickest northern route linking the oceans. There were two "choke points" in the passageway that all U.S. and Soviet submarines had to pass through. Even though the Canadian submarine fleet was small, it guarded and monitored these choke points.

There was more. The Soviet navy kept its biggest fleet of Typhoon-class submarines on patrol in the Arctic. The Typhoon was the world's largest submarine, capable of carrying twenty long-range ballistic missiles armed with a total of two hundred nuclear warheads. The submarines were extremely difficult to destroy because of their maneuverability, silence, and ability to hide in deep water for months. The shortest and fastest route for a Soviet nuclear missile strike against the U.S. was from Typhoons in the polar region. Consequently, the Soviet military was keenly interested in keeping its Typhoon fleet hidden from the U.S. and the Canadians.

In his cable, Sergei explained that the Canadian Parliament was trying to decide how to best update its submarine force. One proposal called for Canada to buy ten to twelve nuclear-powered submarines at a total cost of $8 billion. Another favored using less expensive hybrid submarines powered by a mix of diesel fuel and electricity. Sergei provided the Center with technical information in his cable about both types of submarines — information the Soviet military could use to protect itself from future detection.

Sergei had gotten information about the submarines under review from an arms control expert who worked for an NGO in Ottawa. The expert had given him information about each submarine's underwater capability, stealth, and firepower. The Canadians were negotiating with British and French submarine makers, manufacturers who didn't offer their products to the Soviets. The KGB could extrapolate and apply the technical data to the British and French fleets, since both of them used submarines that were manufactured in their own countries. Sergei's cable also identified which foreign nations had shown an interest in buying Canada's old submarines. Several of the potential buyers were hostile to the Soviet Union.

Sergei's source had given him performance reports, too. These military documents critiqued how well the Canadian navy was policing the Northwest Passage. They contained detailed information about the Arctic Subsurface Surveillance System — acoustic sensors (listening devices) that the U.S. and Canada had installed on the bottom of the seabed to detect and record what was happening around them. Sergei's cable contained statistics that showed where the underwater listening system was weak and often failed to register submarine movements.

"General Trubnikov wrote in his note that my cable was going to be used as an example of excellence for others," Sergei recalled. Word of Trubnikov's note spread quickly through the Ottawa *rezidentura*. Overnight, Comrade Jean's lengthy cable went from being the butt of a joke to being praised.

Sergei quickly followed his submarine cable with dozens and dozens more reports, filing some two hundred within his first year. *Rezident* Ponomarenko, who had become a close friend, proudly declared, "Sergei, you can now ski on your own. You are now the teacher!"

ELEVEN

Who were the Canadians recruited by Sergei in 1990?

According to U.S. intelligence officials, Sergei recruited five *trusted contacts* in Ottawa who provided him with stolen classified military and political information. To date, none has been arrested. The KGB assigned each a code name:

- **Code name: *ARTHUR*.** Sergei said he prepared more than a hundred cables based on information from ARTHUR. The KGB Center considered him an "extremely productive contact." ARTHUR was working as a nuclear weapons expert at the Canadian Centre for Arms Control and Disarmament in Ottawa when he was recruited. He was one of three employees there who spied for the KGB. The Canadian Centre was a private, nonprofit organi-

153

zation established in 1983 to study arms control policies and to promote world peace. It was funded by donations from Canadian philanthropic groups.

- **Code name: *ILYA*.** He was a Canadian government arms control specialist who gave Sergei military reports that described methods Canada and the U.S. used to track Soviet Typhoon submarines in the Arctic. The Soviet Navy was constantly searching for "sanctuary zones" — undersea hiding places where its submarines could avoid detection. Many of these spots were in underwater crevices, similar to fjords, that a submarine could slip into and disappear. "ILYA provided us with classified documents that explained how the Canadians and the Americans were working together to identify sanctuary zones and mark them with underwater listening devices."

- **Code name: *SEMION*.** When recruited, SEMION worked for the Ministry of Northern Affairs and Indians, a branch of the Canadian government. He provided Sergei with information about U.S. activities in the Arctic. The Arctic covers an enormous area — more than one-sixth of the earth's landmass — and despite its often hostile climate, some four million people live there, including more than thirty different indigenous tribes. As part of Gorbachev's democratization efforts, the Kremlin agreed to participate in international meetings about the region. Most of them dealt with protecting the Arctic environment and monitoring land development. "SEMION was our eyes and ears in the Canadian delegation at these talks. He would tell us what the U.S. was planning to do. Our experts would then look for ways to exploit our differences with the U.S. and disrupt whatever the U.S. was trying to promote. Our goal was always to drive a wedge between the U.S. and other Arctic nations. We used SEMION as our shill."

Canada, Denmark, Finland, Iceland, Norway, Sweden, the U.S., and Russia eventually agreed to form an international legislative body called the Arctic Council to oversee issues that affected the region. The KGB used SEMION to undermine U.S.-backed proposals when that group's governing rules were being drafted.

- **Code name: *LAZAR*.** This was a coworker of ARTHUR's at the Canadian arms control and disarmament center in Ottawa. "He had an excellent relationship with members of the Canadian Parliament." LAZAR's expertise was in international environmental law, and the KGB used him whenever it could to cause headaches for the U.S. "The Center in Moscow provided LAZAR with scientific information that was specifically written to disrupt relations between Canada and the U.S. over environmental issues. LAZAR would deliver these anti-U.S. reports to his political connections in the Canadian Parliament. They, in turn, would cite them when drafting legislation about environmental concerns. LAZAR never believed he was committing treason against Canada. He thought he was protecting the Canada environment and helping the Soviet Union at the same time. This was because we were able to meld his interest in the environment with our desire to disrupt relations between the U.S. and Canada."

Although Sergei handled LAZAR, he was not credited by Moscow with recruiting him as a trusted contact. A KGB *rezident* in Ottawa during the 1980s, Sergei Aleksandrovich Labur, had already turned LAZAR into a spy — or, at least, that is what the Center believed. After Sergei and LAZAR became friends, Sergei asked him about Labur, and LAZAR said he had never spoken to him.

"This was what I called an 'Agatha Christie' recruitment," Sergei said later. "I call them this because they were the products of a KGB officer's imagination."

Every KGB foreign intelligence officer was expected to develop trusted contacts, but most had trouble recruiting spies. "LAZAR was an example of a fake recruitment by Labur, similar to the trick that Aleksandr Fokin had pulled where he was sending back 'intelligence' that he'd read in newspapers. Labur was putting his own words into LAZAR's mouth and LAZAR had no idea that he was being used this way."

Sergei did not tell the Center that Labur had lied about his relationship with LAZAR. By this point, Labur had become a KGB general and he would eventually be named the head of the First Chief Directorate's First Department, overseeing all North American KGB operations. "He was powerful, but I knew his secret."

Of Sergei's five trusted contacts, the most important was given the code name *KIRILL*. His KGB moniker would later be changed to *KABAN* to provide him with an even thicker layer of cover. KIRILL was the third employee who worked at the Canadian Centre with ARTHUR and LAZAR.

"My superiors referred to KIRILL, ARTHUR, and LAZAR as 'the bridge' because they became so important. When a Russian officer can obtain intelligence from several sources in the same city, it means he had created a network, and that is the highest, the best, that an officer can do. It was considered a tremendous achievement."

Trained as a political scientist, KIRILL had first been noticed by the KGB when he became embroiled in a political scandal. In the early 1980s, KIRILL had worked for Prime Minister Pierre Trudeau in a clandestine program called Op Watch, which stood for "Opposition Watch." Trudeau's most trusted advisers had created Op Watch to dig up dirt on his political enemies to discredit them. Much as in the U.S., two major political parties traditionally have controlled Canada. For decades, the Liberal Party was in charge, but in 1957, the Progressive Conservative Party won a majority.

Since then, the two sides have traded the prime minister post and seats in Parliament.

Trudeau was a member of the Liberal Party, and one of Op Watch's first targets was Brian Mulroney, a rival member of the Progressive Conservatives. Op Watch began snooping into his past when he was elected leader of the conservatives in June 1983. At the time, Mulroney was unusual in Canadian politics because he was a former businessman, not a professional politician. Op Watch learned Mulroney had benefited from a sweetheart deal with his former employer, a mining company with U.S. ties, before he entered politics. The company had sold him a million-dollar home for a dollar. Although there was nothing illegal about the transaction, Mulroney had not revealed it to voters, and when Op Watch tipped off a Montreal newspaper, the public lambasted him.

A short time later, a reporter at the *Toronto Globe* revealed that Trudeau was using Op Watch to smear his opponents. Trudeau came under fire, Op Watch was disbanded, and its employees were reassigned to other government jobs.

When Trudeau retired in 1984, Mulroney became prime minister and took revenge on the government employees who had participated in Op Watch, including KIRILL, who lost his job.

"The KGB had targeted KIRILL for recruitment when Trudeau was in office because the Center believed he was an up-and-coming Canadian political figure," Sergei said later, "but after he was kicked bare-ass on the asphalt by Mulroney, his career and usefulness appeared to be over. The Center lost interest, but when I approached him, I discovered he still had many important connections in the Liberal Party."

Sergei found KIRILL to be an eager spy. It was KIRILL who provided Sergei with classified military information about the government's plans to replace its aging Canadian submarine fleet. He'd gotten it from his politically connected friends in Parliament. In addition, Sergei used KIRILL to obtain copies of RAND Corporation studies that were supposed to be for Canadian and American eyes only. The KGB Center was especially interested in RAND military assessments written by James L. Lacy, an American naval expert. At one point, the KGB sent Sergei to a military conference because Lacy was scheduled to speak. Sergei approached him, but Lacy showed no interest in talking with him.

"My superiors at the Center were over-joyed that my five Canadian trusted contacts had access to information about the Arctic," Sergei later explained. "When Americans think about this region, they visualize ice, polar bears, and penguins. But for the Soviet military, it was a crucial area because our Typhoon-class submarines were concentrated in sanctuary zones there and they were the strongest arm of the Soviet triad, which included land-based and airborne missiles. For Russians, the Arctic was much, much more than polar bears."

Sergei would later describe how he recruited the Canadian spies. "In the beginning, they had no idea they were going to be used as spies. They thought they were simply sharing information with their Soviet friend — Sergei — thinking they were contributing to the international debate about politics, disarmament, and the environment. But all of them were soon accepting with great pleasure expensive lunches, dinners, and gifts, and over time they each felt comfortable enough to provide me with classified military and political information, knowing fully that I was sending it back to the Center."

All of Sergei's spies worked in jobs that required them to tell the RCMP about any conversations they had with foreign officials. "I knew this law and *I* was the one who urged them to do exactly that," Sergei said later. "I wanted them to tell the RCMP we were talking because I didn't want the Mounties to think we had anything to hide. And it worked beautifully. The RCMP and CSIS assumed they were on top of the situation because my sources were reporting our meetings to them, when, in fact, I was obtaining information from my trusted contacts right under the RCMP's noses."

Was it possible that ARTHUR, ILYA, SEMION, LAZAR, and KIRILL were double agents? "The type of sensitive information I was receiving — both political and military — from each of them was too valuable to be used in such a game," Sergei said later. "It was not the sort of information Canadian intelligence wanted the Soviet Union to have."

In addition to his five trusted contacts, Sergei developed more than a hundred sources in Ottawa during his stint there, but they were *information contacts:* diplomats, journalists, college professors, and public officials who simply answered questions that he posed, oftentimes about Canadian politics. Nothing these sources said was thought to have harmed either Canada or the U.S.

In January 1991, Sergei finished his first year in Ottawa and it was time for him to take his annual home leave. Every KGB foreign intelligence officer was entitled to return to Moscow at the KGB's expense once a year. Moments after Sergei and Helen landed at Moscow's Sheremetyevo Airport, Sergei hurried to the Center. He had been told that General Trubnikov wanted to see him as soon as possible. Trubnikov was the general who had written him a complimentary note about the Canadian submarine cable, but Sergei had not heard from him since and he had no idea why he was being summoned to the Center. He was nervous.

Trubnikov greeted him warmly, asked a few general questions about the Ottawa *rezidentura,* and then wished him a pleasant holiday. There was no hint of an emergency. Two weeks later, however, Sergei received a panicked call from a Trubnikov aide ordering him to report back to the Center.

Sergei raced to the perimeter of the Center in a taxi. Cabs were not allowed to enter a two-mile-wide buffer zone between the outer gate and the main KGB building, so Sergei ran the distance on foot and arrived sweating, breathing heavily, and clearly worried. He went to the fifth floor without changing his shirt and was whisked in to see the general.

"Have I ever asked you to destroy the Canadian federation?" Trubnikov asked.

"What do you mean?" Sergei stammered.

"Did I instruct you to encourage the breakup of Canada into two pieces, one French- and the other English-speaking?"

"No, I don't remember you ever giving me that assignment."

Trubnikov handed Sergei a sheet of paper to read. It was a letter of complaint that had been delivered to the Center by Alexander Nikolaevich Yakovlev, the Soviet Union's former ambassador to Canada. Ambassador Yakovlev had served in Ottawa between 1973 and 1983, before returning to Moscow, where he had become a close adviser to Gorbachev and had emerged in the Soviet Politburo as a driving force for *glasnost* and *perestroika*.

"We are worried about the activities of Sergei Tretyakov, second secretary at the Soviet Union's Ottawa embassy," the letter stated. It had been written by a group called the Soviet-Canadian Friendship Society. The letter explained that Canadian intelligence had identified Sergei as a KGB officer and had discovered that his assignment in Ottawa was "to destroy the Canadian federation" by instigating dissent between French- and English-speaking Canadians. The letter asked Ambassador Yakovlev to use his political influence to "facilitate the removal of Mr. Sergei Tretyakov from his KGB post in Canada and return him to Moscow." Ambassador Yakovlev had forwarded the complaint to KGB chairman Vladimir Kryuchkov, who, in turn, had passed a copy to General Trubnikov.

Sergei was stunned. Ambassador Yakovlev was one of the Soviet Union's most influential Politburo members.

"What do you think of this letter?" Trubnikov asked him.

"It's bullshit!" Sergei replied. "The Canadians are upset because I am doing my job."

Trubnikov handed Sergei a second letter. It was a handwritten response from General Kryuchkov to Ambassador Yakovlev, and it was several pages long. In his reply, Kryuchkov defended Sergei and accused the Canadians of trying to oust him because he was an effective KGB operative. After Sergei read that note, Trubnikov gave him another letter. It was a revision that Kryuchkov had made of his first draft. Trubnikov then gave Sergei a copy of the final, edited note that Kryuchkov had actually sent to Ambassador Yakovlev. It simply said: "Comrade Yakovlev, please don't pay attention to this complaint. It is a provocation by Canada against an active KGB officer."

"Are you afraid to return to Canada?" Trubnikov asked.

"No, but I promise you that because of that complaint, I will be a hundred times more active."

"Well, when you return, please remember to add to your list of duties the destruction of the Canadian federation," Trubnikov replied. Then he laughed and told Sergei that he could finish out the rest of his vacation.

TWELVE

Two months after Sergei returned to Ottawa from his home leave in Moscow, one of his colleagues didn't report to work. A security officer found a handwritten note that Anatoli Gayduk had left in his apartment that said he and his wife, Larisa, had defected. Larisa had been the physician at the Soviet embassy and had been well liked. Her husband had not been.

Rezident Ponomarenko ordered an immediate damage assessment. Gayduk had worked for Line X, which was responsible for stealing scientific and technological information. Every cable Gayduk had written in Ottawa and every document he might have read was examined. His colleagues and their families were questioned. Sergei felt certain Gayduk didn't know about his five trusted contacts. The only person who knew their identities was Ponomarenko. Even so, there was always a chance that Gayduk might have inadvertently overheard or seen something.

After a painstaking investigation, Ponomarenko decided Gayduk's defection had caused zero intelligence damage. Of course, Gayduk had known the *rezidentura's* daily routine and could identify which KGB officers were posing as diplomats. But he hadn't had any access to any meaningful secrets.

Sergei had become a close confidant of Ponomarenko's and the veteran *rezident* predicted trouble. "Someone must be punished," he explained. "It is the KGB way." He suspected the generals at the Center would accuse him of poor management, even though he had inherited Gayduk from a predecessor. Gayduk's peers also would be criticized. "The Center will ask: 'How could you sit next to him and not know?'"

Ponomarenko thought the Canadians also might cause a fuss. "They could expel all of us," he fretted. Being declared persona non grata and booted from a foreign country was deadly to a KGB officer's career, because it meant he had been exposed in the West. It would be difficult for him to work anywhere outside the Soviet Union again.

That night, Sergei told Helen: "Buy whatever Western goods you need as quickly as you can and pack our bags." For the next several days, they waited anxiously along with their colleagues. A month passed without incident and then Ponomarenko called Sergei into his office. The Soviet-Canadian Friendship Society had sent another letter to former Canadian ambassador Yakovlev in Moscow asking that Sergei be sent home. As before, Yakovlev had passed the letter to KGB chairman Kryuchkov. "There is tremendous pressure on the Center by Yakovlev to appease his Canadian friends," Ponomarenko warned. "I am sure, my friend, you are going home soon, but please don't worry. You will receive my highest recommendations." A worried Sergei told Helen that their fate seemed sealed.

Two months later, in June 1991, Ponomarenko summoned Sergei into his office again. The Center had sent him a private cable. "They've made a decision," he declared, thrusting the message forward. It was addressed to Comrade *Petr,* which was Ponomarenko's code name.

Sergei read it quickly. It said that Comrade *Petr* — not Sergei — was being recalled. The Center had given Ponomarenko two weeks. He was told that Sergei would immediately assume all of his duties. Ponomarenko was instructed to hand over all secret codes to Sergei, including his "belt code" — a special code that *rezidents* were required to carry with them at all times for use during emergencies. (It was called a "belt code" because it was normally hidden inside the lining of the *rezident's* belt.)

Instead of being kicked out of Ottawa, Sergei had been promoted to acting *rezident*. At age thirty-five, he was the youngest KGB officer ever to take charge of a Canadian *rezidentura*.

News of his promotion did not sit well with KGB officers who had more experience and seniority, nor with the ambassador, Aleksandr Belonogov. "Belonogov felt I was too young and inexperienced," Sergei recalled, "but that was an excuse. The truth was that he absolutely hated the KGB and me."

Early in his diplomatic career, Belonogov had been forced by the KGB to snitch on his colleagues at the Soviet Ministry of Foreign Affairs. He had been a "co-optee" and had deeply resented it. He and Sergei had butted heads from the moment Sergei came to Canada.

"He knew the Canadians wanted me out and I knew that Ambassador Belonogov wanted me gone, so I immediately set out to neutralize him."

Sergei convinced Vladimir Seleznev, who was Belonogov's personal code clerk, to slip him copies of every message Belonogov sent to Moscow. "I was reading about his every move without him knowing. This way I could counter it with cables of my own to the Center."

Infighting between the KGB and the Soviet diplomatic corps had escalated in many embassies, Sergei later explained, because of Gorbachev and his democratic reforms. "These diplomats were not as afraid of the KGB or of the party."

Ambassador Belonogov soon got his chance to attack Sergei. An official from the Canadian Ministry of Foreign Affairs delivered a "non paper" complaint about Sergei to the embassy. "Non papers" were letters from one government to another that were delivered but not signed. This made them unofficial communications. They were used to resolve issues informally. As soon as Belonogov read the non paper, he summoned Sergei and showed it to him.

"We appreciate the great breakthroughs in cooperation that our two nations have made in recent years," the non paper letter stated. "However, there are still some points that continue to impede our mutual interests and harm bilateral dialogue, including the excessive use of Soviet intelligence in Canada. . . . We expect the Soviet government to take our point of view seriously and reduce foreign intelligence in Ottawa. . . ." The non paper then specifically identified Sergei Tretyakov as an "active KGB officer posing as a diplomat," and it asked that he be recalled to Moscow to avoid "future embarrassment."

Ambassador Belonogov was beaming by the time Sergei finished reading.

"Sergei, your time is over," he declared. "You see, we are becoming a democratic society and the KGB is in the past."

"Comrade Ambassador," Sergei replied in a somber voice, "let's not rush history."

Belonogov forwarded the Canadian non paper to Moscow. A short while later, he received a reply: "Do not react to Canadian hysteria." There was no mention of recalling Sergei.

What Belonogov didn't know was that Sergei had already undermined his credibility. "I had secretly investigated him and had discovered Belonogov was accepting valuable gifts from foreigners — other ambassadors and diplomats — and he was selling them in Ottawa for cash. This was illegal. But because of his political power —

all ambassadors are sort of untouchable —
I knew he would never be prosecuted. Still,
I used this evidence to ruin his reputation
at the Center, and I convinced the generals
there that Ambassador Belonogov was a
Canadian puppet who was acting in his own
best interests — not the KGB's. They didn't
pay attention to him or the Canadians' complaint."

That first "non paper" was followed by
thirteen hand-delivered complaints during
the next two years. All of them asked that
Sergei be replaced. It was a record. In
Sergei's mind, the unsigned letters proved
he was doing an effective job.

THIRTEEN

Because Helen had grown up in Poland as the daughter of a diplomat and later traveled across Europe as an economist working for the Soviet Ministry of Foreign Trade (MFT), she had no problem adapting to Canadian culture. For her, the most difficult change in Ottawa had been giving up her career. In Moscow, Helen had steadily risen through the MFT ranks and become a senior economist, while Sergei was slogging his way through the NIIRP and Komsomol. The move to Canada forced her to resign and relegated her to pedestrian overseas assignments. She was hired as a clerk at the embassy press office, but that actually was a cover assignment. Secretly, she became a KGB employee with the code name Comrade *Clara*.

From 9 a.m. until noon each day, Helen worked inside a closet-size room on the third floor of the embassy, where she listened to tape recordings. The conversations had been plucked from the airwaves by Line RP officers who used antennas on the embassy's roof to randomly sweep a several-mile swath in search of promising telephone calls. "It was tedious work," Helen said later. Most recordings were meaningless chatter by ordinary Canadians who had no idea their conversations were being overheard. Only once did Helen hear something promising. A U.S. military officer was recorded talking to a secretary in Europe at NATO. Helen flagged the conversation and Line RP officers zeroed in on the frequency and later recorded several more overseas calls by the officer, but they were about his expense reports and he never revealed any useful secrets.

Helen spent her afternoons in the embassy's press office, where she mailed out propaganda, mostly KGB-prepared publications that were disguised as factual research and sent to university libraries and organizations that had shown an interest in Russian affairs.

Because she spoke Russian, French, and English, Helen eventually worked as a receptionist at the embassy, but none of her jobs was as interesting or as satisfying as her economic studies had been. Her focus shifted in Canada to taking care of Ksenia, who was nine years old in 1990, and to supporting Sergei's KGB career. She regularly attended diplomatic functions and, when asked, hosted private dinners in their apartment.

"I had to begin looking at myself from a much different angle in Canada," Helen later noted. She was now "Sergei's wife" and "Ksenia's mother." As a graduate of the Institute of International Relations, Helen had been schooled in diplomatic courtesies, and she moved easily in the diplomatic community. "If there was a possibility that a person I met was a foreign counterintelligence officer and I was introduced to him or his wife, of course I would drop this contact. But that rule was no different for clean diplomats and their wives."

Neither Sergei nor Helen ever felt their family was in danger. "There was an unwritten understanding that neither side bothered the other's spouses or their children," Sergei said. Helen believed it. "My husband had diplomatic immunity, so the worst thing that could happen to him was that Canadian authorities would ask Sergei to leave within twenty-four hours. Not a pleasant thing to do, but not really a tragedy."

The only role Helen played in helping

Sergei's KGB recruitment efforts was hosting dinner parties for his Canadian spies. "I was introduced to all of his sources and their families, and I did my best to develop really good friendships with them. We celebrated holidays together and I felt absolutely at ease. I knew they were helping Sergei, but that was not my concern."

Sergei, Helen, and their daughter followed several commonsense rules. "You did not panic. You did not become paranoid. You did not let fear destroy your morale," Helen later explained. "You were always careful and cautious and you always thought before you took any actions. Mostly, you realized there were secrets to be kept."

Not long after the family settled in Ottawa, Ksenia mentioned that one of her Russian friends had shown an unusual interest in Helen's job at the embassy.

"Your mother comes into the embassy every morning and then disappears for several hours before she goes to the press office," the child had volunteered. "Why does she go in so early?"

Sergei and Helen suspected the girl had overheard her parents talking about Helen. Without hesitating, Ksenia had replied: "My mother has a lot of girlfriends and she visits them because she feels lonely at home."

Helen was thrilled that her daughter had been shrewd enough to handle the question without revealing any family secrets.

It wasn't fear of outsiders that complicated Helen's life. It was the daily dramas of working inside an overseas embassy and the familiarity of its employees. "My husband was a high-ranking intelligence officer, so I had to constantly analyze my behavior. You must never seem snobbish or rude or unsociable, otherwise people can start plotting against you, which can affect your husband's work. You must keep in mind that clean diplomats' wives are usually not eager to be friends with KGB wives, and you must keep a certain distance and not become sentimental or best friends with them or really anyone. This was not difficult for me because, first of all, my husband was my best friend and my second-best friend was my daughter. But I know that some wives had trouble accepting this."

Like most workplaces, the embassy was riddled with gossip, and because of Sergei's job, he was informed of every scandal and was dragged unwillingly into many. One weekend, the embassy's security officer was stopped late one night returning from a party. He and his wife were drunk and became so belligerent with the Canadian police that officers sprayed them with pepper gas. When the embassy's duty officer arrived to resolve the matter, he also was so intoxicated that he fell out of his car. In another incident, a code clerk returned home from a late-night fishing trip and left a large catfish on the kitchen floor before going to bed. His wife went into the kitchen, saw the still-alive fish flopping, and tried to kill it by smashing its head with her bare foot. The blow tore a huge gash in her foot, and because code clerks and their spouses didn't speak English, someone had to race them to an emergency room. Sergei got a panicked call. Such was their life.

Living in Canada was the toughest on Ksenia. Most other parents enrolled their children in the Russian embassy school or English-speaking public schools, but Helen chose a French-speaking elementary school because she wanted Ksenia to learn French and Canadian culture. The Canadian children didn't welcome the new Russian intruder, especially when she arrived wearing the wrong-style clothes and shoes. Helen bought her tearful daughter five different pairs of sneakers before she found the right one. Even though Ksenia was attending a school with a good reputation, Helen felt the classroom assignments and pace were too simple. She had Sergei's mother send her the materials that Ksenia would have been studying in a Moscow school, and each day after Ksenia returned home from her Canadian school, her mother taught her from the Russian textbooks.

"We lived in a suspended state of mind," Helen said later. "When you live overseas, everything is temporary. In Canada and in the U.S., we had ridiculously small and poorly furnished apartments. Sergei could have had something considerably bigger and nicer because of his position, but he was too modest to spend an extra penny from the KGB for himself, and he used to repeat the same thing to me and Ksenia: 'Girls, be patient. This is all temporary. Our home is in Moscow.'"

FOURTEEN

The center sent word in mid-1991 that a special delegation from Moscow headed by Anatoli Kulakov would soon be arriving in Ottawa. Kulakov was the chairman of a commission created by Secretary Gorbachev to investigate ways the Soviet Union could convert its military industries into civilian factories. Sergei was told to introduce Kulakov to Canadian business leaders and tell the Center about his contacts.

The Center said two Soviet businessmen would be traveling with Kulakov. Vladimir B. Dmitriev was president of the newly formed International Chetek Corporation of Moscow, and Dr. Aleksandr K. Chernyshev was a department head at Arzamas 16, the formerly top-secret Soviet nuclear bomb–design laboratory. Sergei was ordered to watch them, too.

Private corporations in Moscow were rare in 1991 and the ones that were permitted were tied in some way to the Soviet government. Sergei discovered the Chetek corporation was being funded by three Soviet agencies: the Soviet Military-Industrial Commission (VPK), the State Planning Committee (GOSPLAN), and the Ministry for Atomic Power and Industry. The VPK coordinated and controlled all research, design, development, and production of military equipment and systems. GOSPLAN formulated five-year defense plans for the Soviet military. The atomic power ministry oversaw all nuclear bomb testing. These three bureaucracies had formed Chetek to raise money privately because the Soviet treasury had cut back on their funding. While investigating Chetek, Sergei noticed a familiar name. One of the corporation's top executives was Aleksandr Fokin, the former KGB officer in Ottawa who had pretended to be his friend while sending negative reports about him and Ponomarenko to Moscow.

"When I saw Fokin's name, I became extremely nervous," Sergei said, "because I knew Fokin was a lowlife."

Sergei asked the Canadian Centre for Arms Control and Disarmament to arrange meetings between the Soviet delegation and Canadian business leaders. He wanted the center involved because its members fraternized with the Canada-USSR Business Council, a group that had been formed specifically to help the Soviets convert their military factories.

Sergei also wanted the center's help because his spies — ARTHUR, LAZAR, and KIRILL — worked there. "This meant I had all possible sides covered. I would know what the Moscow delegation was doing because I would be escorting them in Ottawa. I would know from the Canadian side what was happening because my three trusted contacts would tell me."

Sergei met the Moscow delegation at a restaurant inside the downtown Marriott Hotel in Ottawa after their flight landed. He told them that he had already secured a meeting for them with a top executive from a Canadian communications company at eight o'clock the next morning in the hotel's Toulouse Bistro. He then spent several hours answering their questions about Ottawa. At that point, the two Chetek executives went to bed, leaving Sergei and Kulakov alone. Sergei had noticed that Kulakov was toting a large briefcase with him — even when he excused himself to go to the men's room. Curious, he asked him what was in the case.

Patting it, Kulakov whispered: "I am holding the financial salvation of our nation." But he refused to elaborate. Several drinks later, Kulakov offered to show Sergei some of the case's contents. He carefully opened it, revealing a number of thick files. "Kulakov told me the case contained exactly one hundred top-secret documents," Sergei recalled. "He said they contained detailed information about Soviet technology developed by our very best scientists. Kulakov said Gorbachev had authorized his commission to sell this technology to the West for millions of dollars to help save the Soviet economy."

Sergei was surprised. "I must have had a look of total disbelief on my face because, at that point, Kulakov reached inside the case and removed several pages for me to examine. I could see where the words *Top Secret* had been covered with Wite-Out."

The document that Kulakov flashed contained drawings of an electrical device used on a Soviet nuclear submarine. "I said to Kulakov, 'How can you be selling military secrets?' And he immediately snatched back the document, closed the case, and said, 'Comrade, when the Canadians see this, just wait, they have spent years trying to learn our military secrets and now that we are an open country, they will pay millions and millions for them. It will be a great thing for us and our economy.' "

Kulakov said that one of the reports in his case described how to manufacture semiconductors in a completely sterile environment. Kulakov had decided it was the document that he would show the Canadian communications official in the morning.

Sergei arrived at 7:45 a.m. and introduced himself to the Canadian businessman who was waiting in the lobby. They moved to the coffee shop. A half-hour later, they were still waiting for the others. Sergei went to find them. Kulakov answered the door half-asleep and still in his pajamas. The two others were asleep, too. It took them another half-hour before they were ready.

"This was a business meeting, so I ordered only orange juice and our guest had coffee, but these three pigs ordered pancakes, eggs, bacon until the entire table was covered. They kept our guest waiting while they gorged themselves."

Finally, Kulakov opened his case and took out the semiconductor drawings. Kulakov spoke only Russian, so Sergei translated. "Kulakov was explaining how semiconductors had to be made in a completely sterile environment and how Soviet scientists had developed a top-secret method for making them inside a glass tube to keep them sterile," Sergei recalled. The Canadian suddenly interrupted the pitch. "This businessman tells me that the technology Kulakov is showing him had already been tried and discarded at least twenty-five years earlier. He said the Japanese had perfected clean rooms where workers wore space suit garments to make semiconductors."

Sergei translated his comments. "Kulakov was completely bewildered and he frantically began rummaging through his case, pulling out sheet after sheet of papers that were twenty-five years old and were completely worthless." Meanwhile, the two executives from the Chetek corporation continued eating. "I thought, What kind of morons are these?" Years later, the Canadian executive who attended that meeting would verify Sergei's account, but would ask that his name not be cited in this book.

The businessman left the hotel empty-handed, and Sergei sent a cable to the Center describing what had happened. That night, he invited Dmitriev, the president of Chetek, to dinner. The Center had asked him to investigate what sort of technology Chetek hoped to sell in the West.

"I flattered Dmitriev," Sergei said later,

"making his ego grow bigger and bigger, until he proceeded to tell me about his company's ultimate moneymaking scheme."

Dmitriev said Chetek was going to earn millions by offering to destroy chemical wastes from foreign nations. It planned to get rid of them on the Arctic island of Novaya Zemlya, where the Soviets had tested their nuclear weapons. The company planned to drill five thousand holes, each 2.4 meters (eight feet) in diameter and 300 meters deep (984.24 feet). Nuclear and other chemical wastes would be lowered into each hole. After they were filled, a single 50-kiloton nuclear bomb would be lowered into another 300-meter-deep hole drilled in the exact center of the cluster. Chetek would then detonate the bomb. Soviet scientists theorized a nuclear blast would melt all the surrounding holes and fifty thousand tons of rock, completely vaporizing the wastes while creating a huge crater.

In addition to getting rid of chemical wastes, Chetek hoped to use that same procedure to rid the Soviet Union of some thirty thousand nuclear weapons that it had promised the U.S. it would destroy. "Fifteen to thirty nuclear bomb blasts should be sufficient to get rid of all our old weapons,"

Dmitriev predicted.

Chetek was already negotiating to buy a second disposal site in south-central Siberia near the city of Dodonovo. It was home to three nuclear reactors, and they needed an inexpensive way to destroy their nuclear wastes.

Sergei wanted to make certain that he understood what Dmitriev had just explained.

"Comrade," he said, "did you just say you are planning on detonating nuclear bombs to destroy chemical wastes?"

Dmitriev nodded, indicating yes. Continuing, he said Chetek would charge $300 to $1,200 a kilogram to vaporize toxic materials. "We will all become rich," he declared. Dropping his voice, Dmitriev then added a juicy tidbit. The scientists who were financing Chetek had given him a nuclear bomb as payment for his services because none of the governmental agencies involved in Chetek could afford to pay him a salary. He kept the bomb in a shed at his dacha outside Moscow and was trying to decide how to sell it.

Sergei thought he was joking. His entire scheme sounded insane. "I said, 'Are you serious? Brother, are you telling me you have your own nuclear bomb?' And Dmitriev laughed and said, 'Don't be so naive. With economic conditions the way they are in Russia today, anyone with enough money can buy a nuclear bomb. It's no big deal really.' "

Sergei drove directly to the *rezidentura* after their dinner and sent a cable to the Center describing Chetek's plans and how Dmitriev had claimed to have his own personal nuclear bomb. Sergei received a coded reply a few hours later. Chetek was being supported by "persons of influence" in Moscow, the cable warned. Because of this, Sergei was not to interfere directly with the company or its plans. However, he was instructed to tell Kulakov that he needed to distance himself from the two Chetek executives because he was an official Soviet representative sent to Ottawa by Gorbachev. Sergei was instructed to tell Kulakov that he needed to make it clear in his conversations with Canadian reporters that he had nothing to do with Dmitriev and Chetek.

Sergei read between the lines. The KGB officially could not interfere with Chetek, but the generals at the Center were obviously nervous about its plans.

Sergei met Dmitriev for breakfast that morning and, in a calculated move, told him that Chetek's idea was "brilliant." He urged him to talk openly about the nuclear bomb venture in his meetings with Canadians that day. Dmitriev took his advice when he briefed executives from the Canadian disarmament center. They were horrified and immediately backed out of their promise to introduce Dmitriev to potential Canadian investors. Acting on orders from Moscow, Kulakov also severed his ties with the two Chetek businessmen. The delegation returned to Moscow embarrassed and empty-handed.

But that was not the end of Chetek.

A short while later, the corporation released a promotional brochure in Moscow that cited the Canadian trip as a huge success and claimed the Canadian disarmament center had "discussed and approved" its plans. Viktor N. Mikhailov, the Soviet deputy minister of atomic energy and industry, sent the company's brochure along with a formal letter to the United Nations. Mikhailov asked the UN to endorse Chetek's plan to use nuclear bombs to eliminate wastes.

When Sergei learned that Chetek was claiming the Canadian Centre had endorsed its plan, he tipped off Tariq Rauf, one of the center's senior executives in Ottawa. In late 1991, Rauf published an exposé about

Chetek in the *Toronto Star* newspaper. His report was headlined: "Soviet Nuclear Deals: A New Time-Bomb?" Reporters at the *International Herald Tribune* and *The New York Times* read Rauf's story and decided to do their own investigations. A *New York Times* reporter contacted John M. Lamb, the executive director of the Canadian Centre, and later quoted Lamb describing the presentation that Dmitriev and his cohort, Dr. Chernyshev, had made during their Ottawa visit. "Everybody in the room thought they were nuts," Lamb told the newspaper.

The *Times* story embarrassed the Soviet government. Dmitriev abruptly resigned from Chetek, and Aleksandr Fokin, who was identified as the corporation's vice president of external relations, announced that Chetek had abandoned its plan to use nuclear bombs to vaporize wastes.

Sergei was thrilled, but there was still a loose end. In a cable to the KGB Center, he reminded the generals that Dmitriev had bragged about having his own personal nuclear bomb stored in his dacha. The Center assured him that the appropriate officials in Moscow had been alerted about Dmitriev's claim.

"I don't know what, if anything, was ever done," Sergei said later, "but I believe today this was an incident where the KGB did something good for the world by undercutting Chetek."

Continuing, he said: "The Moscow delegation's visit to Ottawa in 1991 was for me a most embarrassing fiasco. I remember wondering to myself: What is happening that would make our Soviet leadership get involved in such irresponsible and desperate acts — first by having Kulakov sell old military secrets and then by encouraging these Chetek thugs?"

FIFTEEN

Sergei was not alone in wondering what was happening in 1991. The whole world was watching Moscow.

On June 17, 1991, KGB chairman Kryuchkov and a group of conservative Communist Party officials led by Prime Minister Valentin Pavlov tried to put a stop to Gorbachev's reforms. They attempted a political coup inside the Supreme Soviet, the country's highest legislative body during Communism. Kryuchkov and the other hard-liners were desperate because, several months earlier, Gorbachev had permitted Czechoslovakia, Hungary, and Poland to withdraw from the Warsaw Pact. Overnight, independence movements had surfaced in all of the Soviet Union's fifteen republics.

Initially, Gorbachev had tried to curb the demonstrations. He sent troops to squash peaceful marches in three Baltic states: Estonia, Latvia, and Lithuania. But the troops' violent attacks only seemed to strengthen the demonstrators' resolve while hurting Gorbachev's image in the West. In a last-minute effort to hold the Soviet Union together, Gorbachev negotiated a treaty with the republics that would give them limited independence but require that they remain under the Soviet umbrella with a common president, a single foreign policy, and one military. That so-called Union Treaty was scheduled to be signed on August 20, 1991 — and Kryuchkov and his supporters wanted to stop it. They saw no reason why the Soviet Union needed to break apart. If they were successful in undercutting Gorbachev in the Supreme Soviet, they would use their newly gained power to force the republics back into line.

Kryuchkov's peaceful coup attempt, however, failed. Having tasted the reforms sparked by *perestroika* and *glasnost,* Soviet legislators were not willing to turn back the clock. This left the KGB chairman and his cronies with only one option. If they wanted to stop the Union Treaty, they had to remove Gorbachev with military force before the August treaty was signed.

On June 20, 1991, Jack Matlock, the U.S. ambassador to the Soviet Union, sent a frightening top-secret message from Moscow to the White House. A copy was delivered simultaneously to Secretary of State James Baker, who was attending an economic summit in Europe. Matlock had met earlier that day with Gavriil Popov, the reformist mayor of Moscow, and during their session Popov had slipped him a hand-scribbled message because he was afraid the KGB had bugged the room where they were meeting. The note warned that Kryuchkov, Defense Minister Dmitri Yazov, and Chairman of the Supreme Soviet Anatoli Lukyanov were planning to use KGB troops to overthrow Gorbachev and seize control of the empire. Mayor Popov urged the U.S. to warn Boris Yeltsin, who had been elected only a few days earlier as the first-ever directly elected president of the republic of Russia. Yeltsin happened to be in Washington, D.C., visiting President George H. W. Bush. Mayor Popov also asked the White House to get word to Gorbachev. Popov was afraid the KGB would stop him if he attempted to warn the Soviet president on his own.

President Bush telephoned Baker in Europe and they formulated a plan. Bush would personally warn Yeltsin. Meanwhile, Baker would get word to the Soviet Union's foreign minister, Aleksandr Bessmertnykh, who was attending the same European economic conference as he was. Ambassador Matlock would try to contact Gorbachev in Moscow. Surely one of them would be successful in warning Gorbachev about Kryuchkov's takeover plot.

In his 1998 presidential memoir, Bush would later recall that he had selected his words carefully when he spoke in Washington to Yeltsin. Bush knew Yeltsin and Gorbachev were political rivals, and Bush wrote that he was nervous that Yeltsin might think the U.S. was passing misinformation to him in hopes of stirring up political unrest.

"Yeltsin discounted the [plot] rumor entirely," Bush wrote in *A World Transformed,* "saying there is no way it could happen." Just the same, Bush persuaded Yeltsin to place a call to Gorbachev from the White House. When they tried, however, the White House operators could not reach him.

According to Mayor Popov's warning note, the KGB-backed coup was supposed to happen June 21, and when that date arrived and passed without incident, the mayor's alarm was dismissed as just another nervous rumor.

One month later, on August 18, U.S. intelligence analysts noticed strange happenings outside Gorbachev's dacha near the Black

Sea where he and his wife had gone for the weekend. At the time, the U.S. used its spy satellites to track Gorbachev's movements and the photo images that the National Security Agency took were so exact that its analysts could tell Gorbachev's presidential limousine had not left the compound for his return trip to Moscow as scheduled. He was supposed to sign the new Union Treaty in two days — on August 20. Even more unsettling, the NSA images showed that a caravan of cars had arrived at the Gorbachevs' dacha and blocked it off from the main road.

The next morning, August 19, a group that called itself the State Emergency Committee announced over Moscow television and radio stations that Gorbachev had become "ill" and was being relieved of his post as Soviet president. The Soviet Union's vice president, Gennady Yanayev, had been named acting president by the committee, whose members included Kryuchkov, Yazov, Pavlov, Internal Affairs Minister Boris Pugo, and four others, soon to be known as the "Gang of Eight." A military coup was under way.

Having put Gorbachev under house arrest, Kryuchkov ordered KGB special military troops into Moscow to confront protesters. Mobs of demonstrators had gathered outside a building called the "White House" because of its gleaming white marble facade. It was where the Supreme Soviet met. Russian president Yeltsin and other democratic reformers had congregated inside to decide how to react to the coup. KGB tanks encircled the White House, and in a dramatic moment, Yeltsin fearlessly marched outside, climbed onto the top of a KGB tank, and used a megaphone to condemn the "junta" and rally protesters. Yeltsin's impassioned speech was so persuasive that the KGB troops who had been sent to intimidate the crowd switched sides. They refused an order to fire on the White House and instead turned their guns around and pointed them in defense of the building.

By August 21, the majority of the KGB's troops in Moscow had joined the demonstrators. Kryuchkov's coup collapsed. Gorbachev was released, and Kryuchkov and his fellow conspirators were jailed.

Although Gorbachev acted as if he were oblivious to the political changes that the coup had caused, historians would later note that a significant power shift had occurred in Moscow. Gorbachev was still president of the Soviet Union, but Boris

Yeltsin was now clearly taking charge. As president of the largest republic in the unraveling Soviet Union, Yeltsin seized control of the Soviet central television broadcasting and radio system, as well as key Soviet ministries. Meanwhile, he and Gorbachev set out to neuter the KGB.

The day after the failed coup, Gorbachev appointed one of his political allies, Vadim Bakatin, to replace Kryuchkov as KGB chairman. A reformist, Bakatin fired the KGB's "ideologues" — the iron-fisted generals and Communist Party members who Bakatin claimed had been responsible for expelling controversial writers, sending dissidents to mental institutions, and destroying the lives of the intelligentsia opposed to the party. Bakatin announced that he wanted to begin a new era of cooperation between the KGB and the U.S. As proof, he gave the U.S. a set of top-secret KGB blueprints that revealed the location of every electronic eavesdropping device hidden inside the walls of the newly constructed American embassy building in Moscow. He demanded nothing in return for his dramatic disclosure.

The KGB's legacy of political repression and covert warfare against Western democracies was over, Bakatin declared at a news conference. In the coming weeks, Bakatin recommended splitting the KGB into several different pieces and creating a system of checks and balances to prevent any of the parts from rejoining and regaining the tremendous power a unified KGB had wielded. On October 24, 1991, Gorbachev signed a decree that officially abolished the KGB. A number of different name changes would take place during the coming months, but the tasks of the KGB would eventually be broken into separate government services.

- The Foreign Intelligence Service, known by its Cyrillic initials SVR, assumed control of all foreign spying operations formerly done by the First Chief Directorate. The SVR took charge of the Center at Yasenevo.
- The Federal Agency for Government Communications and Information, called FAPSI, became the Russian counterpart to the U.S.'s National Security Agency. FAPSI controlled communication security and satellite signals intelligence.
- The Federal Protection Service, FSO, assumed command of the ten thousand KGB troops that had guarded the

Kremlin and protected high-ranking Communist officials. The FSO also took over the Presidential Security Service, which was the Russian equivalent of the U.S. Secret Service.

- The Federal Security Service, FSB, absorbed the KGB's Second, Third, Fifth, and Seventh directorates, creating a new 75,000-member police force responsible for providing internal security within Russia's borders, including counterintelligence investigations. In many ways, the FSB acted much like the FBI.

Because the KGB's foreign intelligence service had not been responsible for persecuting dissidents, it was not as hated or feared by reformers as other KGB directorates. The Center also was outside Moscow, far away from Lubyanka, which was the KGB building that most Soviets identified with midnight arrests, torture, and other KGB cruelty. Consequently, Gorbachev and Yeltsin did not fire all the generals who ran the Center. Nor did they put an outsider in charge of foreign intelligence and order him to clean house. Instead, Gorbachev promoted a former KGB lieutenant-general, Leonid Shebarshin, to take charge of the

SVR. Shebarshin had been one of Kryuchkov's protégés but had opposed the armed coup. His tenure, however, proved short-lived. Shebarshin quarreled with Chairman Batakin and one month later was pushed out. His successor at the Center was Yevgeniy Primakov, a close friend of Gorbachev's and a rising power inside Russia.

Primakov had started his career as a journalist, working in the 1950s as a deputy editor at the newspaper *Pravda.* As such, he was a KGB "co-optee" who had served two masters — the newspaper and Soviet intelligence. Primakov had eventually been elected to the Central Committee of the Communist Party and to the Politburo, which were important bodies before Gorbachev's democratic reforms. Primakov had tried to warn Gorbachev about the August KGB coup and had not supported Kryuchkov and his comrades.

In October 1991, Primakov officially took charge of the SVR Center at Yasenevo, and he quickly proved that he was a shrewd operator. Before making any changes, he sought advice from several KGB godfathers — former intelligence officers who were highly respected by their peers. One was retired KGB General Boris Aleksandrovich Solomatin, the Cold War operative who had run the John Walker spy ring. Another was Sergei's former boss, General Dmitri Yakushkin, who had been fired by Kryuchkov after the Yurchenko-defection fiasco. Solomatin and Yakushkin both told Primakov that the Center at Yasenevo was a well-oiled machine. They urged him to leave it alone and, more important, they begged him to protect it from Chairman Batakin. Solomatin and Yakushkin were both furious that Batakin had told U.S. intelligence about the microphones hidden inside the U.S. embassy — especially since he had not gotten any useful intelligence from the U.S. in return.

Having castrated the KGB, Gorbachev and Yeltsin scrambled to maintain order. Between the August coup and December 1991, they met repeatedly with delegates from the fifteen rebellious Soviet republics to discuss a peaceful dissolution of the USSR. By year-end, all the republics had declared their independence from Moscow, and on December 25, Gorbachev voluntarily resigned as president and the Soviet Union officially ceased to exist. The red hammer-and-sickle flag was lowered and replaced at the Kremlin with the tricolor flag of Russia. President Yeltsin, as the elected leader of the largest successor state, took charge. A new era had begun.

In Canada, Sergei and his colleagues had watched the dramatic events unfolding in Moscow on Soviet television. During the August coup, Sergei had considered unplugging the satellite link that fed Soviet broadcasts into the Ottawa embassy because the images were so upsetting.

"When the coup was happening," Sergei recalled later, "the State Emergency Committee [Kryuchkov's Gang of Eight] sent coded cables to every Soviet ambassador abroad, demanding that they swear allegiance to the new government. Several of them got scared so they called in sick or announced they were on vacation to avoid declaring their loyalty. All of the ambassadors who did swear allegiance to the State Emergency Committee were later fired by Gorbachev and Yeltsin."

The confusion about who was in charge at the Kremlin showed itself in other ways at the Ottawa embassy. "There was a huge statue of Lenin in the lobby. In the spring of 1991, this statue was taken into the basement because Communist symbols under Gorbachev had fallen from favor. Still, it was kept there intact, just in case Communism was embraced again. That happened in August when the coup took place.

Workmen dragged the statue back upstairs and returned it to the main lobby — for four days. After the coup failed, they dragged it back into the basement. I am confident it is still somewhere in the Ottawa basement — just in case there ever is another coup."

Sixteen

At the start of 1992, President Yeltsin took charge of a Russia that was in political disarray and disastrous economic shape. In the coming months, inflation would rise 2,500 percent and a nose-diving economy would post a "negative growth" of minus 14.5 percent. Those figures were reflected in human suffering on Moscow's streets. The government announced it did not have sufficient funds to pay pensions for the elderly. Salaries of many government workers were deferred, often for months. Money for food and heat was scarce.

But in Canada, Sergei and the SVR officers under his command didn't miss a paycheck. The KGB no longer existed, but the SVR had no trouble meeting its financial obligations. Nor did Sergei notice any dramatic procedural changes in how foreign intelligence operated. The SVR announced it was replacing the KGB term *main adver-*

sary with the phrase *main targets.* But those targets were exactly the same as during the Cold War: (1) USA, (2) NATO, (3) China.

As the acting *rezident,* Sergei ran the day-to-day tasks. "The Cold War is over," he told his officers, "and this is something we can use to our advantage." Canadians, he predicted, would now be eager to speak to "democracy-minded" Russians.

In the spring of 1992, one of Sergei's officers asked for permission to pitch a promising target. Vitali Domoratski, whose code name was Comrade *Yurgis,* was a vice consul in the consular department, but his real job was working for Line VKR (*counterintelligence*). A year earlier, he had been attending a reception in Ottawa being held to honor Ukrainian immigrants. Much like the U.S., Canada is largely a nation of immigrants and more than a million of its citizens could trace their roots to the Ukraine, making it the seventh most common ethnic group. Domoratski had been born in the Ukraine and, more important, had once been a member of the Ukrainian state gymnastics team, which gave him some cachet at the reception. Alex Kindy, a prominent member of the Canadian Parliament, also was at the reception and the two had struck up a conversation.

According to his official résumé, Kindy was born in 1930 in Warsaw, Poland. But his parents were Ukrainian, and Kindy, who had immigrated to Canada as a young man, was proud of his Ukrainian ancestry. According to Sergei, Domoratski and Kindy met several times after the reception and became friends.

Sergei wasn't fond of Line VKR officers because their main job was tattling on their coworkers. In addition, Domoratski was not fluent in English, had not been trained how to recruit a spy, and didn't have much knowledge about Canadian politics.

"Going after a sitting member of the Canadian Parliament was an extremely, extremely risky proposal," Sergei explained later. President Yeltsin was counting on the West for billions of dollars in financial aid, and only a few months earlier, Chairman Batakin had declared that the spy wars between Russia and the West were over. "I knew Yeltsin would be at our throats if we caused an international scandal, and I wasn't sure Domoratski could handle this assignment."

Kindy seemed an unlikely target. A conservative and strident anti-Communist during the Cold War, Kindy had made his first run at politics in 1962 in Quebec, but had come in last out of five candidates. He ran again in 1968, 1972, and 1974, but didn't win any of those elections. At that point, Kindy moved to a less populated region of Alberta, where he was elected in 1984 to the Canadian House of Commons, a body of 308 members, similar to the House of Representatives in the U.S. Congress. Kindy represented Calgary East, home to about 120,000 voters, and was a member of the Progressive Conservative Party.

He quickly made a name for himself. Kindy strongly opposed allowing homosexuals to serve in the Canadian armed services or in the Mounties. He was an ardent supporter of the death penalty. In 1987, Kindy accused the government of trying to hide information about a spy case that had rocked Canada some thirty years earlier. A Canadian diplomat named E. Herbert Norman was accused in the 1950s by a U.S. Senate subcommittee of being a Communist spy. His name had been exposed by Senator Joseph McCarthy. But before Norman's case could be fully investigated, he committed suicide in 1957 in Cairo, where he was stationed. Rumors soon began to circulate that he had been shoved from a rooftop and had not jumped, as the Cairo police claimed. Nearly thirty years later, a

Canadian newspaper set out to investigate Norman's case, but Canadian intelligence officials refused to cooperate, citing privacy reasons. Kindy jumped into the dispute. He told reporters he didn't understand why the Canadian government was trying to protect a former KGB spy, and he added that he had no sympathy for traitors, arguing they deserved to be publicly outed regardless of how much time had passed since their crime.

Three years after that outburst, Kindy made even bigger headlines. He was expelled from his own political party after he voted against a controversial 7 percent goods and services tax that Prime Minister Mulroney had endorsed. An unrepentant Kindy called his former colleagues "robots" and said he would seek reelection as an independent in the 1993 elections.

Kindy had been raising campaign funds at the Ukrainian reception when Domoratski first met him. According to Sergei, when the two men talked later, Kindy mentioned he was having trouble raising money for his 1993 reelection.

"Domoratski thought Kindy was vulnerable because he needed cash," Sergei recalled.

Sergei sent a cable to the Center explaining the situation and asking for permission to approach Kindy. After a series of lengthy exchanges, the Center gave Sergei permission to move forward, but it warned him that if the attempt became a public scandal, it would be his career that would suffer.

Sergei had no choice but to use Domoratski. "We decided Domoratski would tell Kindy that he personally wanted to contribute ten thousand dollars to the reelection campaign. We thought this might give Kindy an out if the contribution was made public. He could say it was from a friend. Of course, the truth was that it really didn't matter. Canadian politicians can't take money from Russians — regardless of whether they are diplomats or SVR officers. Besides, every dog in Ottawa knew Domoratski was an SVR officer." Domoratski would invite Kindy to lunch and make the pitch at the end of their meal.

The Center approved the plan with one requirement. It insisted Domoratski secretly tape-record the entire meeting. "Penetrating the Canadian Parliament would be a major coup. President Yeltsin would be immediately informed if we were successful, so there could be absolutely no mistakes made. The Center wanted it all tape-recorded because it needed to make certain that this operation was not simply some good story that Domoratski and I had conjured up to promote our careers. And it wanted evidence to use to blackmail Kindy."

Sergei sent Domoratski to buy a wallet big enough to hold $10,000 in $100 bills. The cash arrived from Moscow inside a sealed package in a diplomatic pouch. The money did not appear to have ever been circulated, and for a moment Sergei wondered if it was counterfeit. Wearing gloves to hide his fingerprints, Sergei unwrapped the cash and slipped it into the wallet to make sure it fit. Worried that Domoratski might leave his fingerprints on the billfold, Sergei had him practice leaning forward and whipping the wallet from his interior jacket pocket so it would drop on its own onto the table. He did this by touching only the wallet's edges. Sergei had an SVR technical expert wipe the wallet clean of fingerprints after Domoratski finished practicing.

Domoratski had Kindy's private phone number. He called and suggested they meet for lunch at a restaurant near Gatineau Park. The SVR did not believe Canadian intelligence listened to Kindy's personal phone calls because he was a member of Parliament. Sergei had chosen Gatineau Park for the lunch because it was only a five-minute drive from downtown Ottawa, but it was a 225-square-mile nature reserve filled with trails, lakes, and panoramic lookouts. The restaurant was named Les Tulipes and was in a wooded area at the rim of the park.

On the morning of the lunch, Domoratski drove to a shopping mall where he visited several stores, pretending to shop. Ottawa has an extensive public bus and rail system and Domoratski used both transports next. When he was certain that no one was following him, he took a bus to Gatineau Park. He was carrying a change of clothes with him in a knapsack and he went into the woods and slipped into his jogging outfit. Domoratski hiked through the trees for about two miles until he reached the area where the restaurant was located. He changed into his regular clothing and emerged from the woods.

Sergei, meanwhile, was waiting at the embassy with a code clerk. A secure satellite channel was being held open between Ottawa and the Center, the equivalent of dialing a telephone number and staying on the line even though no one was speaking.

The lunch was set for noon. If Kindy pocketed the money, Domoratski was to say that he would be in touch and then immediately leave the restaurant. The Center

213

did not want to give Kindy time to change his mind, nor did it want Domoratski to wait in case Kindy called the RCMP. Domoratski was expected to return to the embassy after he hiked back through the woods and caught a bus. If everything went according to schedule, he would be returning shortly after 2 p.m., which was 10 p.m. in Moscow.

Sergei paced. "When two o'clock came, I stared at the entrance, waiting for him to appear. Then three o'clock came. Nothing. Then four. Nothing. Then five and six, and the code clerk said, 'We have to send something to the Center. The head of the North American department is waiting. The head of the SVR is waiting. We have to tell them what is happening.' "

"No," Sergei replied. "We will not speculate."

At 7 p.m., there was still no sign of Domoratski. "Eight o'clock came, then nine o'clock, and finally ten o'clock and I was half dead. The code clerk said, 'Sergei, this operation is a failure. You must tell the Center.' Of course, I suspected Domoratski had been arrested. Why else had he not arrived back? All sorts of thoughts rushed through my head. Perhaps Kindy had fooled my operative and this was part of a provocation by the Mounties."

A few minutes after 11 p.m., Sergei told the clerk to hand him a special yellow pad with numbered sheets that he used to handwrite messages for the clerk to encrypt. He wrote: "YURGIS didn't return. Disappeared. We assume the operation is a failure. Request information about how to minimize damage."

He gave it to the clerk. At that moment, Domoratski burst through the embassy's door. "His face was scratched and he looked exhausted. He was so distraught he couldn't speak. Neither could I. I handed him a glass of strong Canadian whiskey without chips [ice] and he drank it as if it were a Coke and I drank one, too. After taking several breaths, he blurted out: 'It was a total success!' Because I had not eaten all day, the whiskey hit me and I yelled to the code clerk to bring me my pad. I wrote: 'Operation success. Details tomorrow.' It was extremely rude, but I knew no one would complain because we had just won a huge victory. Domoratski had successfully recruited a member of the Canadian Parliament! No one at the Center would dare criticize us. I told Domoratski we would leave immediately to celebrate. We went to an all-night strip club and drank. The next day, my code clerk showed me the yellow pad I had written on. I had been so excited and then the whiskey had hit me. The writing was nearly impossible to read."

Domoratski explained that he had gotten lost for several hours in the woods at Gatineau Park. "The tape recording that he made with Kindy was exceptionally clear," Sergei said. Domoratski had flipped the billfold with the cash inside it onto the table just as he had practiced. "On the tape recording, you could hear Kindy say, 'Oh no, I can't take this,' and Domoratski said, 'Yes, you can. You can because it is for your reelection campaign and we need people like you in the Parliament because people like you will help us to rebuild Canadian relations with the Ukraine and . . . blah, blah, blah. And then you can hear Kindy say, 'Okay,' and Domoratski said he snatched up the billfold."

Sergei sent a transcript of the tape and the original cassette to the Center. Kindy was given the code name *GREY,* according to Sergei. "The Center sent us countless cables asking us to get GREY to tell us about various intrigues inside the Canadian Parliament and government. This was intimate information about his colleagues and also details about internal maneuvers that were going on."

Sergei said the Center wanted to know what Ukrainian leaders were telling Western leaders. After the breakup of the Soviet Union, the Ukraine seized control of 1,320 nuclear warheads. Russia demanded the Ukraine return them, but in 1992 the first Ukrainian president, Leonid Kravchuk, refused. He was using them as bargaining chips to obtain promises of foreign aid. "There was a lot of hostility and mistrust between the former Soviet republics and Moscow," Sergei said later, "and it was not unusual for leaders in the Ukraine and the republics to speak more openly about their ambitions and goals with the U.S. and the West than they did with us. They would say things to a Canadian Parliament member that they would never reveal to a Russian."

According to Sergei, Domoratski had a difficult time handling Kindy. "Domoratski had few analytical skills and was not intellectually equipped to ask Kindy the complex questions that we needed answered." Despite this, Sergei said that Domoratski met Kindy several times between the summer of 1992 and mid-1993. "The information Domoratski received — both orally and from documents that GREY gave him — was used in more than one hundred cables to the Center, and I can tell you that in the Center today there are two volumes that each contain four hundred and fifty pages that describe GREY's recruitment and Domoratski's meetings with him. GREY received at least two more payments of five thousand dollars each."

Domoratski's tour ended before the October 1993 Canadian elections. He returned to Moscow, and his replacement, Valeri Barayev, was supposed to become GREY's new handler. But when the Russian called, Kindy refused to speak to him. For three months, Barayev tried unsuccessfully to make contact. Finally, he confronted Kindy outside the Parliament building. Kindy reportedly said he had no interest in speaking to him.

"I was furious when I heard what Barayev had done. He had disobeyed my orders. I had told him never to approach Kindy in public, especially outside a government building. We always had surveillance teams following us."

Sergei sent a cable to the Center recommending that Barayev be removed as GREY's handler. "As a human being, Barayev was a nice, kind person, but professionally, he was a zero. He was also an accomplished alcoholic with trembling hands," Sergei said later.

The Center agreed and decided that only Domoratski would contact Kindy in the future, and only when the politician was traveling outside Canada. The Center was afraid Barayev's blunder had put Kindy at risk, Sergei said.

Kindy lost reelection in October, but Sergei said Domoratski met with him at least one more time when the ex–Parliament member was invited to the Ukraine. According to Canadian newspapers, Kindy visited the capital city of Kiev to participate in a roundtable with senior Ukrainian government officials who were curious about Canada's parliamentary system and whether it could be adapted for use in their government.

Sergei said Domoratski received a medal from the SVR in a private ceremony because he had recruited Kindy. Sergei also got a commendation. Meanwhile, Barayev's career was finished. "Helen and I gave him a small parrot as a gift one year, and his greatest accomplishment in Ottawa was teaching the bird how to drink beer."

According to Sergei, the Center considered Kindy a "highly valued agent." Now in his late seventies, Kindy did not return telephone calls or respond after being sent copies of Tretyakov's account.

SEVENTEEN

Sergei became convinced in Ottawa that Canadian intelligence tried to trap him at least three times. "Local counterintelligence agents are like a band of wolves chasing a deer," he later explained. "They travel in packs, their ultimate goal is to feast on your bones, and they are relentless."

The first attempt happened after Sergei enrolled in a summer class at the School of Public Policy and Administration at Carleton University. The course was entitled "The Canadian Policy-and-Decision-Making Process," but Sergei was more interested in his classmates than the course. He had grown up hearing stories about the legendary British traitor Kim Philby, who became a closet Communist in 1929 while studying at Trinity College, Cambridge. Sergei thought he might be able to recruit a naive Canadian student to groom as a future spy.

About twenty students were enrolled, but none seemed promising, and then, halfway through the course, a new student arrived. He said his name was Gordon Smith, and like Sergei, he was older. He also appeared to be more interested in Sergei than in studying. He invited Sergei to join him for drinks after each class, but Sergei refused. "The Canadians had been sending non papers to the ambassador about me, so I assumed this fellow was a worm on a fishing hook."

After the semester ended, Gordon still badgered Sergei until finally he agreed to meet him for dinner in Ottawa's Chinatown district. "As soon as Gordon arrived, he began to blurt out how he needed to speak to me about something extremely important, but I told him, 'No, I am Russian. I eat first, drink first, and then talk business.' But he was so nervous he couldn't eat. He was sweating, and after torturing him for an hour by talking about nothing but the weather, I finally let him give me his pitch, which he had clearly memorized."

Gordon said his family had always supported trade unions in Canada, which traditionally had been sympathetic to Socialism and Communism. He said Canadian officials had warned him that Sergei was not really a diplomat, but was an SVR officer. Gordon said he was willing to work for Sergei in return for $5,000.

"His approach was so direct, so obvious, I was offended the Canadians would send such a buffoon," Sergei recalled.

Sergei acted dumb. He said he would ask Helen if they had enough savings in their personal bank account to loan Gordon the money. "Gordon said to me, 'No, no, Sergei, you don't understand. I don't want your money. I want money from your government.'"

Sergei replied: "Well, brother, I don't know why my government would pay you." At that point, Sergei left the restaurant and never heard from Gordon again.

Not long after that, Sergei was at a reception when an attractive woman named Uran introduced herself. She spoke Russian without an accent and explained that she was from Mongolia. Her parents had belonged to the Communist Party and had sent her to the Moscow Institute of Foreign Languages to study, which is why she was fluent in Russian. It was the same university that Sergei had attended. She had defected to Canada to escape from the Mongolian secret police, who were persecuting her family.

Once again, Sergei was suspicious, but rather than avoiding Uran, he introduced her to Helen and encouraged them to become friends. "If she was supposed to be watching me, then I wanted her to see that I was not doing anything suspicious. I was simply a Russian diplomat. Helen knew how to act, and they ended up spending a lot of time together. In fact, the three of us became friends — even though I suspected she was reporting everything back to Canadian intelligence. In this way, I used her."

Sergei sent photographs of Uran to the Center, where a file was created. One day, Uran disappeared. Her phone had been disconnected.

The third encounter that struck Sergei as strange involved a well-known socialite named Bhupinder Liddar, a Canadian citizen of Indian descent who was publisher of *Diplomat & International Canada,* a magazine that covered Ottawa's diplomatic and parliamentary social scene. One of Sergei's predecessors, Vladimir Novoselov, had noticed Liddar shortly after he launched his magazine in 1989. Novoselov had suggested in a cable to the Center that Liddar might be a good target because his job required him to attend diplomatic receptions and gossip with politicians. The Center had given Novoselov permission to approach Liddar, and the KGB had assigned him the code name *ALADDIN*. But Novoselov decided after meeting with Liddar several times that he didn't really have any useful information.

Sergei had read Novoselov's cables about Liddar, and when they met by chance at a diplomatic social function, Sergei decided Novoselov had been correct. "Liddar was a friendly fellow but useless as a recruit," Sergei said later. After that, the two men would bump into each other at diplomatic events, but Sergei did not seek him out.

In December 1992, Sergei saw Liddar on the street near Parliament Hill, the site of the Canadian government buildings in Ottawa, and the journalist asked if Sergei wanted to accompany him to a private reception. The party was being hosted by office workers employed by Herb Gray, a powerful Canadian politician. Gray served as Opposition House Leader from 1984 to 1990, and then as the Finance Critic for the Official Opposition, another party post. He would later be put in charge of all federal law enforcement activities in Canada.

"I was surprised Liddar was willing to take me — a Russian diplomat — to a New

Year's party in one of Mr. Gray's private offices because this area of the Parliament building was strictly off-limits to Russians. I said to him, 'Is it okay for me to go with you?' And Liddar laughed and said, 'No one will even notice because you are with me and there is a party going on.' "

Liddar introduced Sergei to about a dozen of Gray's aides, but Gray wasn't there. At one point, an aide asked if Liddar and Sergei would like to see "one of the most secret rooms in Canada." According to Sergei, several of the partygoers left Gray's office and walked to a chamber that was used by members of the House of Commons when they needed to talk about national security. "I couldn't believe it! I was taken into this room where all the windows were covered with heavy metal blinds. I am not sure these people were thinking straight, but Liddar was along, and because I was with him, they apparently thought I could be trusted. I could never have gotten access to this room or even to this part of the Parliament building without Liddar. Imagine, giving a Russian intelligence operative a private tour of the chamber where Canadian politicians discussed intelligence. It was a major security breach."

After the party, Sergei did not hear from Liddar for several weeks. Then Liddar telephoned and invited Sergei to lunch at Le Café, a popular restaurant beside the Rideau Canal. When Sergei arrived, Liddar wasn't there, but another man was. He said Liddar was running late. The man was a member of the Sikh religion and explained that he was a businessman from India. He told Sergei that a Moscow bank had acquired several million Indian rupees in a business deal and was now having a difficult time exchanging them for Russian currency. The businessman wanted Sergei to help him buy the rupees at a reduced rate. He would then use them in India and pay Sergei a commission for helping arrange the deal.

Sergei had read that Sikhs were required to follow a rigid dress code. Men had to wear turbans and a steel bracelet, and carry a small ceremonial sword. They were forbidden from cutting their hair. The businessman appeared to have shaved part of his face. He wasn't wearing a bracelet or carrying a dagger. Sergei's instincts told him it was a trick. His first thought was that Canadian intelligence had heard about Liddar escorting a Russian to Gray's party. Someone in Gray's office had probably reported Sergei's private tour of the secret chamber. Sergei figured Canadian intelligence had contacted Liddar and used him to arrange today's lunch in an attempt to trap Sergei.

"I began yelling in the restaurant. I said: 'Are you attempting to bribe a diplomat? Is that what you are doing?' At that point, Liddar suddenly appeared from another part of the restaurant. He rushed up and tried to quiet me because I was making a public scene. I tossed some money on the table to pay for the drink I had ordered and I walked out."

When contacted for this book, Liddar said he remembered meeting Vladimir Novoselov, but he had no memory of Sergei Tretyakov or "ever taking him to a party on the Hill or for that matter to a secret chamber." Nor did he recall arranging lunch at Le Café. In 2003, Liddar was nominated by the Canadian government for a diplomatic job in Chandigarh, India. Before he could accept, he was required to sell his magazine and obtain a security clearance. Liddar sold his publication, but the CSIS refused to grant him a clearance. In a carefully worded statement, the CSIS said it was uncertain about Liddar's "loyalty and reliability." A furious Liddar accused the CSIS of besmirching his character and appealed its decision. After an independent panel examined the case, it ruled there was no reason why Liddar couldn't be trusted, and he was issued a top-secret clearance. By that time, the post in India had been filled. In October 2005, the Canadian government appointed Liddar to a senior diplomatic post in Nairobi, Kenya.

"It is possible these three persons — Gordon Smith, Uran, and the Sikh — were exactly who they said they were and were not sent by Canadian counterintelligence to spy on me. It's possible, but I don't believe it. When you are an SVR officer, you must assume everyone you meet — every foreigner who contacts you — is probably a counterintelligence officer who is secretly trying to destroy you. It is not personal. It is simply the life you have chosen."

EIGHTEEN

Sergei's mother, Revmira, was coming to Ottawa to visit and he was excited to see her. It had been two years since his home leave in 1991. He hadn't been back to Moscow because the SVR Center was afraid Canada might not let him return if he left the country. The Canadian government was still hand-delivering non paper complaints about him to the Russian embassy on a regular basis. Sergei's father, Oleg, had died from a massive heart attack in 1985 at age sixty-four, and Sergei fretted about Revmira living by herself — especially now.

His mother did little to calm his fears when she arrived and began telling him about life in Moscow under President Yeltsin. "People are starving," she reported. One morning, Revmira had gone to buy bread at a store close to her apartment and overheard an elderly man, who was wearing World War II medals, ask if he could buy one-quarter of a loaf because it was all he could afford. The clerk said no. Shocked that a "hero of the Soviet Union" had been turned away empty-handed, Revmira stepped forward and offered him money. But he'd been too proud to take it. His plight had made her cry.

Sergei and Helen knew from Russian newscasts that many Russians were having a tough time, but Revmira's account put a human face on the problems. They also knew not everyone in Moscow was in such dire circumstances. A select few were becoming instantly rich.

President Yeltsin's shining moment had come when he climbed atop the KGB tank outside the Russian White House and thwarted the August 1991 attempted coup against Gorbachev. Since then, his leadership and his personal health had both faltered. Early on, Yeltsin turned over much of the day-to-day running of the nation to Prime Minister Yegor Gaidar. Rushing to dismantle the Soviet system, Gaidar ended price controls, legalized private businesses and private ownership of land, made drastic cuts in military spending, and introduced commercial banking to Russia. These hurried reforms caused havoc.

And then matters had gotten worse.

Yeltsin put one of his supporters, Viktor Gerashchenko, in charge of the nation's central bank, and he showered Russia with cheap credit. Inflation exploded. By the end of 1992, Yeltsin's "economy reforms" were being called "shock without therapy." The exchange rate for rubles had skyrocketed. When Yeltsin first took power, 400 rubles were equal to one dollar. Under his leadership, that rate soared to 3,081 rubles per dollar. Savings and wages were gobbled up by runaway inflation. But not everyone was going broke.

With Yeltsin's approval, Gaidar had started selling off the Soviet Union's vast natural resources. The rights to oil, gas, and timber formerly owned by the Communist state were doled out. Overnight, a new breed of Russian business magnate surfaced. They were called *oligarchs,* and all of them were relatives or close friends of Yeltsin. They bought the nation's assets at badly undervalued prices or in some cases by getting them free during the privatization process. For the first time ever, *Forbes* magazine began adding Russians to its list of the world's most wealthy. By the time *Forbes* had a tally, there were thirty Russian businessmen who had personal assets worth more than a billion dollars. The oligarchs gorged themselves while ordinary Russians went hungry to bed.

Yeltsin's policies came under such fierce political attack that he was forced to fire Prime Minister Gaidar, who would later be accused of stealing government funds for himself. Yeltsin replaced him with Viktor Chernomyrdin, one of Russia's first oligarchs. Yeltsin had awarded Chernomyrdin the rights to much of Russia's vast natural gas reserves, and his company, Gazprom, had increased Chernomyrdin's net worth overnight to an estimated $5 billion.

Despite the prime minister switch, conditions in Moscow continued to decline and in March 1993 Yeltsin's critics moved to impeach him. He survived their political attack in the new Russian Parliament by a slim 58.5 percent majority vote. Yeltsin exacted revenge by dissolving both elected chambers — a clear violation of Russia's infant constitution.

On October 3, 1993, Yeltsin's political opponents stormed the Moscow mayor's office and seized control of the city's largest TV broadcasting station. Twenty-three persons were killed during the melee. His critics announced over the airwaves that Vice President Alexander Rutskoy had succeeded Yeltsin and was now Russia's new president. Yeltsin's supporters broadcast reports from a secret underground bunker built at the Kremlin for use in case of a nuclear war. They called on "democracy-loving" Muscovites to take to the streets.

The next day, October 4, troops loyal to Yeltsin arrived in Moscow and encircled the White House legislative building where Rutskoy and his cohorts had clustered. Russian tanks aimed their guns at the building — just as they had done during the first attempted coup.

Sergei and Helen attended a diplomatic reception on the night of October 4 in Ottawa, and as soon as they arrived, they were surrounded by concerned Canadians pelting them with questions about the standoff in Moscow.

"We are a civilized country with civilized politicians who will never physically threaten their opponents," Sergei declared. "The trouble will be worked out peacefully in Moscow."

When they returned that night to their apartment, Sergei and Helen watched CNN until 3 a.m. The picture on the screen was the same: a light-armored vehicle moving back and forth in front of the Russian White House. Finally, they went to bed.

The next morning, Sergei left his apartment without checking the news. A gaggle of Canadian television reporters was pressed against the embassy's front gate. As he approached, one yelled: "How do you feel about what's happening in Moscow?"

Sergei gave an impromptu press conference. "Everything is under control," he declared. "This situation is developing as it is supposed to develop in a civilized country. We are showing the world that we want to be part of a modern democratic society."

Just then, Vassili Dmitrievich Sredin, a member of the Russian ambassador's staff, hurried out of the embassy to fetch him.

"Are you insane?" Sredin asked incredulously as soon as they broke free from the reporters. "How can you say such things about the atrocity that has happened?"

"Don't try to tell me what to say to reporters," Sergei snapped. "I am a trained officer. I know how to deal with reporters."

"Switch on the TV!"

The broadcast showed Russian tanks firing at the White House. Fire and smoke poured from shattered windows. The newscaster said a hundred people had been killed. Sergei, who had no idea, was dumbfounded. That attack ended the coup against Yeltsin. Its organizers were arrested.

Years later, Sergei would recall his emotions that morning. The attack on the Russian White House, he said, marked a turning point in his life. "I understood at that very moment that my country had never been even close to becoming a civilized, democratic society. We were not ready for democracy."

Once again, Sergei found himself wondering: "Who are these people I am protecting and why I am serving them? What sort of man is this Yeltsin — that he turns Russian tanks on his own people?"

The failed coup happened during Revmira's five-month-long visit in Ottawa and on the night of October 4, she, Sergei, and Helen stayed up late talking about what was unfolding in Moscow. During their conversation, Revmira made a comment that became forever etched in the couple's minds. "I hate that my granddaughter will be brought up in this new Russia," she declared. "My granddaughter deserves a better future than this."

The statement surprised Sergei. "My mother was a patriot who loved Russia passionately, yet she was telling us she didn't want her granddaughter, our beloved Ksenia, to be brought up in her native land. At that moment, all of us realized the significance of what she was saying and what had happened that day in Russia. As a people, we were showing the world that Russians would never be able to run a country that was free of corruption and chaos. It was simply beyond our capabilities. And Helen and I had to ask ourselves: Is this what we wanted for our daughter's future?"

The Center sent word to Sergei that it was time for him to return to Moscow. His Canadian tour was coming to an end. He was being made head of the Canadian section in the North American Department of the SVR — an important promotion that would put him in charge of overseeing all foreign intelligence operations in Ottawa and Montreal.

One Sunday, before they left Ottawa, Sergei and Helen went for a walk along a path that edged the Ottawa River. Helen said, "Sergei, look at all of these people." She nodded toward others who were enjoying the park that afternoon. "They live in comfortable houses, not mansions, yet they seem happy. They have okay jobs, not important ones like generals, but they seem okay. They send their children to public schools and their children seem fine and have a future. But us, what do we really have in Moscow?"

Then she added, "Tell me, Sergei, what if

we didn't go back?"

Whenever he would later remember their conversation that day, Sergei would recall that he hadn't been "mentally ready" at that point to take such a drastic step. But as they talked while strolling along the path next to the river, both of them began to lift the lid on a Pandora's box and peek inside. Their conversation that day would be the first of a seemingly endless line of conversations that would follow. The words between them would be spoken softly and only when they were absolutely certain no one else could hear them. Defecting was still a faraway, remote idea. First, they would examine their alternatives. What if Sergei retired early from the SVR and found a job in Moscow working for a private business with international offices? What if he simply resigned and tried to emigrate? Where would they go: Europe? Latin America? Canada? How would they support themselves? What about Sergei's promising SVR career? What would happen to their luxury Moscow apartment and their two dachas? What about Revmira? Sergei's mother would never leave Moscow and they could not abandon her there. But how long could they wait? Each day, Ksenia grew older. There were so many things to discuss, so much to digest — too much at times. The daily demands of their lives would interrupt. Time would pass without either of them making a mention. But like a half-finished crossword puzzle that can't be put down, the discussions would nag at them.

It was in Ottawa, then, that the seed was first planted.

■ ■ ■ ■

Part Three:
Fake Diplomats and
UN Thefts

■ ■ ■ ■

What is the difference between an
optimist and a pessimist in Russia today?
Answer: A pessimist believes that things
in Russia can't possibly get any worse.
An optimist is confident they can.
— *Common joke in Moscow
during Boris Yeltsin's presidency*

NINETEEN

Sergei Tretyakov knew something was wrong when he reported to work at the SVR Center in April 1994 and walked across its parking lot toward the main entrance. Years earlier when he had first worked at the foreign intelligence service headquarters as a fresh-faced KGB officer, he had felt a sense of awe, as if he were entering, in his own words, "a five-star, luxury hotel." The main building's marble facade had sparkled in the morning sunlight. The lobby's wooden floors had been hand-scrubbed and brightly buffed. The Center had been a working shrine.

Now the main building's exterior was grimy. Pieces of marble had broken loose and not been replaced. Inside, the lobby was filthy. It was not just the building's lack of cleanliness that caught his eye. On the elevator ride to the fifth floor, Sergei noted many of his coworkers were shabbily dressed in badly wrinkled clothing. Their faces were unshaven, their eyes bloodshot and watery.

As the head of the Canadian sector, Sergei was assigned a spacious office protected by a thick oak door. The room had a panoramic view of the forest that edged the compound with the Moscow skyline rising in the distance. Sergei opened the room's windows to rid it of a musty smell and took stock of his new surroundings. There was a safe bolted into the wall. Sergei already knew the security procedure. Anytime he left the room, he was required to put all secret documents into the safe, lock it, and seal it with a metal tab that had a plastic strip attached. The tab, which looked like a thick button, was imprinted with a personal number assigned specifically to Sergei, showing that he had snapped the seal onto the safe's handle. Once that was done, it was impossible to open the safe's door without breaking the plastic. Sergei could tell instantly whether anyone had tampered with the door while he was gone. He would hand the keys to the safe and to his office door to a duty officer in the hallway. The officer would sign a paper accepting them and then lock both sets in yet another safe. When Sergei returned, he would sign a logbook and reclaim his keys. He would unlock the office door and check the safe's plastic strip.

His office contained a wall of file cabinets that also could be locked and sealed, a large wooden table, and a desk with four different-colored telephones. The number of telephones on an officer's desk showed how important he was. The more phones, the higher his rank. The first line was unsecured and could be used like a regular phone to call outside the compound. Next to it was an internal, secure line, used only inside the Center to communicate between offices. The third was connected to all SVR offices in Russia and former KGB departments that had been turned into independent agencies, such as the Federal Security Service (FSB), which was responsible for internal security in Russia. The final phone was a direct link between Sergei and his immediate boss.

Sergei's office did not have a private toilet, and when Sergei went to use the men's room down the hallway that first morning, he was aghast. "Dozens of empty liquor bottles were tossed on the floor or left on windowsills. The place reeked of alcohol and tobacco. There was no toilet paper or paper towels. I was told these paper products were stolen as soon as they were put there. Janitors left old newspapers on the floor for us to use. The bathroom had once been a spotless facility, but now it resembled what you would find in a rural Russian rail station. The cleaning ladies had put handwritten notes above the toilets. 'If you sprinkle when you tinkle, please be a sweety and wipe the seatee.' "

Later that afternoon, Sergei was interrupted by two friends, both high-ranking officers. According to protocol, they were required to wait for Sergei to flip over any papers that he was reading before they approached his desk. Instead, they burst forward. One of them shoved Sergei's work aside as he heaved a briefcase onto the desk. He began removing bottles of vodka and sandwiches from it.

"What's happening?" Sergei asked. No one would have dared to have stopped working at four o'clock in the past. During Sergei's first assignment at the Center, senior officers routinely stayed at work until nine o'clock at night.

"We are celebrating your return," one of his buddies explained.

"But it is only four o'clock," Sergei replied.

His friends told him that no one worked late anymore and there was usually an office party each afternoon. Drinking alcohol on the job had become so commonplace that if anyone needed information from some departments, they were told to call before 11 a.m. Otherwise, everyone who worked there would be drunk.

The KGB's professional standards had been stripped away, Sergei said later. "Nearly all of the best and brightest had resigned from the service and gone into the private sector to become rich. Our headquarters had taken on the appearance of a cheap provincial bar filled with tobacco and drunks."

Everywhere Sergei looked, he saw slough. The deputy head of foreign intelligence, General Aleksey Medyanik, code name Comrade *Makar,* arrived at the Center one morning to give a speech to young SVR officers. His father, Yakov Prokofyevich Medyanik, had been a respected KGB general. In the old days, meeting someone as important and powerful as the deputy head had been considered a great honor. "Such men were living gods inside the KGB," Sergei recalled. But Medyanik had been so drunk that when he tried to stand and address the recruits, he toppled over, hitting his head. It was only 10:30 a.m.

"I received calls every day from my former

KGB colleagues asking me to join them in the private sector. 'Why are you still working there?' they would ask. 'You can get rich if you come work with me.' One close friend was in charge of a shoe manufacturing plant and was a millionaire. Others were working for the Mafia."

Sergei wasn't interested. "I did not see myself as a shoe manufacturer or a member of the Russian Mafia. I had become a KGB officer to become part of the crème de la crème."

News reports during 1994 in Moscow confirmed Sergei's personal observations. Yuri Kobaladze, the official spokesman for Russian intelligence, told reporters that the SVR lost a whopping 40 percent of its senior personnel between 1991 and 1993. Nearly all resigned to enter private businesses. Along with that management mass exit had come a devastating drop in morale. One reason Russian intelligence was at an especially low point in 1994 is that it had lost one of its best U.S. spies. CIA employee Aldrich Ames, who had been spying since 1985 for the Kremlin, was arrested outside his suburban Virginia home. U.S. intelligence said Ames had been caught because of internal detective work. A special team of CIA investigators had noticed Ames deposited huge amounts of cash into his bank on the same days that he was meeting with a Soviet diplomat in Washington, D.C., as part of his job. But no one in Moscow believed that claim. Historically, the only way a Russian spy had gotten caught was if someone working inside the KGB/SVR had tipped off the U.S. The same was true about the KGB catching traitors in its own midst. A snitch was nearly always the source. After Ames was caught, the SVR began searching for a mole inside the SVR Center, and that internal witch hunt made the officers there feel even more under attack.

On April 27, 1994, President Yeltsin made a rare appearance at the SVR headquarters to boost sagging spirits. Speaking to some eight hundred SVR employees, Yeltsin said he needed good foreign intelligence from them as the Russian president, especially since the U.S. and other foreign governments were engaging in "secret diplomacy instead of the practice of international relations." He was referring to U.S. efforts to reach out privately to the leaders of former Soviet republics. "We need to look under the cover of these secrets so as not to be caught napping." Continuing, Yeltsin warned the Center that the SVR had to be even more diligent and productive now because Russia had made deep cuts in the size of its military. "Our national security rests with you."

Despite the sloppiness and drunkenness around Sergei, and his own growing misgivings about Russia's political leaders, he was determined to do an impressive job at the Center. If for no other reason, it would help make his stay in Moscow as short as possible. "I wanted to get another overseas posting — this time in Manhattan." While he and his family had been living in Ottawa, Sergei had gotten permission to visit New York City on vacation. He had been mesmerized by it. He thought it was the most impressive city he'd ever seen. The fastest way for him to get overseas again was by impressing the Center's generals with his performance. His chances of doing that were especially good now because so many of his contemporaries had abandoned the SVR. But there was another reason Sergei thought he could nab a quick promotion. He had an idea that hadn't been tried before by Russian intelligence, and if his scheme worked, he believed it would revolutionize how the SVR was able to recruit and handle its network of spies.

TWENTY

SVR Intelligence Officers were not supposed to tell foreign spies where they lived in Russia or how to contact them after they returned home. But Sergei ignored this rule when he left Ottawa and gave his apartment and telephone number in Moscow to KIRILL. At the time, addresses and phone numbers were difficult to obtain in Russia because there were still few public directories.

Sergei had a motive. KIRILL had helped write government policy documents and speeches for several prime ministers and numerous senior Canadian government officials. He'd provided classified documents that Sergei had used to write more than a hundred cables to the Center. KIRILL was simply too valuable a trusted contact to cut loose, especially since Sergei's new job was overseeing SVR spying operations in Canada. His plan was to discreetly keep tabs on KIRILL.

In 1994, KIRILL was operating a consulting firm in Ottawa, having left the Canadian Centre for Arms Control and Disarmament. He came to Moscow on a business trip and telephoned. Sergei immediately invited him to his apartment, where Helen fixed an elaborate dinner and Sergei introduced KIRILL to Revmira. By the time dessert was served, Sergei had offered to introduce KIRILL to several Russian businessmen.

The next morning at the Center, Sergei sent a written proposal to General Trubnikov, now the second-in-command of the SVR under Director Yevgeniy Primakov. Sergei suggested the SVR arrange a lucrative consulting contract in Moscow for KIRILL. This would enable Russian intelligence to launder its spy payments to him and also would create a reason for KIRILL to travel frequently to Moscow without causing Canadian intelligence to become suspicious. The simplest arrangement would be to use a shell company to hire KIRILL's Ottawa-based firm.

"General Trubnikov loved my idea," Sergei said later. The general showed it to Primakov, who then presented it to President Yeltsin. The reason Yeltsin had to be told is that the SVR was not permitted under Russian law to conduct covert operations inside Russia, just as the CIA was not permitted to do clandestine jobs inside the U.S. President Yeltsin had to sign off on the proposal before Primakov could approach Russia's internal security service. (In 1994, it was called the Federal Counterintelligence Service, or FSK, but it was later renamed the Federal Security Service, FSB.) Yeltsin okayed the plan, and Director Primakov, General Trubnikov, and Sergei's immediate boss met with their FSK counterparts at Lubyanka to work out an agreement. According to Sergei, it became the first joint project undertaken by the SVR and FSK after the KGB was splintered into pieces. Although KIRILL's name was kept secret, Yeltsin's legal staff had to review the SVR and FSK agreement because the president was nervous about the two services working together. The failed August 1991 coup led by KGB director Kryuchkov and the more recent coup against Yeltsin were still fresh memories.

Sergei was brought back into the project after Yeltsin's legal staff approved the working agreement. At this juncture, the SVR changed KIRILL's code name to *KABAN*, which means boar, as a precaution. It would now be sharing information about him with the FSK and it didn't want its officers to link KIRILL to his past spying efforts.

Sergei recommended that KABAN be awarded a contract to consult and help build housing in Tver, which was a town about a hundred miles outside of Moscow. His superiors and the FSK agreed.

In 1994, Russia was in the midst of a national housing shortage. The main cause was the dissolution of the Soviet Union. Russian troops from across Eastern Europe were being called home, but there was no place to house them. Yeltsin had specifically asked President Clinton for help with this problem when they met in April 1993 at their first presidential summit. According to *The Russia Hand: A Memoir of Presidential Diplomacy,* by Deputy Secretary of State Strobe Talbott, Yeltsin had been desperate.

> There was one area . . . where Yeltsin said he needed as much help as possible and as soon as possible, and that was in emergency funds to build housing for the Russian officers whom Yeltsin had promised to withdraw from the Baltic states in 1994.

Clinton had earmarked $6 million for housing, but Yeltsin said he needed much more than that. Yeltsin added that he could only make his plea in private, according to Talbott's book, because it was embarrassing for him to talk openly about the conditions in which the Russian army was living. Talbott quoted Yeltsin saying:

"Tents, Bill! Can you imagine? They're living in tents!"

Clinton promised to increase the figure for housing. In addition to U.S. aid, Yeltsin received loans from Canada, France, Germany, Italy, Japan, and the United Kingdom to help build houses. The World Bank chipped in another $550.8 million loan specifically earmarked for housing improvements in six cities, including Tver.

Sergei suggested that KABAN be given a contract to build houses in Tver because the city was close enough to Moscow for KABAN to meet with the SVR but far enough away to make it difficult for Canadian or U.S. intelligence agencies to keep an eye on him. Tver was located near the confluence of the Volga and Tver rivers and was home to about half a million residents.

According to Sergei, the FSK arranged for KABAN's consulting firm to be hired. On paper, everything appeared completely legitimate. KABAN was paid to hire architects in Canada to design a model home that could be built inexpensively in Tver. Russian-built homes, made of concrete, took too long to construct and were too expensive for returning Russian soldiers. KABAN's firm was asked to come up with a quick and less expensive design based on Canadian building techniques. Once the firm came up with a model, KABAN would be paid to send Canadian craftsmen to Tver, where they could build a sample and begin teaching Russians there how to duplicate it.

"KABAN was generally interested in building affordable housing and, of course, the operation gave us an easy way to pay him," Sergei said. The FSK could hide the additional spy payments in a myriad of ways.

KABAN's firm designed a wood frame house that could be built in only three weeks at a cost of $15,000 per unit. The two-story, four-bedroom home with stucco siding and a tin roof was the least expensive of all the demonstration houses built in Tver, where the average resident earned less than $1,000 per year.

"I was having dinner with KABAN in Moscow and he kept talking about how easy it was for him to do business in Tver when other foreign companies were getting no-where because they had to deal with the Russian bureaucracy and corruption, and I thought, 'Of course it is easy for you because the SVR has made it easy, otherwise you wouldn't last a day in Tver. The mafia there would have your throat cut and you would be buried in the woods by gangsters who were stealing from everyone.' But I kept quiet. I had gone to Tver long before KABAN had ever set foot there, and I had told the local officials that this man and his company were supposed to get everything they asked for. There would be no problems created for him, otherwise the local officials would have to answer to us."

KABAN began traveling regularly between Canada and Russia to supervise the Tver project. According to Sergei, he brought copies of classified Canadian documents with him. "I suggested we reward him by introducing him to a good Russian girl during one of these trips so we could further tighten our control over him."

The FSK arranged a translator for KABAN. "She was very good looking and very smart and he was lonely, so it did not take long before they began having sex." According to Sergei, the FSK secretly videotaped KABAN's sexual liaisons. He had a wife back in Canada. "I was later given transcripts of these sex sessions and I remember reading several pages and thinking the best thing you can do when you are making love to a woman is not to talk at all because you sound rather stupid."

After KABAN's consulting firm completed its demonstration house in Tver, the SVR and FSK arranged for his firm to get a piece of another project, this one in Moscow. KABAN was hired to help manage a $300 million "housing divestiture project" being paid for by a World Bank loan. The cash was supposed to be spent reconditioning more than a million apartments in 15,300 buildings in six major Russian cities. When this project started, Sergei turned the handling of KABAN over to an FSK officer in Moscow.

Sergei said he received a commendation for his dealings with KABAN. "The director of Department A told me that I had single-handedly created an entirely new method of recruitment for Russian intelligence. It was called 'business recruitment,' and it was going to be widely used in Moscow because so many Westerners were rushing into Russia to open businesses. It gave us a way to pay them without anyone becoming suspicious. It was a clever way for foreign intelligence to take advantage of the new democratic and open Russia economy."

According to U.S. intelligence, KABAN

continues to operate a firm in Canada, where he specializes in consulting contracts in Russia and former Soviet republics.

TWENTY-ONE

Inflation and political unrest were not the only troubles Boris Yeltsin faced in 1994. Chechnya, an oil-rich and largely Muslim area of Russia, declared its independence after the Soviet Union ceased to exist. More than three hundred thousand non-Chechens, mostly Russians, fled the region to avoid persecution by the new government's president, Dzhokar Dudayev. When armed rebels, who were being backed by Moscow, failed to topple Dudayev, Yeltsin sent in the Russian army to restore "constitutional order."

Even though Department A at the SVR Center was not directly involved in Yeltsin's military campaign, Sergei and his coworkers were ordered to distribute propaganda to justify Yeltsin's action. The propaganda drive was important to Yeltsin because he didn't know how his Western friends would react to the fighting and he needed their ongoing political and financial support. The Center produced anti-Chechen materials for Sergei to forward to journalists, politicians, and interested groups in Canada. The packets included news stories and videotapes about Russians being tortured, raped, and murdered by Chechen troops. The propaganda emphasized that Chechnya was a part of Russia. It was not a former Soviet republic that had declared its independence. To make this point easier for Westerners to understand, the Center tailored the propaganda materials to fit its audience. In Canada, Chechnya was compared to Quebec. In the U.S., Chechnya was likened to Southern states seceding during the Civil War.

On January 3, 1995, Mike McCurry, the press spokesman for the State Department, compared Russia's invasion of Chechnya to the Civil War. He said:

We have a long history as a democracy that includes an episode . . . where we dealt with a secessionist movement through armed conflict called the Civil War. So we need to be conscious of those types of issues when we look at a new democracy in the former Soviet Union.

In April 1996, during a Moscow press conference, President Clinton used that same comparison.

> I would remind you that we once had a civil war in our country in which we lost, on a per capita basis, far more people than we lost in any of the wars of the twentieth century, over the proposition that Abraham Lincoln gave his life for, that no state had a right to withdrawal from our union.

In his memoir *The Russia Hand*, Strobe Talbott wrote apologetically that he felt responsible for suggesting the Chechnya–Civil War comparison to McCurry and Clinton. It proved to be a "gaffe" that "produced a headline we didn't want out," he noted. Clinton was accused in the international media of shilling for Yeltsin. Clinton himself later quipped: "I really painted a bull's-eye on my butt with that Lincoln line."

The fact that Talbott, McCurry, and Clinton each defended Russia's attacks in Chechnya by comparing the invasion to the U.S. Civil War delighted the propagandists inside the SVR, Sergei said. Whether or not their efforts had planted the idea in the three men's minds didn't matter. The SVR spin masters claimed credit.

The use of propaganda by Russian intelligence dated back to the first days of the 1917 October Revolution. At the Red Banner Institute, Sergei had read dozens of case studies where the KGB used propaganda and disinformation to influence public opinion. But he didn't learn about what was reportedly the biggest case of disinformation ever propagated by the KGB until he returned to the Center in 1994 and had access to some of its most sensitive files. "There was an incident in recent times where Soviet intelligence managed not only to deceive the U.S., but the *entire* Western world, with propaganda," Sergei said later. "It created the myth of nuclear winter."

This is what the KGB did, according to Sergei, who not only read classified reports about the propaganda operation but also spoke to one of the key KGB officials involved in it.

In the 1970s, KGB director Yuri Andropov set out to undermine NATO, which had been created in 1949 by ten Western European nations, Canada, and the U.S. to thwart the threat of a Soviet invasion in Europe. Andropov funneled money into European peace and anti-nuclear organizations that were vehemently opposed to the

U.S. operating military bases in Germany — a key component of NATO. The KGB used the Soviet Peace Committee, a part of the Soviet government, to organize and finance demonstrations in Europe against the U.S. bases.

When NATO members voted in 1979 to deploy 572 Pershing II cruise missiles in Western Europe, Andropov stepped up the KGB disruption campaign. NATO said the missiles were needed to offset more than three hundred triple-warhead Soviet SS-20 mobile missiles that the Soviet Union had pointed at Europe. Andropov ordered the Soviet Academy of Science to produce a doomsday report that would describe the dire consequences that would happen across Europe if both sides began firing nuclear weapons in Germany. His goal was to stop deployment of the Pershing II missiles, which were scheduled to begin arriving in 1983, by scaring Europeans and inciting more demonstrations and resentment in Germany toward the U.S.

Not long after NATO voted to approve the Pershing missiles, the Soviet Union's news service released a story to the West that was picked up by the British Broadcasting Corporation. The story, which had been approved by KGB propagandists, described experiments in the Karakum desert in South Central Asia that were being done by a Soviet specialist in atmospheric physics, Dr. Kirill Kondrayev. He and other Soviet scientists were part of a research team being funded by the Aleksandr Voyeykov Main Geophysical Observatory and Leningrad University, according to the Soviet release. The story said that Kondrayev had made a startling discovery. "Even in the sweltering deserts at the height of summer, the Earth's surface can remain comparatively cold if dust storms are raging in the air," the news report declared. Kondrayev called this phenomenon the "anti-hothouse effect" and explained that the reason why the earth's temperature could be cooler was that dust particles filling the atmosphere during a major dust storm were "capable of shutting out the Sun's rays."

Neither Kondrayev nor his colleagues ever submitted their experiments to the West for scientific peer review. However, their claim — that dust particles could effectively block out the sun, causing temperatures to drop — would later be widely accepted as a scientific fact. Only a few top KGB officials and a handful of Soviet scientists would know that Kondrayev's dramatic discovery was not the result of painstaking research, but the first step in a carefully choreo-graphed KGB propaganda campaign.

The next step forward in satisfying An-dropov's demand for a cataclysmic scenario came from the Institute of Terrestrial Phys-ics of the Soviet Academy of Sciences. It prepared a study drafted by Georgi Golitsyn, a geophysicist; N. N. Moiseyev, a mathematician; and V. V. Aleksandrov, a computer expert, under the direction of Yuri Israel, chairman of the USSR State Com-mittee for Hydro-Meteorology and Environ-mental Control. The scientists claimed they had used a mathematical model to estimate how much dirt and debris would be blasted into the atmosphere during a nuclear attack in Germany. They then applied Kondrayev's "anti-hothouse effect" to see what impact the airborne debris would have on the planet. Their conclusion: The use of nuclear weapons in Germany during a Soviet inva-sion of Europe would lodge so much dirt in the atmosphere that the sun would be un-able to shine through and temperatures across Europe would plunge.

"I was told the Soviet scientists knew this theory was completely ridiculous," Sergei said later. "There were no legitimate scien-tific facts to support it. But it was exactly what Andropov needed to cause terror in the West."

Andropov suspected that Western scientists would be skeptical of a Soviet study that made such a spectacular claim, so instead of publishing it in a scientific journal, the KGB began using *aktivnye meropriiatiia* — covert active measures — to disseminate the doomsday findings. Information from the study's key findings was distributed by KGB officers to their contacts in peace, anti-nuclear, disarmament, and environmental organizations in an effort to get these groups to publicize the propagandists' script. One of the publications that the KGB targeted was *Ambio* — *A Journal of the Human Environment.*

Founded in 1972 in Stockholm by the Royal Swedish Academy of Sciences, *Ambio* prided itself on investigating scientific, social, economic, and cultural factors that, according to its mandate, "influence the condition of the human environment." In 1982 — a year before the first Pershing missiles were set to arrive in Germany — an editor at *Ambio* contacted Paul J. Crutzen at the Max Planck Institute for Chemistry in Mainz, Germany. Crutzen, who would be awarded the Nobel Prize in Chemistry later in his career, had recently moved to the German institute after spending three years as director of research at the National Center of Atmospheric Research in Boulder, Colorado, where he had been investigating how fires and other natural disasters affected atmospheric conditions.

The editor explained that *Ambio* was preparing a special issue that would examine how a nuclear war would impact the planet. The editor asked Crutzen to write specifically about the effect of nuclear blasts on the atmosphere. Crutzen and one of his former colleagues from Colorado, John W. Birks, submitted an article called "The Atmosphere After a Nuclear War: Twilight at Noon." In it, they wrote that a nuclear blast would cause soot and dust to rise in the atmosphere, creating a thick layer of smoke that could alter the world's climate.

There is no evidence or reason to suspect that *Ambio*, Crutzen, or Birks knew the KGB was trying to instigate anti-U.S. feelings by circulating fraudulent scientific data about the atmospheric dangers of a nuclear war in Western Europe.

The *Ambio* article reached the United States even before it was published in Sweden. Audubon Society president Russell Peterson, whose wife was an editor at *Ambio,* was later identified in news reports as having given an advance copy of the

Crutzen story to Robert Scrivner of the Rockefeller Family Fund. Other news reports would credit George Carrier, a Harvard mathematician in charge of a National Academy of Sciences committee studying nuclear war, with spotting the article and deciding to pursue it in the U.S. Regardless, the *Ambio* story ended up in the hands of Carl Sagan, an astronomer and professor at Cornell University, and an ardent antinuclear activist. Sagan was one of the best-known scientists in America because of a thirteen-part televison series called *Cosmos* that first aired in 1980. Hosted by Sagan, the show traced the history of the universe from the time of the "big bang" up to the present. More than 500 million people in sixty countries had watched it.

Sagan would later explain during interviews that he had already been studying completely on his own the possible impact of dust stirred up by a nuclear blast when he read the *Ambio* article. He recruited a team of scientists, including Richard P. Turco, Owen B. Toon, Thomas P. Ackerman, and James B. Pollack, to delve deeper into the impact on the planet of a nuclear war in Europe. They dubbed their report "the TTAPS study," which was the first initial of their last names. Sagan and the others announced that a nuclear blast would cause dust to block out the sun's rays, but they took the scenario even further. They claimed the layer of debris would be so thick that much of Europe would be thrust into a new ice age.

Years later, *National Review* magazine would investigate the TTAPS study and publish a scalding review of it and Sagan's actions. According to the magazine, Sagan first approached the scientific heads of the NASA Ames Research Center and asked them to host a conference in late 1982 so that he and his colleagues could make the results of their frightening findings public. But when the space agency chiefs examined the TTAPS study, they questioned the validity of the mathematical model that the scientists had used. They refused to help Sagan. Undeterred, he used his national popularity to publish the group's findings on his own — on October 30, 1983, in the Sunday newspaper supplement *Parade* magazine. In an unusual step, he released it before the TTAPS findings could undergo scientific review — the normal channel used by scientists to verify findings. One of Sagan's coauthors, Richard Turco, would later be credited with coining the eye-popping phrase that would emerge from the magazine story and captivate the public. Turco said an attack in Europe would cause a "nuclear winter."

The Wall Street Journal would later join the *National Review* in writing critical accounts of Sagan's actions. According to the newspaper, the Washington, D.C., public relations firm Porter, Noveilli and Associates was hired to launch a $100,000 campaign to publicize the threat of a nuclear winter. The Kendall Foundation, which financed environmental causes, paid for the national ad campaign. Sagan appeared on *The Phil Donahue Show* and dozens of other radio and television programs in 1983, explaining "nuclear winter" and denouncing the use of nuclear weapons, especially in Europe. Peace, anti-nuclear, disarmament, and environmental groups, including Common Cause, Friends of the Earth, the Institute for Policy Studies, the International Physicians for the Prevention of Nuclear War, Physicians for Social Responsibility, Planned Parenthood, Scientists Against Nuclear Arms, the Sierra Club, the United Nations Association of the United States of America, and the Union of Concerned Scientists rallied behind him and the TTAPS study.

Incredibly, Sagan and his fellow authors

still had not submitted the study for scientific peer review at this point. Despite this breach of protocol, they appeared at an international conference in November 1983, "The World After Nuclear War," which was hosted in Washington, D.C., by a conglomeration of U.S. environmental organizations and scientific foundations. During their presentation, the TTAPS team released several frightening details from the study, which was officially titled *Global Atmospheric Consequences of Nuclear War.* They said their findings were based on a mathematical model that examined a hypothetical nuclear exchange of 5,000 megatons and a total number of 10,400 explosions. The scientists estimated a 5,000-megaton nuclear exchange would result in the deaths of 1.1 billion people and would leave another 1.1 billion seriously injured. Based on this model, the scientists projected that at least 100,000 tons of soot and dust would be catapulted into the upper atmosphere by each megaton exploded in a ground burst. The dense clouds, held aloft by winds for months, would blanket most of the Northern Hemisphere, cutting off the heat and light. The authors claimed that sunlight would be about 5 percent of normal, causing temperatures to plunge to minus 13 degrees Fahrenheit (minus 25 degrees Celsius). The surface of the earth would remain that way for months.

In addition to Sagan and the TTAPS authors, the conference sponsors asked the Soviet Union to send over a group of its scientists to speak. Moscow sent Moiseyev, Golitsin, and Aleksandrov — the three Soviet scientists who had concocted Andropov's original doomsday report. They confirmed the TTAPS study, saying their research concurred completely with their Western colleagues'. At a news conference Sagan cited the Soviet study as proof that the TTAPS study was valid.

A few weeks after the conference, ABC television broadcast a made-for-television movie entitled *The Day After,* which dramatized what would happen to ordinary citizens living in Lawrence, Kansas, if the U.S. and Soviet Union unleashed a nuclear attack. *Newsweek* magazine wrote: "There's never been a movie like ABC's *The Day After,* nor any video event that has stirred so much ferment in so many quarters. . . . It has already emerged as the single biggest mobilizing point for the anti-nuclear movement." The show caused such a national sensation that after it was broadcast, ABC held a special edition of its popular *Night-*

line program with a panel of experts, including Sagan, who once again discussed the dire consequences of a "nuclear winter."

Sagan and his coauthors finally released the TTAPS study for peer review on December 23, 1983, when it was published by *Science* magazine. But their article did not satisfy their colleagues. Some 136 pages of promised data to back up their "nuclear winter" theory were not included. A notation in the article said those pages were "in preparation." A week after that *Science* article appeared, Sagan published another article, this time in *Foreign Affairs* magazine, titled "Nuclear War and Climactic Catastrophe." In it, he argued that the U.S. and Soviet Union needed a "coherent, mutually agreed upon, long-term policy for dramatic reductions in nuclear armaments." Once again, he declared that a nuclear winter was inevitable if nuclear weapons were launched.

How much influence, if any, the KGB's active measure efforts played in pushing the nuclear winter concept would be impossible to discern. But Andropov and his KGB propagandists were convinced their handiwork had prepared the stage for Sagan, according to Sergei. Sagan's appearances and the TTAPS study did not, however, stop NATO from installing the Pershing missiles.

Sergei's grandmother Lyubov (in Red Army military uniform), when she served in the NKVD, later to become the KGB, 1937.

Sergei's mother, Revmira, with her comrades-in-arms in the Red Army during World War II.

Sergei's father, Oleg, in his secret atomic weapons laboratory in Moscow, 1957.

A group of children greet Nikita Khrushchev and Fidel Castro in the Kremlin park, 1963. Sergei's future wife, Helen, is the girl in the white hat in the lower left corner.

Helen and Sergei's
wedding, 1976.

Sergei's first KGB ID
photo—his rank was
lieutenant—July 1982.

Sergei (right, with blond hair) with Komsomol members bringing flowers to the grave of Konon Molody, aka Comrade Ben, a famous Soviet illegal KGB intelligence officer in the U.S. in the 1950s who stole nuclear secrets.

Sergei, as Komsomol Secretary of the First Chief Directorate (Intelligence) of the KGB, addresses the annual Komsomol Congress at KGB headquarters in Lubyanka Square, Moscow, October 1988.

Полковнику

ТРЕТЬЯКОВУ

СЕРГЕЮ ОЛЕГОВИЧУ

УВАЖАЕМЫЙ

СЕРГЕЙ ОЛЕГОВИЧ!

ДИРЕКТОРАТ СЛУЖБЫ ВНЕШНЕЙ РАЗВЕДКИ РОССИЙСКОЙ ФЕДЕРАЦИИ ПОЗДРАВЛЯЕТ ВАС С ПРИСВОЕНИЕМ ВЫСОКОГО ВОИНСКОГО ЗВАНИЯ ПОЛКОВНИК И ЖЕЛАЕТ ДАЛЬНЕЙШИХ УСПЕХОВ В ДЕЛЕ ЗАЩИТЫ ИНТЕРЕСОВ РОССИИ.

Директор Службы внешней разведки
Российской Федерации
генерал-полковник   В. Трубников

«20» мая 1999 г.

A formal congratulatory letter on the occasion of Sergei's promotion to the military rank of colonel. The front (at top) reads: "Colonel Tretyakov, Sergei Olegovich." The message (at left) reads: "Dear Sergei Olegovich! The Directorate of the Service of Foreign Intelligence of the Russian Federation congratulates you on the conferment of the high military rank of colonel and wishes you further success in the cause of protection of the interests of Russia." It is signed "Director of the Service of Foreign Intelligence of the Russian Federation, Colonel General V. Trubnikov" and dated May 20, 1999.

Sergei, at the controls of the boat requisitioned for the Russian embassy resort at Pioneer Point, Queen Anne County, Maryland. The SVR *rezidentura* used it by night to dump illegally several tons of broken and obsolete equipment in the Chester and Corsica rivers.

At their lunch in Brighton Beach, August 2000: from left to right, Viktor Zolotov, head of Vladimir Putin's personal security; Yevgeni Murov, head of the FSO (Federal Protection Service—the equivalent of the U.S. Secret Service); Sergei Kutafin, the SVR resident in New York City; and Sergei Tretyakov. Tretyakov recounts how Aleksandr Lunkin, deputy head of the FSO, told him that Zolotov and Murov prepared a list of persons whom they wanted to eliminate for standing in Putin's way. When they finished the list, Zolotov reportedly announced, "It's too many to kill—even for us."

Sergei at home in his study with his cat, Matilda, March 2007.

Helen and Ksenia
at home, 2007.

In coming years, several scientists challenged Sagan and the TTAPS results. Princeton's eminent theoretician Freeman Dyson was quoted in the *National Review* article stating: "Frankly, I think it's an absolutely atrocious piece of physics, but I quite despair of setting the public record straight. . . . Who wants to be accused of being in favor of nuclear war?" An MIT scientist, Victor Weisskopf, was quoted by *National Journal* writer Brad Sparks stating, "The science is terrible, but perhaps the psychology is good." In January 1986, the leading British scientific journal *Nature* wrote about the politicalizing of science. "Nowhere is this more evident than in the recent literature on 'Nuclear Winter' — research which has become notorious for its lack of scientific integrity." Russell Seitz, an MIT-trained physicist and visiting scholar at Harvard University, joined in the criticism by writing that nuclear winter was a theory based on a "notorious lack of scientific integrity." Even well-known author Michael Crichton eventually joined the chorus, pointing out that Sagan had appeared on Johnny Carson's *Tonight Show* forty times, pushing his nuclear winter argument as part of a "well-orchestrated media campaign. . . . This is not the way science is done, it is the way products are sold."

Sagan never backed down. In 1991, he appeared on *Nightline* and predicted that fires caused by the burning of 526 Kuwaiti oil wells — set by retreating Iraqi soldiers during the first Gulf War — would send black smoke into the upper atmosphere, disrupt the monsoons, and significantly alter the environment. Sagan's predictions were called "ridiculous" on that same broadcast by Dr. S. Fred Singer, who predicted the smoke would go up only a few thousand feet and then be washed out of the atmosphere by rain. Three days later, black rain began falling over Iran, which essentially put an end to the argument. There were no dramatic temperature drops. Sagan died in December 1996.

"I am not a scientist, nor did I ever meet Mr. Sagan or his coauthors," Sergei said later. "I did have several conversations with the former KGB official responsible for scientific propaganda during this time period, and she told me repeatedly the KGB was responsible for creating the entire nuclear winter story to stop the Pershing missiles. I don't know if Mr. Sagan ever knew the KGB was behind this effort, but inside the KGB, the nuclear winter propaganda was considered the ultimate example

of how the KGB had completely alarmed
the West with science that no one in Moscow
ever believed was true."

Twenty-Two

Sergei and Helen deposited $25,000 in a Moscow bank that was paying 200 percent interest — a rate that didn't seem out of line given that inflation was unchecked. They were impressed. Armed guards stood watch in the ornate lobby and smartly dressed tellers eagerly answered their questions. A month later, they decided to drop by the bank to see how much interest they'd earned. When they reached the building, the offices had been stripped clean. No guards, no furniture, no employees — and no deposits. Their bank was one of 315 financial institutions in Moscow that disappeared overnight during 1994. Most were pyramid schemes. Sergei used his connections at the Center to look for the thieves. "The bank had been run by a Russian mafia clan and I was told it was better to lose the money than to be killed trying to get it back. It was a shock to me. Not losing the money — the change. The KGB had been the most frightening organization in the Soviet Union, but now these Russian criminals were more feared." A study by Transparency International, a German think tank, found that only seven countries in the world were as corrupt as Russia. Contract killings in Moscow hit three hundred per year. A U.S. study warned that the Russian mafia had taken control of half a million businesses, fifty thousand banks, and one thousand corporations.

Sergei and Helen had returned to a Moscow that they quickly came to despise. "You'd see people on the street who couldn't afford bread and then a new, shiny American SUV would race by and you knew it was a criminal."

Sergei began pressing the director of Department A for another assignment overseas. A year after they returned to Russia, Sergei was given a choice. He could pick New York City or Washington, D.C., for his next assignment, but there was a catch. If he chose Manhattan, he could leave Moscow as soon as he trained his replacement and underwent several briefings about SVR activities in the U.S. But the job in Washington, D.C., wouldn't be open for at least two years.

Sergei didn't hesitate. He picked Manhattan.

Based on his recommendation, Sergei's bosses chose Vitali Domoratski, the officer who had successfully recruited a Canadian member of Parliament, to replace Sergei as head of the Canadian section. Sergei began splitting his time between training Domoratski and attending top-secret briefings to prepare him for the combination job of deputy *rezident* and head of Line PR (political intelligence) in Manhattan.

It was during the briefings that Sergei discovered the SVR had identified U.S. deputy secretary of state Strobe Talbott as a SPECIAL UNOFFICIAL CONTACT. Inside the SVR, that term was used only to identify a top-level intelligence source who had high social and/or political status and whose identity needed to be carefully guarded.

For example, Fidel Castro's brother Raúl Modesto Castro Ruz had been recruited by the KGB during the Khrushchev era as a SPECIAL UNOFFICIAL CONTACT and worked secretly for the Russians continuously during the Yeltsin administration, Sergei said.

"Raúl was used by the Center to get access to and to influence the Cuban president during periods when Fidel Castro became hostile toward the Soviet leadership. The KGB/SVR always took special precautions to keep his role as a SPECIAL UNOFFICIAL CONTACT hidden from Castro and the Cuban people." (Raúl Castro took charge of the Cuban government on July 31, 2006, when his older brother became ill.)

Because of the prominence of SPECIAL UNOFFICIAL CONTACTS, the SVR's operational dossiers about them were always closely guarded with top-secret access limited to only a few senior officials in Moscow. Sergei later explained that this was why he could not cite specific examples in this book of information that the SVR claimed it had collected through diplomatic channels from Talbott. Nor could he recall any specifics of how information alleged to have come from Talbott might have been used. "All I can tell you is that the SVR conferred on Talbott the SPECIAL UNOFFICIAL CONTACT designation, and I was told Russian intelligence had tricked and manipulated him."

A SPECIAL UNOFFICIAL CONTACT was identified in cables between the Center and *rezidenturas* as a "11-2" source. That was the same designation used by the SVR to identify sources in its network who were "trusted contacts" (spies).

"Even though the SVR identified Talbott as a SPECIAL UNOFFICIAL CONTACT, I want to underline that he was *not* a Russian spy," Sergei carefully explained later. "In fact, I suspect he was the opposite — an ardent American patriot. But like so many before him, he underestimated his Soviet and Russian counterparts and he overestimated his own knowledge and influence to a point where our intelligence service was able to use him with great effectiveness during the Yeltsin presidency. He became an extremely valuable intelligence source."

A former columnist and Washington bureau chief for *Time* magazine, Talbott befriended Bill Clinton when both were Rhodes scholars at Oxford University. After Clinton won the 1992 presidential election, he asked Talbott to oversee U.S. and Russian relations. In *The Russia Hand,* Talbott would recall that one of his first and, ultimately, his most important contacts in the Yeltsin administration was Georgi Mamedov, the deputy minister of foreign affairs. Talbott noted fondly in his book that Mamedov had both a gift for gab and an ability for straight talk that made him effective in arguing his side's case and in probing for diplomatic give on the American side. Talbott wrote that he and Mamedov frequently worked behind the scenes during Talbott's seven-year stint. They arranged the Clinton–Yeltsin presidential summits, handled dozens of international emergencies, and found ways for the Clinton administration to support Yeltsin politically when his administration was being rocked by charges of massive corruption. Talbott added that he and Mamedov privately negotiated the framework for a controversial NATO-Russian cooperative agreement and personally resolved preliminary matters in the START II treaty talks about arms reduction. Talbott wrote that many of their face-to-face meetings were held with only the two of them being present, and during their exchanges, the two diplomats developed a friendship, trust, and respect that Talbott felt was mutual and mentioned repeatedly in his memoir. In one chapter, Talbott described a scene that typified their warm relationship. He wrote that he and Mamedov decided to take a break after working all day during a meeting in Washington, D.C. Talbott invited Mamedov to go with him to see that summer's blockbuster movie *Independence Day,* along with Talbott's children. Afterward, Mamedov joined the family for dinner at an Italian restaurant, and Talbott and the Russian diplomat playfully joked about whether the aliens in the Hollywood movie would be eligible to join Partnership for Peace (a Clinton and Yeltsin initiative) or if they would be considered for membership in NATO. At the time, the U.S. and NATO were feuding with Russia about NATO expanding its membership.

During the secret briefings that Sergei was given in Moscow before his move to Manhattan, he was told that Mamedov was secretly working for the SVR. "Mr. Mamedov was a longtime co-optee. The KGB and SVR helped him build a very successful career in the foreign ministry. What does this mean? It means he was reporting everything that was said or done by Mr. Talbott directly to us at the Center. *Everything.* It was part of his job." There is no evidence that shows, nor is there any reason to believe, that Talbott knew Mamedov was a longtime co-optee with Russian intelligence.

Sergei was told that SVR director Primakov and his deputy, General Trubnikov, decided early on that Talbott could be "massaged" and developed into a useful source based on a psychological profile that the SVR had prepared. "Mr. Talbott saw himself as an expert on Russia and he thought he knew what was best for the country and its people. The SVR had seen this arrogant attitude before in Western leaders. We understood this, and Mr. Mamedov was instructed to massage Mr. Talbott's ego to suit our purposes," Sergei said. Mamedov was encouraged by the SVR to meet with Talbott in private as often as he could, without any of the two men's aides being present. During these sessions, Mamedov was told to ask Talbott questions that had been prepared specifically for him by the SVR Center. The Russian diplomat posed these questions as if they were coming only from him. "Mr. Talbott was led to believe that many of his conversations with Mr. Mamedov were between only the two of them, when, in fact, Mr. Mamedov was collecting information that had been specifically requested by the Center. This is how the SVR was able to begin manipulating him to the point that it eventually identified him as a SPECIAL UNOFFICIAL CONTACT."

Sergei was told that Mamedov's relationship with Talbott was an "example of how a skilled intelligence agency could manipulate a situation and a diplomatic source to its advantage without the target realizing he was being used for intelligence-gathering purposes."

Sergei's statements are not the first to

raise questions about Talbott's interactions with Russian officials. A U.S. House of Representatives select committee released a three-volume report in 1999 that harshly criticized the Clinton administration for its handling of Russia. Known informally as the Cox Committee Report, after its chairman, Representative Christopher Cox, the study initially was classified top-secret. Several parts of it, however, were later declassified. Representative Cox told reporters at a news conference that the Clinton administration had continuously supported Yeltsin regardless of his actions or his behavior. The Cox report said the Clinton administration's "unchecked" backing of Yeltsin had undermined the development of democratic institutions in Moscow by short-circuiting the legislative process that Russia had put into place and by ignoring the wishes of the country's elected representatives. This partisan and oftentimes parental attitude toward the Russian president had caused Yeltsin and the Russian government to rule by decree rather than by establishing a genuine democratic process, the report concluded. Representative Cox claimed a small group of administration officials, including Talbott, consistently ignored and downplayed U.S. analytical information that contradicted their own personal views of Russia and what was happening under Yeltsin. One criticism was that Talbott had been persuaded by Mamedov and other Russian officials to disregard negative stories about Yeltsin, his presidency, and the oligarchs.

After portions of the Cox report were made public, Talbott noted that twelve of the fifteen committee members who had drafted the critical study were Republicans. He called their findings politically biased and questioned the timing of the report, which was released in the midst of the 2000 presidential campaign.

Talbott became president of the Brookings Institution, a Washington, D.C., think tank, after he left the Clinton administration. His diplomatic counterpart, Mamedov, was appointed Russian ambassador to Canada.

Talbott was shown Sergei's statements while this book was being written and he quickly dismissed them. "Your source's [Sergei's] interpretation of events is erroneous and/or misleading in several fundamental respects," Talbott wrote. "First, there was never a presumption on Ambassador Mamedov's part or mine that what we said to each other in our one-on-one sessions would remain between us alone. Quite the contrary, each of us presumed that the other would report back to his government. Second, your source suggests that, in his many exchanges with me, Ambassador Mamedov 'tricked, deceived, and manipulated' me into helping him and his government advance Russian causes. . . . Your source offers no amplification or corroboration. There can be none, since what went on in my channel with Mamedov in fact advanced U.S. policy goals: getting Russian troops to leave the Baltic states, getting Russia to accept NATO enlargement and join the Partnership for Peace, getting Russia to support us in Bosnia, and getting Russia to help in ending the Kosovo war on NATO's terms."

In a note responding to Sergei's accusations, Ambassador Mamedov wrote: "As a devoted fan of John le Carré's novels, I really enjoyed the fantasy land you and your 'sources' from the CIA created to impress me. . . . Surely, I don't need to tell you what you know already: all of these allegations of my 'manipulation' of Strobe Talbott on behalf of the SVR are blatant lies and nothing else. Unfortunately, old stereotypes die hard and some witch-hunters from the CIA and FBI simply can't make themselves believe in such simple human values as trust and friendship — especially between Russian and American officials. Pity for them!"

Knowing that he and his family would soon be leaving Moscow for New York, Sergei, Helen, and Ksenia went to the Russian countryside as frequently as they could on weekends to enjoy their summer houses. They had inherited two. Sergei's dacha was located outside the village of Tarasovka and had been built in 1932 in a Communist co-operative that had belonged to the NKVD. The dacha had been awarded to the family at the time because Sergei's grandmother had been an NKVD officer. It was a sturdy wooden house in an area that was referred to by many as the "Russian Switzerland" because of its beauty. Helen had inherited a larger summer house from her father located near a village called Zelenogradskaya. It was more prestigious because it was in a region where many Kremlin officials owned homes. Helen's house was across the road from a cottage owned by Galina Brezhnev, the boozy spoiled child of former Soviet leader Leonid Brezhnev.

Sergei considered the two dachas "family treasures" and also permanent headaches. "In May, all Muscovites began restoring their summer houses, making repairs that were always extensive because of the tough Russian winters. By September, the house would be perfect, but then winter would come and destroy all progress that you made. In May, you had to begin again. We often joked that dachas were Stalin's real labor camps."

Sergei wanted to take Ksenia, who was now fourteen, to pick mushrooms in the woods near his dacha before the family left for the U.S. His parents had taught him how to gather mushrooms and he wanted to pass the tradition to her. Sergei and Ksenia had walked about ten minutes into the forest along a dirt road when their path was blocked by a newly constructed guardhouse and gate. Two young men armed with semiautomatic rifles were stationed there.

"Where do you think you're going?" one of them demanded.

"Is it of your business?" Sergei replied, irked that he was being questioned so rudely.

"Yes, it is my business because you're on private property."

Sergei told them that he was a high-ranking officer in the SVR and that his family had hunted wild mushrooms in the forest for several decades. But neither guard was impressed. They said Yuri Luzhkov, whom President Yeltsin had appointed mayor of Moscow in 1992, had purchased the tract that now bordered Sergei's dacha. Luzhkov intended to bring wild animals into the property for his friends and him to hunt.

Sergei would later remember his reaction: "Here were these two men pointing automatic weapons at my daughter and me in our very own backyard, telling us we were no longer welcome in our own woods where my parents and their parents had walked. This criminal community had not only invaded Moscow, but now the countryside. They were taking over. Russia had become a place I no longer recognized. I looked at these two guards and thought: 'This isn't my country anymore.' "

TWENTY-THREE

New York, April 1995

New York fit Sergei like a well-worn slipper.

Familiarizing himself with the consulate, Riverdale apartments, and permanent mission proved easy. Dealing with his colleagues was trickier. They were divided into two camps, even though the Russian Federation claimed they all worked for the Ministry of Foreign Affairs (MFA), the equivalent of the U.S. Department of State.

Legitimate diplomats (cleans) answered to Ambassador Sergei Lavrov, the Russian Federation's UN envoy. Intelligence officers — SVR and GRU — reported to their respective *rezidents*. To confuse the CIA and FBI, everyone was issued diplomatic credentials. As part of this charade, the MFA never used the terms SVR and GRU. Ambassador Lavrov used "close neighbors" whenever he discussed the SVR in correspondence. He used "far neighbors" when referring to GRU. If Lavrov needed to tell the MFA about the SVR *rezident,* he would refer to him as the "rezident of our close neighbors." The terms were grounded in Russian history. During the Stalin era, the MFA was located in Moscow on Vorovskiy Street, close to the KGB's Lubyanka headquarters. The GRU's offices were miles from downtown Moscow. Accordingly, the KGB became "our close neighbors" and GRU "our far neighbors."

In spite of these subterfuges, nearly everyone inside the mission knew who was clean and who wasn't — and, more important, Sergei suspected U.S. intelligence also knew. "The MFA insisted intelligence officers be given very low diplomatic ranks, and once assigned, these slots were never changed," he said later. "Because of this, our officers always had the same covers, and once the FBI or CIA realized an intelligence officer held that position, they knew his replacement was also SVR." Sergei's diplomatic title was First Secretary for Press and Information. Everyone who had held that job in recent memory had been an SVR officer.

When the Soviet Union ceased to exist, the SVR created a new department called VS (*cooperation through partnership*) and agreed to reveal the name of its SVR *rezident* in Washington, D.C., to the State Department in a spirit of post–Cold War cooperation. In return, the CIA identified the head of its Moscow station. Both sides thought it would help to have a known contact so they could exchange mutually beneficial information, especially about international terrorism.

"But the hostility between Russian and American intelligence services never really disappeared," Sergei said. Rather than using the new channel constructively, both sides flooded the other with picky complaints. "I was not privy to what sort of information about terrorism the Americans shared with us, but I knew at the Center there was no sincerity toward helping Americans, in part because of the two nations' difference in defining what is terrorism. Americans decided early on that Russian Caucasus separatists, such as the Chechens, were freedom fighters. But for Russians, they were part of the Al-Qaeda network. Meanwhile, the Russians did not recognize Hamas or Hizbollah as terrorists."

Officially, the SVR *rezident* answered to Ambassador Lavrov, who was in charge of the mission. But under Russian Federation law, the SVR *rezident* was not required to tell Lavrov about SVR intelligence operations. Because of this, the *rezident* rarely shared information with Lavrov and the ambassador rarely asked what the SVR was doing. "This was typical everywhere. Most Russian ambassadors hated the SVR and didn't want anything to do with us." One reason they were contemptuous was that the SVR spied on them. It used "co-optees" — informants who were paid to snitch on their coworkers, including the ambassador. In addition, the SVR was authorized by Russian law to spy on its GRU counterparts, but the GRU could not use co-optees against the SVR. This was a throwback to when Stalin's internal intelligence spied on everyone.

"Clean diplomats and GRU officers at the mission both tried to avoid socializing or having any close contact with SVR officers," Sergei recalled, "because they did not want their coworkers to suspect them of being informants."

The cold shoulder treatment, however, was a facade. Sergei never had trouble recruiting co-optees in the diplomatic corps. "I had one of Lavrov's top deputies and the heads of all three of the MFA *referenturas* [divisions] working for me as co-optees at the mission." They told Sergei who Ambassador Lavrov met with, what was discussed, and what actions Lavrov was taking — information that was sent back to the SVR Center.

"I had dozens and dozens of other co-optees — *every* office in the mission and consulate was penetrated — and because of this, everything that happened was totally transparent to me."

Technically, the SVR *rezident* — not Sergei — was responsible for keeping tabs on the ambassador and the day-to-day running of the *rezidentura*. But when Sergei first arrived in Manhattan as the new deputy *rezident,* the SVR's operations were being handled by an acting *rezident*. He was filling in until Valeri Antonovich Koval, code name Comrade *Karev,* could move to Manhattan from the SVR's Mexico City operations, where he'd been that station's *rezident.*

Sergei had asked several officers at the Center who knew Koval what they thought about him. All of them had been evasive. When he'd finally gotten a source in the Center's personnel department to offer an opinion, it hadn't been good. "You are in deep, deep shit with Koval as your *rezident,*" he warned. "You have my condolences."

"What's wrong with him?"

"You'll discover for yourself soon enough."

Sergei had figured out the problem within hours after Koval got to Manhattan. At age fifty-seven, Koval was only three years from mandatory retirement, and he was intent on not causing waves.

"Koval was afraid of his own shadow," Sergei claimed. "He had nervous tics, was scared to death of the Center, and was mentally and physically incapable of making any major decisions."

Sergei was stumped over how someone as wishy-washy as Koval could have ever become the *rezident* in a post as critical as Manhattan, but he later understood. "He had been promoted when the SVR was losing tons of officers to private enterprise. He happened to be in the right spot at the right time. Plus, Koval was extremely loyal to his superiors." In American parlance, he was the perfect bureaucratic yes-man.

Koval's timidity was noticed by others, too. "Ambassador Lavrov sometimes would forget to invite him to diplomatic receptions and important meetings. Clean colleagues openly laughed at him." During Koval's three-year stint, Sergei took charge.

"I became indispensable to him. He always wanted me close by, even during weekends, because he wanted me to call the shots. He didn't hide it from anyone. 'Do what you wish,' he told me. 'Just don't get me in trouble.' All he ever talked about was surviving long enough to retire and collect his pension."

Koval's replacement was Sergei Kutafin, code name Comrade *Ernst,* who was much more ambitious. But he, too, showed little interest in the *rezidentura's* day-to-day operations. "His entire focus was on finding ways to get promoted because he wanted to become a general. As soon as he arrived, he began buying and sending gifts — bribes — to the leadership of the SVR, beginning with Lieutenant General Margelov, code name Comrade *Mikhail,* who by that point had become a deputy head of the SVR and was overseeing operations in North America, Western Europe, and Latin America."

According to Sergei, Kutafin purchased pricey Montblanc pens, valuable original oil paintings, and cases of American liquors, which he shipped to the Center every month in diplomatic pouches. "Some of his packages were so heavy that two strong men were needed to carry them aboard the Aeroflot jet." Sergei said he knew about Kutafin's bribes because the *rezident* paid for them with SVR operational funds, which came out of Sergei's budget. "I had to find ways to hide these expenses and it was a major headache for me."

Still, Sergei didn't object. "Like his predecessor, Kutafin gave me total control but for a different reason. Koval had been indecisive, but Kutafin didn't really know how to gather intelligence and he wanted someone to blame if things went wrong."

As a result, Sergei ran the *rezidentura* from April 1995 to October 2000. In addition to the sixty SVR operatives working for him, he had twenty-five women employees inside the mission's eighth-floor submarine. All were married to SVR officers. They did clerical, custodial, or other non-spy assignments.

Being an SVR officer was grueling, Sergei said. "During the Soviet period, the KGB expected its officers to do their intelligence job and then twenty-five percent of the work that an ordinary diplomat would do. But that percentage gradually increased. By the mid-1980s, you were expected to do your job and seventy-five percent of your cover job. Beginning in the 1990s, it became one hundred percent for both jobs under SVR director Primakov. I saw this as a very smart move because executing your official functions made it easier for you to establish useful contacts for recruitment and also made it more difficult for your true motivations to be detected — even though some of my men complained endlessly about the hours they had to work doing two separate jobs."

The MFA did not like having SVR officers perform diplomatic work. "Its attitude was, 'Hey, we don't have access to your work and to your reports, why should we give you access to our business?' There was constant friction." Sergei once sent an SVR officer to attend a UN briefing as part of his diplomatic cover. When he got there, the officer was told that a Russian diplomat had already been briefed. The MFA had rushed one of its clean officers to the UN, intentionally undercutting Sergei's man. "Which of you is the real diplomat?" the UN official had asked coolly.

The majority of SVR officers stationed in Manhattan posed as diplomats, but Sergei also had officers working undercover as Russian journalists, and he kept one hidden inside the Aeroflot Airlines office.

At the start of each year, the *rezidentura* received a report from the Center that listed goals that it was supposed to meet. "The SVR was not interested in anything that concerned UN politics, UN resolutions, or other political UN bullshit. Why should we care about how this nation or that one was going to vote? That information was being reported by our clean diplomats."

Instead, Sergei and his men were ordered to penetrate intelligence targets and recruit spies who could steal political, economic, technical, counterintelligence, and military secrets. The Center ranked the targets according to their importance.

1. The U.S. Mission. "Penetrating the U.S. Mission was always our number-one and most important priority."
2. The missions of the five permanent members of the UN Security Council, which included China, France, the U.S., and the United Kingdom. Its fifth member was Russia.
3. The missions of Germany and Japan.
4. Missions operated by NATO members.
5. New York City political circles, especially members of the U.S. Congress and employees who work for political think tanks in Manhattan. The SVR's primary target was the Council on Foreign Affairs, a nonpartisan group of experts who have offered advice about foreign

diplomacy to top U.S. officials since 1921.

6. New York financial institutions, including the New York Stock Exchange and major Manhattan banks.
7. New York University and Columbia University.
8. Russian and Jewish immigration groups, especially immigrants who still had some tie to Russia or showed sympathy to their former homeland.
9. Foreign journalists, especially those who were assigned to cover the UN.

At the end of each year, Sergei was required to submit a report to the Center that explained if the *rezidentura* had met its goals. Much like a factory worker on an assembly line, he and his officers were expected to show an increase in penetrations and recruitments every year.

"When I arrived at the mission, the SVR had a hundred sources. By the time I left, we had more than a hundred and fifty. Most of them were informational contacts, but we also managed to add several significant agents and trusted contacts [spies]."

Sergei's days soon fell into a routine. He

would arrive at his mission office in the submarine before nine o'clock and begin sorting through stacks of requests that had been sent in cables from the Center. The *rezidentura* was never told why or how the information would be used or who had requested it. On a typical day, Sergei would be asked to obtain information about: a study of genetically engineered food being done at New York University, personal information about a UN Secretariat employee in charge of monitoring humanitarian aid to Bosnia, tests being run at the U.S. Department of Agriculture's Animal Disease Center on Plum Island, New York. The questions seemed endless. Some would take only a few hours to answer, others might require months of digging. During his time as deputy *rezident,* there were only two questions that Sergei knew he would be asked over and over. Did any of his sources in Manhattan know anything about the U.S. search for Osama bin Laden? Had the *rezidentura* found any information about Al-Qaeda aiding Chechen rebels?

The cables sometimes contained propaganda the Center wanted spread. Oftentimes it was about the fighting in Chechnya. Sergei would send an officer to a branch of the New York Public Library, where he could get access to the Internet without anyone knowing his identity. The officer would post the propaganda on various websites and send it in e-mails to U.S. publications and broadcasters. Some propaganda would be disguised as educational or scientific reports. These studies would be sophisticated documents that would appear to have been written by European scholars or scientists at universities or respectable-sounding research companies based overseas. In fact, the scholars didn't exist. The studies had been generated at the Center by Russian experts. The reports would be 99 percent accurate but would always contain a kernel of disinformation that favored Russian foreign policy. The reports would be distributed to U.S. groups that criticized the government, especially environmental organizations, opponents of the World Bank, and human rights agencies. "Our goal was to cause dissension and unrest inside the U.S. and anti-American feelings abroad."

In the days following the collapse of the Soviet Union, Russia agreed to stop engaging in *active measures* (disinformation campaigns). But Sergei said that promise had been a ruse. "We said, 'Okay, now we are friends. We'll stop doing this' and the SVR shut down Directorate A [A stood for active measures]. But Directorate A simply underwent a name change. That's all. It became Department MS [measures of support] and the very same people who had run it under the KGB were still doing it for the SVR."

By ten o'clock each morning, Sergei would have assigned the Center's questions and active measures to his officers. They would fan out from the mission to get answers from their informational contacts or spies. Because the SVR assumed all of its phones had been tapped by the FBI, Sergei's troops were not allowed to call their contacts from the mission. Most walked to the Bloomingdale's at Fifty-ninth Street to use pay phones. The department store had several on each floor and most were in locations where an officer had a clear view of the shopping area around him and could see if anyone was watching. The phones were used only for quick conversations, usually to set up a lunch or dinner meeting.

At one point, Sergei sent a Line PR officer, Aleksandr Kayrish, code name Comrade *Pike,* to recruit Padma Desai, a professor at Columbia University. Sergei told Kayrish to first win her trust as an informational contact and then, over time, turn her into a spy. Sergei had picked Desai as a target because of her academic achievements and her connections. She was a member of the Council on Foreign Relations, and during the summer of 1995, the U.S. government had hired Desai to advise the Russian Finance Ministry about ways to improve Russia's sickly economy. Desai had published several well-received books during her career that pinpointed why Communist economies had been doomed to fail.

Sergei had other reasons why he wanted Kayrish to recruit Desai. He had learned that she had recently been invited to brief the CIA about Russia's financial problems and he wanted to discover what she had said. Desai also was married to Jagdish Bhagwati, another professor at Columbia, and the fact that both of them were from immigrant families — at least in Sergei's mind — meant they might be more susceptible.

"We often targeted academics because their job was to share knowledge and information by teaching it to others, and this made them less guarded than, say, UN diplomats."

Sergei's SVR officer, however, bungled the assignment. "Kayrish had waited twenty years in Moscow for his first post overseas and he was so enthusiastic and impatient that when Professor Desai didn't return his first telephone calls, he immediately raced over to Columbia University and literally began chasing her around the campus. One day, he came into my office and said, 'I saw her and her husband in a corridor at the university. When she saw me, she escaped into the ladies' room, but her husband wasn't that fast, so I began asking him questions before he could hide.' "

The two professors became so weary of Kayrish harassing them that they told him to leave them alone, Sergei said. "We got absolutely nothing from either of them, but we were able to report to the Center that we had attempted to recruit her and her husband, which made a good impression in Moscow."

The most infamous story about a failed recruitment by the *rezidentura* involved former secretary of state Henry Kissinger, Sergei said. Kissinger was running his own international consulting firm in Manhattan, and the Center decided it wanted an officer to approach him. "There was some international incident somewhere and the Center thought Kissinger could explain the U.S.'s position and thinking about it to us," Sergei explained. "One of our officers made an appointment with Kissinger's secretary — posing as a diplomat."

The officer arrived early and was seated outside Kissinger's office when his secretary asked: "How do you plan to settle your bill?" She explained that consultants charge by the hour.

"The officer rushed back to the mission and announced that Kissinger charged a hundred dollars a minute for an interview. Our man had run away because he hadn't been told he could spend that kind of money just to chitchat with the great Mr. Kissinger, and he was afraid the *rezident* would be furious at him if he did."

Most days, Sergei's officers would return to the mission before 5 p.m. to write reports for the Center about what they had learned from their sources. But before their summaries could be turned into a cable, they had to be edited by Sergei Shmelyov, code name Comrade *Patrick*, who was called "Turtle" behind his back. He was something of a legend in the New York *rezidentura* because he wore thick, big-framed glasses, was near mandatory retirement, and was methodical. "He sat like a big turtle in the center of a pond waiting for everyone splashing around him to show him their reports." Shmelyov scrutinized every sentence and chastised any officer whose answers were incomplete or unclear. "Patrick was a walking encyclopedia, who was hated because he was always demanding more and more information from my men. He tortured them, but this was his job, and after he had edited and rewritten their cables, he would bring the paperwork to me." Most nights, Sergei would get sixty single-spaced pages to read before they could be encoded and sent. Unless he had questions, he would sign off on each page and take the stack to the SVR *rezident* to read. After he approved, the information was sent to the Center.

Because he was overseeing the daily operations, Sergei could have kept himself occupied at his desk in the submarine. But he hated to be desk-bound and instead spent his afternoons and evenings meeting with sources and seeking new ones to recruit.

He personally oversaw the handling by his officers of the SVR's most important spies in New York during his tenure, and while there were many instances of comic blunders, such as the fumbled pursuits of Professor Desai and Kissinger, the *rezidentura* was not a joker's playground. It recruited and "ran" several important spies — all working against the U.S. Their identities and actions would remain closely guarded secrets in

Moscow and would not be made public —
until now.

TWENTY-FOUR

One of the SVR's most important sources in Manhattan was a deep-cover officer whose identity had been carefully concealed by Moscow for decades. The Center considered him such a valuable source that it had taken extraordinary steps to hide his identity — even from its own officers, including Sergei. In cables between the *rezidentura* and the Center, the deep-cover operative was identified only as "V," and the SVR had sent an officer from Moscow to New York to specifically handle V and only him. The handler and V answered directly to the Center, cutting Sergei and the *rezidentura* out of the loop.

Although Sergei and his men all worked undercover — most of them posing as diplomats — deep-cover officers inside the SVR played much more secretive roles. Sergei credited longtime KGB chairman Yuri Vladimirovich Andropov with expanding their use. "Under Andropov, they became like spores. They were everywhere." Andropov, who ran the KGB from 1967 to 1982, used deep-cover officers to create what became known inside the KGB as the "second layer of defense."

"The Soviet Union and the United States were constantly declaring each other's diplomats persona non grata and booting them out of the country. Andropov began to worry: What if the Cold War suddenly turned hot and all of the KGB's intelligence officers were expelled? Who would be the KGB's eyes and ears? He decided to create a second layer of KGB intelligence officers in every foreign diplomatic post, and he demanded their KGB careers be completely hidden from everyone — other KGB officers, their coworkers, even their wives and children and parents — so the U.S. would never be able to identify them. They would only be called on if our first layer of KGB officers were expelled."

Under Andropov, many deep-cover officers were recruited while they were attending Moscow universities preparing for a career in the diplomatic corps. They were put through a short KGB training program operated independently of the Red Banner Institute. After that, they returned to school and later joined the MFA.

Sergei had never liked deep-cover officers. He considered them freeloaders. They earned a regular salary from the MFA and got an additional paycheck regardless of whether or not they did any actual intelligence work. Even more irksome, they were automatically promoted inside the KGB. Most of them entered as lieutenants and within two years were promoted to senior lieutenants. Three years later, they became captains, followed in four years by the rank of major and four years after that lieutenant colonel. Finally, they became full colonels — all in as little as seventeen years. Their KGB counterparts, meanwhile, frequently had their promotions delayed or blocked.

How many deep-cover operatives had been recruited was, of course, kept a closely guarded secret. But because of Andropov's campaign in the late 1960s and early 1970s, the MFA was riddled with them. Ironically, the hierarchy inside the MFA had no clue that their ranks were swarming with KGB officers because Andropov went to extraordinary lengths to keep legitimate diplomats from discovering their colleagues were deep-cover operatives. After the collapse of the Soviet Union, the Eleventh Department of the SVR continued Andropov's deep-cover program and, according to Sergei, actually became more aggressive at planting its officers in the foreign ministry. "I complained about deep-cover officers being worthless, but the Center told me, 'Sergei, it only takes one to justify a hundred.'"

The officer known as V proved them correct.

Although Sergei was not supposed to know V's identity, he discovered it within a few weeks of reporting to work at the New York *rezidentura*. According to Sergei, V was Eldar G. Kouliev, who was appointed in September 1994 as the permanent representative to the United Nations from the Republic of Azerbaijan.

This meant the Russian government had an SVR colonel working under deep cover for it between 1994 and 2001 as a United Nations ambassador representing a completely different country. His stint coincided with an important period in U.S., Russian, and Azerbaijan relations. This is the first time that Kouliev's secret status as a deep-cover officer has been exposed.

Born in 1939 in Baku, the capital of Azerbaijan, Kouliev entered the Soviet diplomatic service after graduating from Azerbaijan State University in 1963 with a degree in Arabic languages. He found work as an interpreter at the Soviet embassy in Assuan, Egypt, but quickly moved up the ranks. In 1976, he was sent to the Soviet Foreign Ministry's Diplomatic Academy in Moscow and recruited by the KGB. Kouliev returned to Egypt and later served in Turkey. Although Kouliev did well in the diplomatic corps, his value as an intelligence officer didn't emerge until later in his career when Azerbaijan and other Soviet republics began to break free.

In 1991, eleven former Soviet republics formed the Commonwealth of Independent States to, as they put it, "allow for a civilized divorce" from the "motherland." One of the first pacts they signed was called the Collective Security Treaty, and in it they tackled the thorny issue of spying. They pledged not to spy on one another. More important, the new Russian Federation swore that it would not use its old KGB connections in each of their countries to spy on them. This was extremely important, because the new republics did not want Moscow interfering in their internal affairs.

The eleven nations that signed the non-spy pact with Russia were Azerbaijan, the Ukraine, Belarus, Moldova, Kazakhstan, Armenia, Kyrgyzstan, Uzbekistan, Tajikistan, Georgia, and Turkmenistan.

When these republics became independent countries, they turned to Moscow for help in expanding their rudimentary foreign ministries. Seasoned diplomats, who had been trained and worked at the Soviet Foreign Ministry, were invited home to fill each country's diplomatic ranks.

This is when Kouliev became important. He was called back to his native homeland by Azerbaijan's president, Heydar Aliyev, and appointed to serve as the country's permanent representative to the UN. Kouliev and President Aliyev had worked together in Moscow previously, but the president did not know his trusted friend was actually a deep-cover SVR officer. This would later strike Sergei as ironic because President Aliyev himself had been a KGB officer and puppet. The KGB had helped him during much of his political life.

Aliyev's career began in 1944 after he graduated from the Ministry of State Security Academy in Leningrad and returned home to work inside the Azerbaijani KGB branch. He moved up its ranks and became chairman in 1969. Because he obediently carried out the KGB's orders, Andropov arranged for Aliyev to become head of Azerbaijan's Communist Party, making him the republic's strongman. When Andropov left the KGB to take charge of the Soviet Union, he brought Aliyev to Moscow as one of his deputy prime ministers. Aliyev used that position to become one of the Kremlin's top bosses, but when Andropov died unexpectedly in 1984, Aliyev was quickly dethroned. During Gorbachev's presidency, reformists portrayed Aliyev as an example of everything that had been wrong in the Soviet *nomenklatura* system. Under Aliyev's leadership, Azerbaijan had become one of the most lawless republics in the Soviet Union. His family had stolen so much money that Azerbaijan was jokingly referred to as a "kleptocracy" rather than a Communist state.

Aliyev returned to Baku and through a series of fateful events became Azerbaijan's new president in 1993. Bitter about how he had been treated by reformers in Moscow, Aliyev began to court the West, especially the U.S.

As Azerbaijan's UN ambassador, Kouliev was required to surrender his Russian citizenship and swear his allegiance to Azerbaijan. At that point, he could have resigned his SVR military rank. Instead, he agreed to continue working for the SVR as a deep-cover operative, Sergei said.

The SVR moved quickly to shield him.

The Center sent an officer from Moscow named Anatoli Antonov to personally handle Kouliev in New York. It was his only real job. To further protect Ambassador Kouliev, his new handler was assigned a cover job at the Russian Consulate on East Ninety-first Street. He was put in charge of maintaining security inside the building. The SVR gave him that slot intentionally, because it knew the FBI rarely paid attention to security directors, who worked inside a building and seldom came into contact with UN officials or other potential SVR targets.

"It was an excellent plan, but the Center made a huge mistake when it chose Antonov to handle the ambassador," Sergei said later. "Antonov was a chronic alcoholic, had zero professional skills, and was not intelligent enough to handle a diplomat with Kouliev's sophistication."

The Center had told Antonov to keep V's identity completely secret from everyone, including the SVR *rezident* and Sergei. But the first time he went into the submarine to file a cable to the Center from V, he ran into a roadblock. Sergei Shmelyov, the demanding SVR officer nicknamed "Turtle," who edited SVR cables, refused to approve Antonov's. The Turtle had a low opinion of

Antonov, and when he showed him a report that contained inside information about UN operations, Shmelyov became skeptical. He accused Antonov of fabricating the report. Antonov immediately revealed V's name and explained that Kouliev was the Azerbaijan UN ambassador.

Having told Shmelyov, Antonov decided to tell the *rezident* and Sergei, too. "Before he stopped, this idiot had told the *rezident*, myself, the head of the Line VKR, Shmelyov, and a fellow SVR security officer," Sergei recalled. "It was outrageous."

During the coming weeks, Ambassador Kouliev realized that Antonov did not understand much of the information that he was being given. After Antonov garbled several important messages that Kouliev wanted sent to the Center, the deep-cover officer decided to take matters into his own hands. He began writing his own cables and giving them to Antonov to deliver to the mission for forwarding to Moscow. What Ambassador Kouliev didn't know was that Antonov was sharing the handwritten cables with Sergei because he wanted Sergei's help.

"Antonov began begging me. 'Please, Sergei,' he pleaded. 'I don't know what to ask this man. I don't understand UN affairs. Can you please write down questions that I can get him to answer for the Center?' "

The Russian Federation's use of Ambassador Kouliev as a deep-cover officer violated the United Nations' charter. It also broke the Collective Security Treaty that Russia had signed with its former republics, including Azerbaijan. Personally, Kouliev was committing treason against Azerbaijan. But the Center did not hesitate to use him. "If Kouliev were ever exposed, there would be an international incident," Sergei said, "but the SVR thought it had protected Kouliev."

One reason Russia decided to risk using Kouliev was that President Yeltsin was becoming increasingly nervous about Azerbaijan's budding friendship with the Clinton administration. Before 1994, the U.S. and its allies had shown little interest in Azerbaijan because the region was unstable. But that changed, and when Azerbaijan began reaching out to the West, the White House quickly responded.

The reason was oil. Azerbaijan borders the largest landlocked body of water in the world, the Caspian Sea, and it sits atop huge oil and gas deposits. Depending on who does the estimating, the reserves are either the second or the third largest on the planet.

Russia, Iran, Turkmenistan, and Kazakhstan also border the Caspian Sea, but their access to its underground riches has never been as good as Azerbaijan's and none of them has ever been able to exploit the oil.

The Clinton administration wanted access to the Caspian Sea reserves because the oil there could help free the U.S. from its continued dependence on Persian sources. The State Department also wanted to prevent Russia and Iran from getting access to the reserves. The most efficient and cheapest way to deliver oil and gas from the Caspian Sea to tankers in the Persian Gulf was by building a pipeline directly across Iran, and the U.S. didn't want that to happen. Because of its location, Azerbaijan also was important militarily. Moscow operated a major satellite listening post inside its borders. If the U.S. improved its relationship with Azerbaijan, the State Department thought there was a chance President Aliyev might be persuaded to shut down that Russian listening station and allow the U.S. to open one of its own in Russia's backyard.

The Clinton administration was extremely interested in befriending President Aliyev. But their talks had to be handled skillfully. Clinton didn't want to irritate Russian president Yeltsin, nor did he want to stir up a hornet's nest back home. Azerbaijan and its western neighbor, Armenia, were at war and there was a large Armenian immigrant population in the U.S. that was pushing Congress to penalize, not improve, relations with Azerbaijan.

The fighting between Azerbaijan and Armenia had its roots in the early 1900s, when the Soviet Union seized control of the Caucasus region and gerrymandered the borders of Azerbaijan, Armenia, and Georgia. Stalin had used a "divide and conquer" strategy to keep control of the region. He intentionally forced Christians and Muslims to live together, and they, in turn, had focused their hatred at each other, rather than at Moscow.

Stalin put a 1,700-square-mile swath of territory known as Karabakh into Azerbaijan's borders, even though its residents were mostly Christian and predominantly Armenian. He then added another 2,120-square-mile area known as Nakhichevan into the same patch, although it held mostly Muslims and native Azeris — Azerbaijans. His tactic had worked effectively until the Soviet Union had started to unravel. Chaos swept across the region and ethnic fighting erupted. Although the Azeris were better armed, the Armenians seized control of the gerrymandered region. They renamed it Nagorno-Karabakh and declared independence from Azerbaijan. The Armenian government threw its diplomatic support behind the fledgling Nagorno-Karabakh Republic. But Azerbaijan, which had lost 20 percent of its territory, refused to recognize it and the fighting continued. More than thirty thousand persons were killed and economies in Azerbaijan and Armenia were ruined. Both nations asked the UN Security Council for help and three different UN resolutions were adopted, but none stopped the war. Finally, Russia pressured the various sides into signing a truce in 1994, although they still didn't agree on the fate of Nagorno-Karabakh.

It was at this critical point that President Aliyev reached out to the Clinton administration, and the White House saw a chance to get access for Western oil companies into the Caspian Sea.

In October 1995, President Aliyev arrived in Manhattan for the United Nations' fiftieth-anniversary celebration and for a series of private meetings with U.S. officials. The Azerbaijan president met with Madeleine Albright, who was then the U.S. permanent representative to the UN, but soon would become Clinton's secretary of state. Three days later, he met privately with President Clinton.

Within hours of those private meetings, Ambassador Kouliev had secretly passed his handwritten notes to his SVR handler (Antonov) to forward to the Center without knowing that Sergei would be reading them, too.

Six months later, the White House sent Deputy Secretary of State Talbott and Deputy National Security Adviser Samuel Berger to Azerbaijan and Armenia. Once again, Ambassador Kouliev passed along notes to the New York *rezidentura* for Moscow.

In August 1997, President Aliyev made a second trip to the UN, and this time, when he visited Washington, D.C., the State Department hosted a diplomatic reception in his honor. As before, Ambassador Kouliev kept the *rezidentura* informed. When President Aliyev returned to Baku from that trip, he announced that the U.S. was in favor of building an oil pipeline from the Caspian Sea across Georgia and Turkey to the Mediterranean and was willing to help Azerbaijan find Western investors.

By this point, Sergei had started expanding Ambassador Kouliev's reach. "Because he enjoyed the trust of his unsuspecting UN colleagues, who were pro-Western, we were able to use him to obtain information that would never have been offered to Russia."

Kouliev gave the *rezidentura* intelligence about the Clinton administration's intentions in Yugoslavia when fighting began in Kosovo. Eventually, NATO would decide to begin bombing Yugoslav targets — a move that outraged Yeltsin. According to Sergei, Ambassador Kouliev provided the Center with a steady stream of intelligence about the UN and NATO's actions during the Kosovo conflict. The ambassador/deep-cover officer also provided the *rezidentura* with intelligence about U.S. activities in Georgia when that former republic began feuding with Russia. As always, the Center wanted intelligence about Chechnya, and Ambassador Kouliev provided Moscow with intelligence that showed Azerbaijan was permitting wounded Chechen rebels to cross over its borders and receive treatment in Baku hospitals — information that infuriated Russia.

In 1999, the U.S. and Azerbaijan announced they were moving forward with plans to build what was now being called the Baku-Tbilisi-Ceyhan pipeline after the names of the major cities that it would pass through. A month later, Ambassador Kouliev gave the *rezidentura* a secret report about meetings held in Washington, D.C., between Azerbaijan's prime minister and officials at the International Monetary Fund, World Bank, and U.S. State Department.

In February 2000, President Aliyev visited President Clinton, Secretary of State Albright, and other top U.S. diplomats in Washington, D.C. Sergei would later brag that the SVR had been able to deliver summaries about each of those confidential meetings to Moscow within forty-eight hours after they happened. He said that the SVR was convinced that President Clinton, Albright, and Talbott had no idea Ambassador Kouliev was a deep-cover officer.

Two months later, the U.S. and Azerbaijan announced the start of construction of the Baku-Tbilisi-Ceyhan pipeline, the second-longest pipeline in the world, covering some 1,094 miles. It was being financed by a consortium of Western oil companies and would be completed in July 2006. It was a huge victory for the Clinton administration.

Sergei would later have a difficult time explaining why President Yeltsin had not chosen to take advantage of the more than one hundred cables that had been sent to Moscow based on Ambassador Kouliev's insider reports. "I could see no evidence that Yeltsin did anything about the oil deal. He let the U.S. walk in and simply take it."

Because the SVR suspected Ambassador Kouliev would be arrested by the Azerbaijan government and likely executed if his spying was ever exposed, the Center drew up an elaborate escape plan for him. If he ever felt in danger in New York, the SVR would get him aboard a direct flight to Moscow. "He would never have to return to Baku." Sergei said the SVR had purchased two expensive apartments in Moscow for its deep-cover officer and his family. It also had set aside extra cash for him in addition to his SVR military pension.

After Sergei defected, he learned that Ambassador Kouliev had escaped to Moscow and a new permanent representative from Azerbaijan had replaced him at the UN. When contacted, the Azerbaijan government declined to comment about revelations in this book.

"I do not know of any intelligence service of one country in recent times that can brag it had one of its deep-cover officers — a colonel in the military — appointed as a permanent representative to the United Nations from another country," Sergei said. "It was a remarkable tribute to the KGB, the SVR — and to Andropov's foresight."

TWENTY-FIVE

Having a deep-cover SVR officer appointed as a United Nations ambassador was considered a masterstroke by the Center, but Sergei was involved in an even bigger coup while in New York. With his help, Russian intelligence planted an SVR officer inside the United Nations' $64 billion Oil-for-Food Program, a humanitarian relief effort created to provide much-needed food and medical supplies to starving Iraqis. The SVR officer did not steal secrets. Instead, he diverted half a *billion* dollars from the program into the pockets of top Russian government leaders in both the Yeltsin and Putin presidencies. Neither Yeltsin nor Putin made any effort to stop the thefts. The Putin administration did, however, arrange for the SVR officer to be awarded one of the Russian Federation's highest civilian commendations, not because of bravery or honor, but for his role in pulling off one of the richest heists in world history.

The Oil-for-Food Program had its beginnings in Iraq's failed August 1990 invasion of Kuwait. After Saddam Hussein was forced to retreat, the UN ordered him to disarm. When he refused, it voted to prohibit its member states from trading with Iraq. The embargo led to suffering by the Iraqi people. The UN offered Saddam a proposition. It would permit Iraq to sell a limited quantity of its oil as long as the proceeds were used to buy food and medicine and not spent on military hardware. To make certain Saddam followed the rules, the UN said it would monitor the oil sales and the delivery of humanitarian supplies.

At first Saddam wasn't interested, but he agreed later, and on April 14, 1995, the UN passed Resolution 986, authorizing as a "temporary measure" what became known as the Oil-for-Food Program. The humanitarian relief was supposed to last six months, but it could be renewed as many times as necessary. Sergei and his SVR officers kept a close watch on the UN program because they were hunting for ways to exploit it for spying purposes.

From the start, the UN officials negotiating with Saddam made a number of mistakes. The biggest came in the first few days of discussions, when Saddam demanded and won the right to personally decide who would be allowed to buy Iraqi oil and who wouldn't. UN officials didn't realize this was important because they assumed he would sell his oil to major oil corporations. But they later learned that Saddam had something else in mind.

The UN, meanwhile, went blithely forward. It created a separate agency in Manhattan, called the Office of the Iraq Program (OIP), to run the program. In October 1997, UN Secretary-General Kofi A. Annan appointed Benon Sevan, an Armenian Cypriot and longtime UN official, to run the OIP. Sevan reported to the UN Secretariat, the bureaucratic body that operates the UN, and to the five permanent members of the UN Security Council.

This is how the UN program was supposed to work. The Iraqi government divided its oil into "oil units," lots ranging from one million to ten million barrels. The Iraqi Ministry of Oil, through its State Oil Marketing Organization (SOMO), would negotiate a contract with a buyer after conferring with Saddam. If Saddam approved, SOMO would issue the buyer a voucher for a set amount of "oil units." The voucher would be reviewed by a panel of

UN "oil overseers" in New York. Their job was to make certain the price of the oil was reasonable and the contract met acceptable business practices. As soon as the UN oil overseers approved, the voucher was shown to Director Sevan for his review. He then presented it to the Secretariat's office and to the UN Security Council. After everyone signed off on the proposed oil sale, the buyer would be permitted to use the voucher to pick up his oil units in Iraq. The money paid for the oil would not go directly to Saddam. Instead, it would be deposited into a UN-monitored bank account. Funds from the account could only be spent for humanitarian goods, and UN inspectors would follow those products into Iraq to guarantee they were distributed directly to the Iraqi people and not misused.

Because the system had so many safeguards built into it, the chances of anyone stealing money or misusing the program seemed remote. But the safeguard procedures actually had two critical weak points.

Saddam took advantage of the first one as soon as the UN began letting him negotiate oil contracts. Rather than offering to sell his oil to huge companies, he began handing out vouchers to foreign officials, journalists, and even terrorist groups. He selected them, not because they knew anything about oil refining, but because he wanted to bribe them. He was especially interested in buying favors at the UN.

Here is how Saddam manipulated the system. Under the Oil-for-Food Program, anyone who received an oil voucher from Saddam could turn around and sell it to an oil company. If he could sell the voucher for more than what he was paying Iraq (through the UN), he got to pocket the difference. To make the vouchers as lucrative as possible, Saddam undercut the price of Iraqi oil, selling it at a price lower than the world market. This allowed his pals to keep the difference between his sales price and the world price.

At first, the UN's monitoring system kept a thumb on Saddam. Under Resolution 986, Iraq was required to sell its oil "at fair-market value" and the UN's "oil overseers" made certain the price of Iraqi oil stayed competitive. Saddam was only able to sell oil for a penny or two per barrel under the going rate. This meant someone who received an oil voucher from Saddam for a million barrels could sell it to an oil company for a quick $10,000 profit — but because that wasn't an outrageous sum, the UN oil overseers allowed it, and Sevan, the UN Secretariat, and the Security Council rubber-stamped the contracts.

Saddam's actions made the role of the UN oil overseers extremely important, because their job was to keep Saddam on a leash. And this became the second weak point in the checks-and-balances system. There were four oil overseers when the program began. They were hired by the UN Secretariat with approval by the Security Council. As with much at the UN, the four jobs were parlayed out based on the clout of UN member nations. The slots were allocated to the U.S., France, Norway, and Russia.

As soon as Sergei learned Russia could appoint an overseer, he suggested that the Center nominate an undercover SVR officer for the job. Sergei thought an SVR undercover officer working in the UN Secretariat might be able to recruit spies. France, the U.S., and Norway all chose overseers who had worked in the oil business and whose qualifications were unquestionable. France nominated Bernard Cullet, a former executive with France's oil conglomerate Elf Aquitaine. The U.S. appointed Maurice Lorenze, the former head of commercial oil training at U.S. Exxon; Norway appointed Arnstein Wigestrand, a trader with Norway's huge Saga Petroleum Company.

But the Yeltsin administration nominated Alexander Kramar. He was completely unknown in international oil circles, had never traveled outside Russia, and was an economist. At the time, he was working for a Russian insurance firm, Ingosstrakh, estimating the value of petroleum cargoes. Despite his obvious lack of experience, no one at the UN program objected, nor did they dig into Kramar's past.

What no one at the UN knew — and what has remained an SVR secret until now — is that Kramar worked for Russian intelligence, and he was sent to the UN to penetrate the Secretariat.

Sergei was in charge of handling Kramar, identified in cables by the code name Comrade *Sid.* The two had known each other for decades. They first met at NIIRP, where Kramar worked as an economist. Later, Kramar had been assigned to work for Sergei when he became the head of the Komsomol Committee of the First Chief Directorate. "Kramar was my creation," Sergei jokingly later explained, "because I wrote the first report recommending him to become a KGB officer." Their careers had gone separate ways, but they had occasionally bumped into each other. During an encounter at the Center in 1994, Sergei berated Kramar because he failed to stand at attention when Sergei, a higher-ranking officer, entered the room.

"Kramar was excellent with numbers and statistics," Sergei recalled, "but he had zero operative skills and zero people skills as an SVR intelligence officer. I was disappointed when he was chosen for the UN job."

According to Sergei, Kramar was ineffective when it came to recruiting spies. "I was soon constantly badgering him about getting useful information about his UN colleagues and about possible diplomats and he was failing miserably."

Secretariat employees, such as Kramar, were not supposed to associate with diplomats from their native countries or spend time inside their missions. This meant Kramar couldn't simply meet Sergei at the Russian Mission or Consulate whenever they needed to talk. Kramar was, however, permitted to shop at the grocery store inside the Riverdale complex. So Sergei gave him a key and told him what to do. Kramar was to visit the Russian store once each week. After he bought his groceries, he would ride the elevator to the eighteenth floor. It contained apartments. If anyone in the building saw him, they would assume he was visiting a friend, which violated UN

Secretariat rules but was not something that would seem suspicious. If the hallway on that floor was clear, he would hurry down it and duck into the building's staircase. He would walk up a flight to the nineteenth floor, which housed the SVR's second *rezidency*. After checking to make certain its hallway was empty, he would dart from the stairwell and use the key that Sergei had given him to unlock a door to an office directly next to the stairs. He would enter it and lock the door behind him so no one could surprise him. Sergei would enter the room from a different, interior passageway. This way, they could meet without anyone from the UN or other SVR officers knowing about Kramar's undercover status. Kramar would exit the building by retracing his steps.

"Kramar was very careful and no one had any idea he was an undercover SVR officer," Sergei said.

But after several meetings, Sergei became so disgusted by Kramar's failure to produce any useful intelligence that he decided to talk to the *rezident* about sending Kramar home. "I didn't have time to teach Kramar how to be a good spy," Sergei later explained, "and the information he was bringing us from the UN was of no interest because it was only financial information about oil contracts. I told the *rezident,* 'He is giving us nothing.' But the *rezident* said Kramar had important friends in Moscow and I should not take any actions against him because they were extremely happy with what he was producing."

That comment made Sergei curious. He took a second look at the statistical reports Kramar was sending back to the Center. "His cables had no intelligence value, but the figures were important to private Russian oil companies." That made Sergei nervous. "It was illegal for an SVR officer to use his position to steal money, and I could see immediately that this is what Kramar was doing. He was helping the oligarchs around President Yeltsin steal."

Sergei distanced himself from Kramar. He assigned the head of Line ER (*economic intelligence*) to handle him. However, he continued to read Kramar's cables, and he was shocked by what happened next.

In 1997, the Norwegian oil overseer at the UN resigned. A few months later, in July 1998, the American overseer resigned. This left only the French overseer, Bernard Cullet, and Kramar in charge of approving the price of Iraqi oil. Records would later show that Cullet and Kramar immediately began approving oil contracts for Saddam that put the price of Iraqi crude below its true price — by as much as *16 cents* per barrel. This meant that an oil voucher from Saddam for ten million barrels of Iraqi crude could be sold by a middleman to an oil company for an instant *$1.6 million* profit.

Even though the U.S.'s oil overseer had resigned, Sergei warned the UN that Cullet and Kramar were undercutting the price of Iraqi oil. "There was just no excuse for letting it be so profitable," he said later. "The pricing was just outrageously bad."

But no one listened to him.

In July 1999, Cullet, the French oil overseer, also quit, leaving *only* Kramar to set the price. The SVR undercover fox was now completely alone in the henhouse. UN investigators would later discover that from July 1999 until August 2000, Kramar dropped the price of Iraqi crude even further than its already undervalued price of 16 cents per barrel. He began approving vouchers that gave their owners as much as a 35-cents-per-barrel profit, or a whopping *$3.5 million* instant payoff on a 10-million-barrel voucher — just for acting as a middleman.

Thanks to Kramar, Saddam was now positioned to use his vouchers as lucrative bribes. And that is exactly what he did. A review of Oil-for-Food records would reveal that the most active years for Iraqi oil sales by Saddam were 1999 through 2000 — the exact same time period when Kramar was single-handedly setting the sales price. When the program began, Saddam was selling an average of only $30 million worth of Iraqi oil per year. But after Kramar began approving contracts by himself, Saddam began issuing vouchers worth $234 million in oil sales during 1999 and $391 million in 2000.

When the U.S. finally caught on to what Saddam was doing, it tried to hire additional oil overseers, but Russia, France, and China blocked the appointment of replacements for several months.

The Oil-for-Food Program ended when U.S. troops invaded Iraq and an interim Iraqi government took charge on June 28, 2004. At first, UN Secretary Annan praised Benon Sevan's handling of the program, explaining that Sevan had successfully overseen the sale of $64.2 billion in Iraqi oil and the delivery of $39 billion of aid to 22 million people. But news of Saddam's manipulation soon surfaced and the Oil-for-Food Program came under investigation by an Independent Inquiry Committee, headed by former Federal Reserve Chairman Paul A. Volcker, and several separate U.S. congressional subcommittees. Former Iraqi deputy prime minister Tariq Aziz and Vice President Taha Yassin Ramadan were interviewed by Volcker's investigators, and they testified that Saddam had been able to beat the UN's safeguards because of greed and corruption inside the UN.

The first safeguard was supposed to be Sevan, the program's director, but records would later show that he had received vouchers from Saddam for 13 million barrels of Iraqi oil, of which 6.6 million had been sold through a dummy operation for an instant profit of $2.4 million. Sevan insisted that he had done "nothing wrong," but he left the U.S. after federal prosecutors began issuing arrest warrants for executives at a small Texas oil company allegedly involved in Saddam's scheme.

The next person in the UN safeguard system was UN Secretary-General Annan. Investigators would not find any direct evidence that showed he had received vouchers from Saddam, but they did discover that Annan's son, Kojo Annan, had earned as much as $485,000 in "consulting fees" related to Iraqi oil transactions. UN investigators would fault Secretary Annan for inadequately scrutinizing the deal that involved his son, and they would accuse Annan's senior advisers at the UN of misusing Iraqi funds and shredding relevant documents to thwart the UN investigation.

There was still supposedly one safeguard left after Sevan and Annan. It was the UN Security Council. Records would show that Russia, France, and China had approved all of Saddam's contracts and blocked the U.S. and Great Britain from stopping his bribery. Those same records would show a possible reason why: Top officials in Russia, France, and China had all received payoffs from Saddam.

Not surprisingly, Russia received the most oil vouchers from Saddam while Kramar was setting artificially low prices. Records showed that *30 percent* of the oil that Saddam sold at discount went to Russian politicians or Russian organizations. Saddam awarded the first of nine lucrative oil vouchers to a group called the Russian Presidential Council on June 10, 1999. It sold its five-million-barrel voucher for a quick 16-cents-per-barrel profit ($800,000) without ever seeing a drop of oil. The Russian council was made up of advisers and close friends of President Yeltsin at that time. Saddam gave lucrative vouchers not only to the

Russian council but also to Jean-Bernard Mérimée, France's former permanent representative to the UN and a former president of the UN Security Council, and to Charles Pasqua, the former French interior minister, according to UN investigators. Both men have denied wrongdoing, but UN records indicate Saddam approved vouchers for 11 million barrels of oil for Mérimée (worth $1.76 million) and for 12 million barrels of oil for Pasqua (worth $1.9 million).

As soon as Kramar took control of oil pricing, Saddam began doling out hundreds of vouchers to Russians, including contracts worth 85 million barrels to Alexander Voloshin and Sergei Issakov, both key presidential advisers and members of the Russian Presidential Council. These vouchers represented a whopping *$29.7 million* in instant profits for the two Russians. Voloshin was one of the Kremlin's most influential powerbrokers. He served as President Yeltsin's chief of staff and later ran Putin's first political campaign and helped him create the pro-Kremlin Unity Party. When Putin became president, he kept Voloshin as his chief of staff, and he remained in power until he was caught in yet another oil scandal involving Yukos, Russia's second-largest oil company. At that point, Voloshin was forced to resign. His buddy, Sergei Issakov, meanwhile, reportedly traveled regularly between Moscow and Baghdad carrying bags of money for Saddam that the Iraqi president had demanded as kickbacks from the Russians.

During an interview with investigators, former Iraqi deputy prime minister Aziz said Saddam had personally decided to reward Russia with oil vouchers because its leaders were taking positions at the UN that were favorable to Iraq. In one instance, Saddam ordered his aides to give the Russian Presidential Council extra vouchers because Russia's permanent representative at the UN had threatened to veto a UN Security Council resolution that would have restricted illicit trade between Iraq and the nations that border it. The threat of a veto by Russia had killed the resolution before it was formally considered. According to Aziz, Saddam believed he could manipulate the UN Security Council through the bribes that he was paying to the Kremlin and France. He later increased the amount of cash that he was giving Russia in return for having the Kremlin consistently oppose the U.S.'s efforts to get the UN to invade Iraq.

In some cases, investigators found that straw men were used to protect the real identities of Saddam's benefactors. This proved true in Moscow, where vouchers were awarded to unnamed officials in the Russian "president's office" during both the Yeltsin and Putin presidencies. The unnamed recipients received vouchers for 84 million barrels of oil, netting them *$30 million* in instant profits. Whether or not this cash was paid to President Yeltsin and Putin has been impossible for UN investigators to discern, in part because Russia has steadfastly refused to cooperate with a UN audit. In addition to the $30 million that Saddam awarded the Russian president's office, records in Baghdad have revealed the Russian Foreign Ministry (MFA) got vouchers for 55 million barrels, and a front man believed to be the son of the former Russian ambassador to Baghdad got another 13.5 million barrels. Several Russian politicians were given vouchers, including Vladimir Zhirinovsky, a former presidential candidate who espoused an ultranationalist agenda. He personally netted $8.7 million in turn-around profits. Two members of the Russian Parliament, including Nikolayi Ryshkov and a politician identified in Baghdad only as Gotzariv, got 6 million barrels of oil each. The speaker of the Supreme Soviet Parliament (Duma), the former head of the Communist Party, the chairman of the Russian Solidarity with Iraq organization, the chairman of the Russian Federation of Trade, and a former Yeltsin deputy chief also got oil vouchers. Saddam even awarded the Russian Orthodox Church vouchers.

In all, Saddam gave vouchers to forty-six individuals or organizations in Russia, giving them the right to buy 1,366 *billion* barrels of Iraqi oil. Thanks to Kramar's undercutting of the market price, the holders of these vouchers made instant profits of between 16 cents and 35 cents per barrel and pocketed as much as *$476 million!*

The *al-Mada* newspaper in Baghdad would later report that Saddam had distributed vouchers to 270 individuals or organizations worldwide, turning the Oil-for-Food Program into the world's biggest boondoggle of corruption in mankind's history. Politicians from nearly every country at the UN — except the U.S. — received money from Saddam's scam. Many of them were UN diplomats. Saddam approved vouchers for persons living in: Algeria, Austria, Bahrain, Bangladesh, Belarus, Brazil, Britain, Bulgaria, Canada, Chad, China, Cyrus, Egypt, France, Hungary, India, Indonesia, Ireland, Italy, Jordan, Kenya, Lebanon, Libya, Malaysia, Morocco, Myanmar, Netherlands, Nigeria, Oman, Pakistan, Palestine, Panama, Philippines, Qatar, Romania, Saudi Arabia, Slovakia, South Africa, Spain, Sudan, Switzerland, Syria, Thailand, Tunisia, Turkey, Ukraine, United Arab Emirates, Vietnam, and Yugoslavia.

Two U.S. citizens received vouchers from Saddam, according to the newspaper. Both were Arab-Americans.

When Saddam realized how much profit Kramar was enabling the recipients of oil vouchers to earn, he began demanding a kickback on every barrel of oil. Records would later show that this "surcharge" was assessed between September 2000 and March 2003, earning Saddam $228.6 million in illegal payoffs. The Iraqi government was careful to hide these illicit payments, but investigators were able to trace the source of at least $61 million back to Russia. Most of the cash was delivered to Iraq's embassy in Moscow, a dilapidated three-story building of yellow chipping paint a few blocks from Russia's foreign ministry. Sport-utility vehicles would roll to a stop in front of the embassy every few days and bodyguards would carry duffel bags of bundled $100 bills into the embassy, where they were stuffed into a safe and then loaded into diplomatic pouches and sent to Baghdad.

"I was reading all of Kramar's reports and I knew he was flying back to Moscow first class on flights that were being paid for by oil companies," said Sergei. "It was clear that he also was getting rich from his role in all of this."

As a UN employee, Kramar was earning $12,000 per month in salary. "He was notoriously cheap. I personally knew he was not paying any taxes on his salary," Sergei said. "He told the U.S. that he was paying taxes in Russia and he told Russia that he was paying them in the U.S." Because Kramar was an undercover SVR officer, Sergei was paying his rent, providing him with a car, paying for his gasoline, covering his utility bills, taking care of his long-distance phone calls to Moscow, and picking up the tab for expensive lunches that he was having with potential sources. "If his wife bought cleaning supplies or even bath soap, he would bring me receipts and demand reimbursement," Sergei said.

Kramar also was collecting his SVR salary because he was a military officer. "He paid for nothing out of his own pocket, and yet Kramar was paranoid when it came to money. I used to laugh at him because he had a raincoat that he shared with his son. It was too big for his son and not big enough for him, but he refused to buy a new one. Once, I told him that we were taking a collection for retired KGB officers who were suffering because they didn't have enough money to eat or buy medicine in Moscow, and he told me, 'Sergei, I don't have a penny, every penny is spent. I can't contribute.' He was a huge cheapskate."

When Sergei first realized what Kramar was doing, he expected someone at the Center to reprimand him. Instead, the New York *rezidentura* received a cable that announced Kramar had been awarded the Russian Federation's Order of Honour, the highest award given to civilians for outstanding service in the field of economics, culture, or the arts. The cable was signed by General Trubnikov. It said the Order of Honour was being given by a decree in the Russian Parliament and had been authorized personally by President Putin. The Center ordered the New York *rezident,* Sergei, and the head of Line ER to meet Kramar in secret to tell him about the order, congratulate him, and drink a toast in his honor. Kramar also was promoted to the rank of military colonel in the SVR.

"I was disgusted," Sergei recalled later. "I

had officers who were recruiting people as spies and obtaining important political information for our leaders. They risked their lives every day. And then here was Kramar. Everything he did was handed to him. Fate made it possible for him to be the only one in charge of pricing. He was making tons of money for these crooks in Moscow, but what was he really doing for the people of Russia? Nothing."

One thought kept recurring in Sergei's mind. "Thieves are more respected and appreciated by Moscow — if they steal for top officials and oligarchs — than hardworking SVR operatives."

In November 2005, the *New York Post* reported that Kramar had fled Manhattan after cleaning out a personal bank account that held more than $1 million — one step ahead of federal investigators. Kramar resurfaced in Moscow working for Zarubezhneft, a Russian oil and gas company that had close ties to Iraq during Saddam's reign. The *New York Post* did not know Kramar had been working at the UN as an undercover SVR officer. Just the same, its reporter was curious about how Kramar had accumulated $1 million in personal savings while living in New York and drawing a $144,000 annual UN salary. When he telephoned Moscow to ask, Kramar sarcastically replied: "I'm sorry. Why should I answer you?"

Sergei said he decided to reveal that Kramar was an SVR officer because he wanted to provide the public with a "smoking gun" that showed how Russian intelligence had been directly involved in looting the UN program with the blessing of both Yeltsin and Putin. "This had nothing to do with intelligence work, it was about stealing money, about Yeltsin and Putin grabbing every possible dollar they could. It was a shameful day for Russia."

Twenty-Six

Sergei would later boast that his tenure as deputy *rezident* in New York was one of the most productive for Russian intelligence in recent memory. Under his tutelage, the SVR would successfully recruit two UN ambassadors as Russian spies. Unlike the case of V — the Azerbaijan ambassador Eldar Kouliev — these were not deep-cover SVR officers who penetrated the UN as part of Andropov's second layer of defense. They were foreign diplomats who were recruited by an SVR officer named Andrei Lagunovski.

In the mid-1990s, the UN decided to create a "situation center" where members of the UN Security Council could exchange information about terrorist groups. "The Secretariat told our ambassador that a Russian representative was needed to work in this special command post," Sergei later recalled. "The candidate had to be a retired former intelligence officer who had never risen higher than lieutenant-colonel in rank. His job at the UN would be to serve as an official contact person from Russia so countries could disclose information to him about terrorism and he could tell other countries about what Russia had learned. I immediately saw this as an opportunity to penetrate the Secretariat."

Sergei notified the Center and it arranged for Lagunovski to be presented to the UN as Russia's pick for the job. "We were breaking the rules by submitting the name of an active SVR operative. At the time, Lagunovski was a colonel, which also was a higher military rank than what the UN allowed, but none of us worried about the UN or its rules. We never did. Our interests were not in protecting other countries or the UN. Our only interest was to do whatever we could to help Russia."

Out of respect to UN members, the Secretariat did not investigate the background of candidates who were presented by their countries for jobs. Lagunovski was hired and immediately set out to recruit spies.

According to Sergei, the first ambassador whom Lagunovski successfully nabbed was Rashid Alimov, the permanent representative from Tajikistan. The Center assigned him the code name *EMIR*. He had been appointed to the UN in 1993 after Emomali Sharifovich Rahmonov seized control of Tajikistan following a civil war between Muslims and non-Muslims that had started after the Soviet Union dissolved. Rahmonov's government was pro-Muslim and the new president began turning Tajikistan into a more conservative Muslim state. This political swing concerned Russia, which was growing increasingly nervous about a number of radical Muslim regimes gaining power along its borders.

Ambassador Alimov became a valued spy, Sergei claimed, because he had access to intelligence from two differing factions. At the UN, Alimov was elected deputy president of the UN General Assembly, a prestigious position that put him into regular contact with the Secretariat's top leadership and members of the UN Security Council. This, in turn, gave him access to information about the U.S. and NATO, and their intentions. As the Tajikistan ambassador, Alimov also had access to his country's communications with the Taliban and other Islamic extremists because of his nation's pro-Muslim views.

Russia was not alone in being alarmed by an increase in Islamic fundamentalism. In

1996 the Taliban movement took charge of Afghanistan, and Osama bin Laden moved his Al-Qaeda organization there from Sudan. A year later, fighting between Afghanistan warlords led to an explosive incident in the town of Mazar-a Sharif, where the Taliban executed the entire diplomatic corps of the Iranian consulate. Iran reacted by mobilizing its army. In the midst of this squabble, President Clinton ordered the U.S. Navy to fire cruise missiles on four sites in Afghanistan that U.S. intelligence believed were terrorist training camps, including one run by bin Laden.

The Center pushed Sergei and Lagunovski during this international crisis for information from Ambassador Alimov. The Kremlin wanted to know what the U.S. was telling its Western allies and if it planned to take military action against the Taliban. It also wanted Ambassador Alimov to tell it how the Taliban was reacting based on intelligence that Tajikistan, which borders Afghanistan, was receiving from its pro-Islamic sources.

It was easy for Lagunovski to meet with Ambassador Alimov without attracting attention, because the Tajikistan diplomat lived in one of the apartments housed inside the Russian Mission. The Russian-provided accommodations were a holdover from the past when Tajikistan had been under Soviet control.

In Canada, Sergei had recognized that it was easier to get diplomats to betray a third country, such as the U.S., rather than their own. This proved true with Alimov. He did not want to harm Tajikistan's national interests, but he was eager to provide Lagunovski with information about the U.S., NATO, the UN, and other Muslim countries, including Afghanistan.

Sergei said Alimov agreed to spy, in part, because he eventually hoped to retire in Moscow. "He was too much Westernized and civilized," Sergei said. "He didn't want to return to a Muslim country that was being very much influenced by Taliban ideology." Alimov's wife, a medical doctor, also was "completely emancipated," Sergei added, and would not have done well moving back home.

The SVR told Alimov that he could have a teaching job at the Moscow State University of International Relations anytime he wished. He was given a deed to a Moscow apartment and the SVR arranged for Alimov's wife to be hired as the physician at the Riverdale complex in the Bronx so that she could earn extra income.

The second UN ambassador whom Lagunovski recruited was Alisher V. Vohidov, the permanent representative from Uzbekistan, according to Sergei. At first, Ambassador Vohidov refused, but he had a secret in his past that Lagunovski used against him. As a promising Uzbekistan student in the 1970s, Vohidov had been sent to the Academy of Sciences Institute of Economics in Moscow. From there, he had moved quickly to the Soviet Ministry of Foreign Trade and then to the Soviet Ministry of Foreign Affairs. The KGB was pulling strings for Vohidov because he was a co-optee who regularly reported on his colleagues. After the Soviet Union ceased to exist, Vohidov returned home and helped Uzbekistan expand its own Ministry of Foreign Affairs. In 1994, he was named Uzbekistan's chargé d'affaires in New York and shortly thereafter its UN ambassador. He thought he was done with Russian intelligence. But he was mistaken. "Once you were a co-optee, it was not so easy to erase what you had done from your biography," Sergei said. The SVRs threatened to disclose Vohidov's past actions unless he helped it.

The Center wanted information from Vohidov about his country's emerging relationship with the U.S. As an independent nation, Uzbekistan had taken a completely different stance toward Islamic revolutionaries than its neighbor Tajikistan. The Uzbekistan president, Islam Karimov, arrested Muslim radicals, denounced the Taliban and Osama bin Laden, and reached out to the U.S. and other Western nations for economic and political support. Uzbekistan shares a border with Afghanistan, and the U.S. saw Uzbekistan as a logical staging area for launching future military operations against the Taliban.

Moscow depended on Ambassador Vohidov to keep it posted about the U.S.'s flirtation with Uzbekistan and ongoing U.S. military and diplomatic efforts to topple the Taliban in the late 1990s.

After Lagunovski's tour in New York ended, the SVR sent another one of its colonels to the UN situation center. He continued to handle Alimov and Vahidov. As this book was going to press, Alimov was the Tajikistan ambassador to China and Vahidov was still Uzbekistan's UN ambassador.

Sergei said that Alimov and Vahidov were designated as SPECIAL UNOFFICIAL CONTACTS. "This was because we knew there would be an international scandal if their names were ever made public. Not only had we violated UN rules by penetrating the Secretariat with Lagunovski, but Russia had officially promised not to spy against Tajikistan and Uzbekistan. Yet here we were with both of their ambassadors working for us."

TWENTY-SEVEN

The United Nations was like a big candy store.

"If one of my operatives couldn't find someone to recruit in the UN, what good was he?" Sergei later asked rhetorically. "It was a nest of spies and scoundrels."

Sergei's officers brazenly met their sources inside the UN's main building. They drank coffee with them in the Vienna Café, located in the basement, and had lunch together in the North Delegates' Lounge, next to the General Assembly Hall. "Diplomats were expected to meet other diplomats for coffee and lunches, so there was nothing suspicious."

Those meetings, however, violated the SVR's own rules, which prohibited an intelligence officer from meeting an agent or trusted contact in the same restaurant more than once every six months. "We ignored this rule because we had so many sources at the UN that even in Manhattan — with its thousands of restaurants — we wouldn't have been able to find enough to follow that restriction."

The SVR taught its officers to prey on anti-U.S. sentiments. "America was seen inside the UN as an international bully. Even among its NATO allies, there was deep resentment. We looked for diplomats who disliked the U.S. even though they were from countries that were considered by America to be a friend. This anti-U.S. attitude was easier to find than many Americans might think."

One country where Sergei's officers found resentment was Turkey. Between 1995 and 2000, the SVR had three Turkish diplomats spying for it, Sergei said. One, identified by his SVR code name, *KOSACK*, was a councillor in Turkey's permanent mission.

"Turkey is half Asian and half European, and it's a nation that has never been satisfied with its Western allies. On a national level, it is a close friend of the U.S. and a member of NATO, but on a personal level, many Turks are anti-American. They feel the U.S. does not appreciate them. But many Russians spend time in Turkish resorts and Turkey shares a border with Russia, so there is no allergy between the two nations."

KOSACK provided the SVR *rezidentura* with classified diplomatic cables being exchanged between the U.S. and its NATO allies. He also gave copies of reports prepared by Turkish intelligence — the MIT (Milli Istihbarat Teskilati) — to his SVR handler. Because Turkey shares borders with two European and six Asian countries, these intelligence reports were highly prized. "Turkey is not a country many Americans think of when you mention espionage, but its location as a cross point and its membership in NATO made it an extremely useful source."

Some of the cables that KOSACK regularly supplied the SVR were called COREU, which stands for CORrespondance EUropeenne. They were classified reports used by NATO members to keep one another informed. "NATO was not going to send its war plans out in COREU, but COREU cables were never shared with Russia, Cuba, the Chinese, or others who were not U.S. allies, and the Center was able to study the ongoing dialogue in COREU and use it to our advantage. For example, it helped us gain a very clear understanding of U.S. and European policy in Yugoslavia during the UN bombing of Serbia."

(NATO forces bombed Serbia for seventy-nine days in 1999 between March and June in a campaign to force Serbian president Slobodan Milosevic to end his war against Albanians in Kosovo. The bombing forced Milosevic to withdraw, and NATO forces moved in. The Center in Moscow was nervous about NATO forces occupying a former Communist state, and it used COREU to keep tabs on NATO and U.S. intentions.)

The SVR considered KOSACK such a valuable spy that it instructed his handler, Sergei Federyakov, code name Comrade *Allen,* to meet with him as often as once a week during the Turkish diplomat's three-year UN stint. Federyakov, who worked under the guise of being a second secretary of the Russian Mission, was one of Sergei's most productive officers. In addition to handling KOSACK, Federyakov recruited an Iranian diplomat assigned the SVR code name *MONK.*

"MONK was bringing to us top-secret documents from the Iranian Mission about conversations Iran was having with its Islamic neighbors, mostly concerning the U.S. and Israel. This intelligence was extremely useful to the Center in understanding and keeping track of Islamic radicalism." Sergei recommended Federyakov for a promotion, and after his tour in Manhattan ended he was sent to London as the SVR deputy *rezident.*

Sergei pushed his SVR officers to find ways to financially reward their sources. Free lunches and dinners in expensive Manhattan restaurants and smaller gifts, such as Montblanc fountain pens, were common. If a source began delivering classified documents, the gifts turned expensive.

"We gave KOSACK and MONK plenty of gold. But still, I was always amazed at how cheaply we could get UN diplomats to work for us," Sergei recalled. "We would buy jewelry at Wal-Mart and they would gobble it up as if it were some precious treasure when they were actually betraying their countries and risking being caught and executed as spies for a few hundred dollars' worth of gold trinkets."

Sergei arranged for an SVR spy who worked in the Swedish permanent mission to receive a rare book published in the 1800s about Russian history. Its cover was made of forged metal and the book weighed more than ten pounds. The diplomat had been recruited by Lieutenant Colonel Vadim Lobin, code name Comrade *Lorens,* another of Sergei's officers. The Swedish spy was known by the code name *SILVESTER.*

"SILVESTER was older, very refined, an intellectual, and he and Vadim Lobin met at a UN function and became friends. Slowly but surely we began pressuring him for intelligence, and he was so gentle and polite he couldn't refuse." SILVESTER provided the SVR with classified materials about the Balkans — Bulgaria, Romania, Kosovo, Croatia, Bosnia, Macedonia, Albania, Serbia, and Montenegro. As always the Center wanted to know about each of those countries' relationships with the U.S. and NATO. At the time, several of the Balkans were trying to join the European Union, a group of European countries that had banded together to promote economic and political unity. Moscow used SILVESTER's spying to keep tabs on their efforts.

"SILVESTER had been a Swedish diplomat for a long time, so I sent a cable to the Center requesting information about him from its files. There was nothing there even though he had once been stationed in the Soviet Union. Because of my request, the Center began digging and found embarrassing documents that revealed that SILVESTER had actually been married in Russia to a homosexual. This made him even more vulnerable to helping us."

Although Sergei found sexual blackmail

364

distasteful, it was another tool. "If I could, I would have given KOSACK, MONK, and SILVESTER a million dollars. I was always in favor of reinforcing the financial factor. I was always trying to raise KOSACK's appetites. The more I gave him, the more I could demand."

Lieutenant Colonel Vladimir Zemlyakov, code name Comrade *Nelson,* was another SVR officer stationed in Manhattan who proved adept at recruiting spies. He reeled in a German diplomat, given the code name COUNSEL, Sergei said.

COUNSEL hated the U.S. "He was exactly what we looked for — a diplomat who felt no allegiance to the U.S. even though he worked for a country that was a U.S. ally."

Although COUNSEL provided Zemlyakov with a steady stream of classified political and military materials, Sergei became suspicious. The German never asked for money and none of the documents that he provided his handler were about Germany. Sergei began to suspect that COUNSEL was an officer in the Bundesnachrichtendienst (German Federal Intelligence Service) who was posing as a UN diplomat.

"Just because COUNSEL may have been a German intelligence officer did not mean he was not giving us helpful materials about the U.S.," Sergei said later. "Nor did it mean we couldn't use him as a spy. This frequently happens inside the UN. You set out to recruit someone and then you discover they were trying to recruit you. It is ironic, but in many cases you can both end up satisfied if you can find common areas where you can exchange information."

A Polish official given the code name *PROFESSOR* was another example of the murky world that Sergei operated in. "For us, Poland was of significant interest because of its history and close relationship with the former Soviet Union." Between 1940 and 1990, Poland had been a Communist country, but that changed when the Solidarity movement, led by Lech Walesa, broke Poland free from the Kremlin's rule. The Poles, however, did not purge Communists from their government. In fact, Aleksander Kwásniewski, a former Communist Party leader, defeated Walesa in 1995 to become Poland's president.

"Poland always had a dual personality," Sergei said. "While it embraces the West, works hard to maintain an excellent relationship with the U.S., and is a member of the European Union, it remains a nation with deep Socialist roots."

The PROFESSOR had been reared during Poland's Communist period and still had a strong feeling of loyalty toward Russia, or so it seemed to Sergei. The PROFESSOR became such a valued spy for the *rezidentura* that Sergei's boss asked to meet him. They decided the best time would be during a diplomatic reception so Sergei could introduce them without drawing attention. "We went to a reception, and when the opportunity presented itself, I took the *rezident* over to the PROFESSOR to say hello. He made a very positive impression on both of us."

When the PROFESSOR's New York assignment ended and he returned to Warsaw, Sergei wondered what had happened to him. "Because he was older, I decided the PROFESSOR had gone home, retired, and was enjoying his grandchildren." But a year after the PROFESSOR left Manhattan, Sergei received a cable from the Center with surprising news. The SVR had agreed to open a "partnership channel" in Warsaw with Polish intelligence by disclosing the name of a senior SVR officer to the Polish government in return for the Poles identifying one of its officers. The cable said the PROFESSOR had been introduced as being the deputy head of information for the

State Protection Office, which at the time was Poland's intelligence service. "I had genuinely believed the PROFESSOR was a clean diplomat, but again, the fact he had turned out to be a Polish intelligence officer didn't diminish the value of the information he provided us. As far as I could tell, he never lied to us. I believe he had made his career during the Communist period and when it ceased to exist, he was reemployed by a new government and began working for them, but he still wanted to help us, too. The world consists of paradoxes. On one hand, he was working against Russia — if Poland required him to do that. On the other hand, he was gathering information for Russia against the U.S. and European countries because he wanted to help Russia. Either way, he was not really betraying Poland. This is the life of a real intelligence officer. You work with many different kinds of people who have many different kinds of motivations, including sources who are themselves spies for other nations but are willing to scratch your back on occasion."

Sergei claimed the SVR *rezidentura* had recruited other spies during his tenure in addition to KOSACK, MONK, SIL-VESTER, COUNSEL, and the PROFES-SOR. His list included two diplomats from

Greece who worked at the UN between 1995 and 1999, and were providing the Russians with COREU.

At one point, Moscow told Sergei that a longtime spy from Helsinki was being sent to New York to serve as Finland's consul general. Because that was such an important diplomatic position, Sergei had high expectations. The Center identified the alleged spy as Jukka Leino, Sergei said later, a career diplomat who was well known and popular in Finland. His Russian code name was *PHOENIX.* The Center sent along background information and when Sergei read it, he knew why PHOENIX seemed familiar.

In 1994, while Sergei was working at the Center, he was asked to review an old case file. At the time, the SVR was sorting through its lists of spies and was clearing the rolls of those who had not produced any useful intelligence since the end of the Soviet Union but were still being paid. Completely by chance, Sergei had been given PHOENIX's case.

According to the case history, as later recalled by Sergei, PHOENIX had been recruited in the 1970s when Finnish president Urho Kekkonen was in office. Kekkonen served as president from 1956 to 1981, and during his long tenure, he worked hard to maintain good relations with the Soviet Union since the two nations share a long border. In 1979, the Kremlin awarded Kekkonen the Lenin Peace Prize, the Communists' equivalent of the Nobel Peace Prize. The KGB had taken advantage of Kekkonen's friendliness by recruiting scores of Finnish bureaucrats in his administration, Sergei said.

"The Socialist movement was strong in Finland and Finland had its own equivalent of a Soviet Komsomol," Sergei said. "PHOENIX belonged to the Finnish Komsomol, and the Socialists and our KGB contacts in Finland were helping him make a career in the diplomatic corps. He got one promotion and then another, according to KGB records."

The Center's files portrayed PHOENIX as being eager to help Soviet intelligence. He never missed a meeting with his KGB handler. "But when I reviewed his file at the Center, I realized something was missing," Sergei recalled. "PHOENIX got everything he wanted from the KGB — money and indirect help with promotions — but during his entire diplomatic career, he had never given us any useful intelligence. None. He gave us only what you could read in newspapers." After studying PHOENIX's case file, Sergei had recommended that the Finnish official be dropped as a paid contact. However, the Center had decided against it, and now Sergei was being told that PHOENIX was en route to Manhattan.

"I thought maybe the reason PHOENIX had been ineffective was because he had not been handled correctly, so I assigned one of my best officers, code name Comrade *Douglas,* to contact him." Sergei later identified Douglas as Lieutenant Colonel Vladimir Zagoskin.

Zagoskin met with Jukka Leino when he arrived in Manhattan, Sergei said. "Zagoskin said that Leino had embraced him and announced: 'I've been waiting for you. I miss my Russian friends! You are great people. I love Russians!' He had assured my officer that he would be willing to do anything asked of him."

Sergei was skeptical, but Zagoskin sent a cable to the Center gushing about Leino. "Everyone was excited because Leino was the consul general and would have tremendous access to documents. But each time Zagoskin met with him, the diplomat said, 'Oh, I'm sorry, but I can't bring you those documents because I don't have access to them,' or 'So sorry, but I don't know the answer to that question.' He was giving us absolutely nothing and he never had."

Sergei said that Zagoskin met with Leino three times without receiving any useful intelligence. At that point, Sergei got the Center to revoke Leino's trusted contact status. "This case was instructional for my officers because it showed how sometimes even the SVR can be taken advantage of. Sources had to produce and they had to be people with meaningful access."

In a written statement issued for this book, Ambassador Leino stated that he had never engaged "in any kind of spying." He was never a member of a Finnish Komsomol and he did not know Lieutenant Zagoskin, Leino wrote. Still a senior diplomat in Finland's Ministry for Foreign Affairs in Helsinki, Leino said that he frequently met with Russians while he was stationed in Moscow between 1976 and 1979 as a diplomat and later in New York as Finland's consul general. However, he said there was nothing inappropriate about those meetings and he stated that he never received any favors from the KGB or its successor. All of Sergei's allegations, Leino wrote, were "false and misleading."

Sergei told his officers about a famous KGB incident. An ambitious officer had successfully recruited a government official in an African country. When the KGB officer arrived at work the next day, there was a line of Africans waiting outside the embassy and all of them wanted to become KGB spies. "Our new African spy had gone home and told everyone in his tribe that the Soviet Union was paying people to become spies. This was a poor African nation where people were starving, so everyone in the village had come to the embassy. I told my officers, 'The SVR is not the Salvation Army.' If you are a spy, you must deliver."

There was an exception. It involved Americans.

Vladimir Zemlyakov, the officer who had recruited COUNSEL, announced one day that he had met a U.S. diplomat at the UN who seemed open to recruitment. "Recruiting Americans was extremely difficult because they were very cautious when it came to dealing with us," Sergei said later. "It was hard to get close to them and we always suspect that any American who seemed interested in meeting with us was actually an FBI agent, so I advised Zemlyakov to proceed carefully, and I closely monitored every aspect of the case."

Zemlyakov invited the American diplomat to lunch and then dinner. Eventually, they met enough times that the Center assigned the diplomat the code name *SAM.*

"SAM was giving us information, but it was not secret nor was it especially useful," Sergei recalled, "but we were making SAM appear in our cables to the Center to be a tremendous source. If needed, we would put information from a genuine spy into SAM's mouth. Why did I allow this? Because the New York *rezidentura* needed statistics. Recruiting SAM was important to our prestige. All of us wanted promotions, and it was in our interest to create a case even where there was no case — to make SAM a bigger source than he was — because if we didn't have any American contacts, especially one inside our main target — the U.S. permanent mission — then we would be under criticism by the Center as a failure."

On the basis of the documents SAM gave Zemlyakov, Sergei decided the American was working for the FBI. "I watched Zemlyakov closely because I wasn't sure who was recruiting whom and who was using whom." Continuing, Sergei explained, "This is a side of intelligence work that neither the U.S. nor Russia ever openly discusses, but I believe it is quite common. It is false intelligence. It is when you fake things, when you have imaginary agents, or agents in whose mouths you put intelligence. You do this to justify your existence, to make your operation appear successful. To not have had an American as a source in Manhattan would have been humiliating — so we provided one to Moscow. It was simply how the game was played."

TWENTY-EIGHT

While nearly all SVR officers under Sergei's command were posing as diplomats, he had four who were journalists. For a brief period after the Soviet Union ended, the SVR stopped using journalism as a cover. But the prohibition didn't stick, and by 1995 the Center had dropped all pretenses.

In his first month in New York, Sergei found himself embroiled in a tricky situation that involved Aleksey Berezhkov, a veteran correspondent for ITAR-TASS, the official Russian news service and successor of the Soviet-era TASS. Berezhkov had officially retired from the KGB when it was closed down by Gorbachev and Yeltsin. He'd even shown his editors a letter from the Russian government that officially declared he no longer was an intelligence agent. But that document was bogus. The SVR created it as a subterfuge so Berezhkov could continue working without his colleagues knowing he was an SVR officer.

Sergei had received a panicked call from Berezhkov requesting an immediate meeting in the second *rezidency* at Riverdale. Sergei told him to go to the eighteenth floor and if the hallway was clear, dart into the staircase and up a flight to the nineteenth floor, where Sergei would be waiting. Berezhkov, who was in his forties, arrived breathless. As soon as Sergei locked the office door behind him, the correspondent began jabbering.

Berezhkov said he had attended a clandestine meeting that a fellow ITAR-TASS colleague, Mikhail Kolesnichenko Jr., had arranged that morning in a Manhattan hotel. Sergei recognized the name. Mikhail was the son of Tomas Kolesnichenko, a popular Russian news correspondent — a Moscow version of Mike Wallace. The senior Kolesnichenko was a close friend of Yevgeny Primakov, the head of the SVR, and he often hobnobbed with top Kremlin officials.

A clearly rattled Berezhkov said the junior Kolesnichenko had introduced him to a Russian who had not revealed his name but claimed to be representing Sergei Vadimovich Stepashin, the Russian Federation's security minister. The Russian said Stepashin needed Berezhkov's help in handling a "delicate proposition." Stepashin had chosen Berezhkov because he had spent nearly twelve years in New York and had useful contacts. The Russian then dropped a bombshell. He claimed Stepashin wanted to sell a top-secret Russian "counterintelligence manual" to the FBI or the CIA. It contained step-by-step instructions that explained how counterintelligence investigations were done in Russia. Continuing, the Russian said Stepashin needed Berezhkov to negotiate a multimillion-dollar sales price with the Americans.

Sergei now understood why Berezhkov was afraid. At the time, Stepashin was one of Russia's most promising Democratic leaders. President Yeltsin had handpicked Stepashin to someday be his successor. Selling a counterintelligence manual to the FBI or CIA would be an obvious act of treason. If what Berezhkov was told was true, Stepashin was willing to betray Russia for cash.

Sergei pressed Berezhkov for details, but the nervous reporter had no idea who the mysterious stranger was. However, Kolesnichenko had vouched for him. Berezhkov said both men had warned him not to tell anyone what Stepashin was proposing. "If word leaks out, we will know who was the source," the Russian said, "and we will know how to silence him."

"Go home and keep quiet," Sergei told his frazzled officer. "Let me look into this."

After Berezhkov left, Sergei briefed Yuri Yermolayev, code name Comrade *Teryokhin,* who was the acting *rezident.* (The permanent one had not yet arrived.) Yermolayev decided to send a hand-coded "TA" (for your eyes only) cable directly to Director Primakov, bypassing the chain of command. A TA cable was a special message encrypted with a one-time code that could only be deciphered by Primakov's personal code clerk. It was only supposed to be used during emergencies. Contacting Primakov directly was a risky move. The generals at the Center would be furious at Sergei and Yermolayev if they discovered that they'd been cut out of the loop. Sergei and Yermolayev also were nervous about how Primakov might react because he was a close friend of the elder Kolesnichenko.

Having just come from Moscow, Sergei didn't doubt Berezhkov's story or that a high-ranking Russian politician such as Stepashin was willing to sell Russian secrets. Sergei had seen firsthand the drunkenness and disarray at the Center, and he was aware of the widespread corruption among oligarchs in President Yeltsin's administration. "Everyone cared only about themselves."

Sergei and Yermolayev waited, but Primakov didn't reply — at least not to them. The next day, Berezhkov once again met with Sergei at Riverdale. He said that Primakov had telephoned his friend Tomas Kolesnichenko, who, in turn, had called his son and warned him. "Somehow Berezhkov convinced Mikhail that the story about Stepashin had leaked out in Moscow and that is how Primakov had heard it. Otherwise, Berezhkov believed he would have been murdered."

Neither Berezhkov nor Sergei heard anything more about Stepashin's alleged plan. That incident, however, didn't seem to harm his political career. In 1997, Yeltsin chose Stepashin as Russia's justice minister, the equivalent of the U.S. attorney general. A year later, he was named Russian interior minister, and in 1999, Stepashin was appointed prime minister. Yeltsin was keeping his promise of preparing Stepashin to become Russia's next president. However, in August 1999, Yeltsin had a change of mind and picked a different candidate to succeed him: Vladimir Putin. When asked, Yeltsin gave an evasive explanation for why he had dropped Stepashin. After being removed as prime minister, Stepashin became a director in the Russian bureaucracy that oversees government audits. Mikhail Kolesnichenko, meanwhile, became president of U.S. operations of ITAR-TASS, and then reportedly returned to Moscow.

Because everything Sergei had heard about the meeting between Berezhkov, Kolesnichenko, and the stranger was secondhand, there was no way for him to know for certain that Stepashin had really been involved in the plot. But this lack of direct evidence didn't stop the incident from thoroughly disgusting him.

"This entire affair was another example to me of how corrupt the leadership in Moscow had become," Sergei said later. "I believe Stepashin was doing what the oligarchs were doing. They were stealing Russia's natural resources and he was offering the U.S. a different kind of asset — the one at his disposal. It was shocking. Imagine in the U.S. if a member of the president's cabinet or a vice president contacted Moscow and offered to sell it secrets."

ITAR-TASS correspondent Berezhkov returned to Moscow in 1999, and that time he did retire from the SVR, Sergei said.

The other SVR officers posing as journalists in New York during Sergei's tenure were Yevgeny Maksimovich Rusakov, Sergei Ivanov, and Andrei Baranov.

Sergei said Russian newspapers didn't object to providing cover for SVR officers because of governmental intimidation and financial reasons. "Russian newspapers never had enough money to afford posting legitimate correspondents overseas." In the 1990s, the second-largest-circulation newspaper in Russia, *Komsomolskaya Pravda,* had more than a dozen foreign correspondents abroad. Only one of them didn't work for the SVR, Sergei said. The Center used its operatives to get access to U.S. public officials and academicians. "They could never be certain if they were speaking to a legitimate reporter or to one of my officers." At news conferences, the SVR used its journalists to ask questions that would embarrass the U.S.

Even though they were reporters, Sergei expected his officers to recruit spies. Yevgeny Rusakov, whose code name was Comrade *Taras,* recruited two sources while he was a correspondent with *Rabochaya Tribuna,* Sergei said. He claimed one of them was James O. C. Jonah, a former top UN official and one of the most influential African diplomats in Manhattan before he retired to become an academic at a New York college. "We used him to foster anti-American feelings among African delegations," Sergei said.

A native of Sierra Leone, Jonah joined the UN Secretariat in 1963 and during the next three decades moved steadily through its ranks, eventually becoming its under secretary general for political affairs. In 1994, he returned to Sierra Leone to help it make the transition from military to civilian rule. In 1996, Jonah became his country's permanent UN ambassador. According to Sergei, Jonah spied for Russian intelligence between 1996 and 1998, until he was called home to become Sierra Leone's minister of finance. Sergei said Jonah provided the SVR with diplomatic cables being exchanged between his country and other African nations, "but mainly we used him to agitate other members of the African caucus against the U.S." The SVR assigned Jonah the code name *GANNIBAL*. He eventually moved back to the U.S. and became a senior fellow at the Ralph Bunch Institute for International Studies of the City University in New York.

When told about the claims in this book, Jonah replied with a written statement.

It is indeed laughable that I could have

been recruited as a Soviet agent. I recall Mr. Rusakov very well. We first met when he requested an interview as a correspondent. He informed me that he had been told by his Soviet colleagues in the Secretariat that I was well informed about international politics. I found him very knowledgeable about current developments in the Soviet Union. Specifically, he was good at clarifying certain details about leading personalities in Moscow. As a student of international politics, I found our conversation very stimulating. At no time did I pass on to him any confidential information nor did he ever hint that I should create anti-American feelings among the African delegations. It never happened. If he had reported such things then they are only figments of his imagination. As someone who served for over thirty years as an international civil servant, there is no way I could have been recruited as a Soviet spy.

The second official whom correspondent Rusakov allegedly recruited was given the code name *TIBR*. He was a top administrator at the Trilateral Commission in New York City. Formed in 1973 by David Rockefeller, the commission comprised 350 leaders in business, media, academia, public service, labor unions, and other non-government organizations. The commission hired experts to research international issues. In 1977, Rusakov had been hired to write a study titled *Managing Global Relations: Avenues for Trilateral-Communist Collaboration.* While researching that report, he had become friends with a senior administrator at the commission and eventually turned him into a trusted contact. "TIBR rubbed shoulders with international business and political leaders and the Center was very interested in what he learned from talking to them. He gladly passed this information to Rusakov, who sent it to Moscow. Although it was not classified material, it proved to be very helpful."

Rusakov was not only an excellent SVR operative, he was an accomplished journalist who was able to develop sources the same way any skilled newspaper reporter does. Only in Rusakov's case, he used his connections to ask questions posed by the Center and to ferret out information for Russian intelligence. Sergei later identified Fred Eckhard, the official spokesperson for the UN, as one of Rusakov's favorite sources. Eckhard was in charge of briefing international reporters, but Rusakov intimated in his cables to Moscow that Eckhard frequently shared "background" information with him that others didn't get. Most was about NATO's decision to bomb Yugoslavia. Russia opposed the use of NATO forces there. "Mr. Eckhard was never paid anything nor did he divulge any classified information," Sergei said later. "He was not a spy, but the Center congratulated Rusakov several times because of his excellent relationship with Eckhard. It made it possible for the Center to ask Eckhard specific questions without the true source of those questions being exposed." There is no reason to believe or evidence to suggest that Eckhard knew he was dealing with a Russian intelligence officer and not a bona fide journalist.

Because the SVR wanted its journalists to blend in with legitimate reporters, Russian correspondents were also expected to write stories that had nothing to do with gathering intelligence. At one point, a correspondent from *Komsomolskaya Pravda* asked for permission to fly to Miami. The newspaper was drafting a story about wealthy Russians who owned houses abroad, and it wanted to confirm that Alla Pugacheva, Russia's highest-selling recording artist, and Valery Leontyev, a popular Russian pop singer, owned property in Florida. The newspaper couldn't afford the trip, so Sergei was asked to finance it. "Of course I agreed, and my SVR journalist used his skills to get inside Pugacheva's condominium, where he took photographs. Then he located land and sales records."

Sergei worked with two *Komsomolskaya Pravda* correspondents. He'd known Sergei Ivanov, code name Comrade *Martin,* in Moscow, and the reporter assumed their past friendship would cause Sergei to go easy on him. "Ivanov was nice, but he was lazy, inaccurate, and a lousy journalist. I always felt I had a moral right to demand excellent work and long hours from my men. I was working twelve-hour days and my blood pressure was racing all of the time." When Ivanov misplaced a decimal and wrote "five hundred thousand" in a cable to the Center rather than the correct figure, which was "five million," Sergei erupted. He complained to the Center. "I said he has zero, zero, zero intelligence value, but they said, 'You don't have the right to choose who you work with, you should work with who we send you, so teach him to become a decent operative.' "

Sergei tried, but failed. One day, Ivanov's boss, Yelena Ovcharenko, from *Komsomol-*

skaya Pravda, came to evaluate the Manhattan bureau. Sergei happened to be near her in the UN press gallery when she started berating Ivanov. "She didn't know her own correspondent was one of my operatives because the SVR had made it appear he was a totally clean journalist. He was being beaten by both sides — the SVR and the newspaper."

Eventually, Ivanov found a foreign exchange student from England attending New York University who seemed a likely target. Ivanov told Sergei the student had been hired by the German government to install computer software inside its permanent mission. "We were looking for someone exactly like this," Sergei said. "We always wanted to recruit computer experts who would be trusted by another country. This student didn't have access to any secrets, but he did have access to the Germans' computer systems and it was an entryway we could exploit. Our technical experts could provide him with the necessary tools."

The SVR assigned the student the code name *CHIP*, and Sergei began pressuring Ivanov for more biographical information about the student spy. "When I studied Ivanov's reports, I noticed something odd." There was nothing about CHIP's studies at

NYU. "Ivanov finally admitted CHIP was a literature major at school and computers were merely a hobby. CHIP hadn't been hired to work for the Germans — he knew someone who worked there. I began yelling at Ivanov so loudly in the submarine the *rezident* came running out of his office to see what was the matter. Ivanov turned completely pale, and after he left my office he went outside to smoke a cigarette. Other officers were afraid Ivanov might kill himself. Obviously, Ivanov had made CHIP more interesting than he was."

Ivanov was recalled to Moscow, but was offered another chance to return to New York as a journalist a short time later. When he was told that Sergei was still there, he declined. Despite Sergei's low opinion of him, Ivanov eventually became the spokesman for the SVR and, as this book goes to print, frequently can be seen on television talking to Western reporters about intelligence operations.

Ivanov's replacement at *Komsomolskaya Pravda* was Andrei Baranov, known as Comrade *Lars,* and he immediately impressed Sergei by recruiting a fellow foreign correspondent. He worked for *Yomiuri Shimbun,* Japan's largest newspaper. The SVR gave him the code name *SAMURAI.* "We never paid him. He was helping us purely for ideological reasons. He hated the U.S."

SAMURAI spoke Russian fluently and was fascinated by Russian culture and history. "He had good contacts with the Japanese ambassador and his staff. The Japanese ambassador was close to the U.S. diplomatic delegation. This allowed us to use SAMURAI to get information about the U.S. and also documents the Japanese were getting from the U.S. Plus, SAMURAI was popular in New York diplomatic circles, so he was a wonderful source for collecting information from other diplomats about the Balkans and even Chechnya. Because SAMURAI was a Japanese correspondent, no one suspected he worked for the Russians."

TWENTY-NINE

In addition to running the *rezidentura*'s day-to-day operations and overseeing the handling of its agents and trusted contacts, Sergei handled two spies by himself.

The first was a familiar face from his past.

While attending a disarmament conference at the UN one afternoon, he spotted ARTHUR, one of his five trusted contacts from Ottawa. When Sergei had recruited ARTHUR, he worked at the Canadian Centre for Arms Control. Now he was a project director at the Center for Nonproliferation Studies, which was part of the Monterey Institute of International Studies, a California think tank. Sergei hurried over to greet him as soon as the conference meeting ended, and they agreed to meet later that night for dinner.

Although the two men had not spoken in several years, Sergei felt confident that ARTHUR would start spying again. The reason was simple. "ARTHUR hated the U.S.," he said later. ARTHUR also had gotten so deeply involved in helping the Russians in Canada that it would be difficult for him to say no. The last time they had met was in 1993 in an Ottawa restaurant called Hy's Steak House. ARTHUR had just returned from a fact-finding trip to the Ukraine and Moscow was eager to hear his report. At the time, Russia and the Ukraine were still squabbling over the five thousand nuclear missiles that the Ukraine had inherited when the Soviet Union dissolved. The U.S. was trying to broker a settlement between them, and as part of the negotiations, the Ukraine had agreed to allow an inspection team from Canada and the U.S. to inventory the nuclear arsenal and recommend ways to keep the missiles safe from terrorists while the two nations argued about the weapons' fate. ARTHUR had been part of the inspection team, and during their lunch, Sergei asked him for a draft copy of its findings.

"Are you crazy?" ARTHUR replied. "I can't give you a copy of it. I could be put in prison for life."

"Okay, then just tell me about it," Sergei said, taking out a fountain pen so he could make notes on a napkin.

Later, Sergei would recount what happened next. "ARTHUR began dictating to me and I was writing on this napkin. After a few seconds, I stopped and said, 'You know, brother, I am a stupid guy. All of these technical terms and details, they are beyond my knowledge. Can you put these words down for me?' I pushed the napkin across the table to him and handed him the pen and he began writing the highlights of his report on the napkin."

It was a trap. "I understood everything he was telling me, but I wanted him to write it down. I wanted it to be accurate, but I also wanted to have his handwriting on that napkin. It was evidence and he would know I had it."

Sergei had forwarded ARTHUR's report and napkin scribbles to the Center. "ARTHUR was one of the best arms control and military-political experts in Canada, and his name was becoming very well known in the international community," Sergei said. "He was an excellent source."

Before Sergei left Canada, he urged the Center to stay in contact with ARTHUR. But when the Canadian moved to California, the SVR decided against contacting him. "The U.S. was pressuring Russia to reduce its intelligence presence in America, and for the SVR to send someone to Monterery to meet ARTHUR was simply not an option because of the risk involved. That is why I was so delighted when I spotted him at the UN conference."

When they met in New York at dinner, ARTHUR picked up where he had left off. "He began telling me about classified studies he had read about Star Wars." ARTHUR told him that the U.S. military had failed to hit a single target when it tested the technology that it needed to make the Star Wars system work. "He called Star Wars a huge fiasco and said Russia didn't need to be concerned about its effectiveness."

ARTHUR promised to back up those comments with documents, and eventually Sergei filed a detailed cable to the Center about the kinks in Star Wars. In response, General Trubnikov sent Sergei a personal congratulatory note. ARTHUR's analysis had been shared with President Yeltsin, the general said.

The timing of Sergei's reunion with ARTHUR proved perfect. Not long after they met, ARTHUR quit his job in California and went to work for the International Atomic Energy Agency, headquartered in Vienna, Austria. Formed in 1957 to promote safe, secure, and peaceful nuclear technology, the agency was referred to in the media as the United Nations' "nuclear watchdog." ARTHUR's new job, as a UN senior verification expert, was to keep track of nuclear weapons owned by the world's five admitted nuclear powers and the five other nations suspected of possessing them. "As soon as I told the Center that AR-THUR was in Vienna, I was ordered to arrange an introduction between him and one of my comrades in Europe. I was later told ARTHUR had excellent access to American and European secrets and that he had made the transition to being handled by another operative without difficulty. I know that he still is employed at the agency and I have no reason to believe he has stopped working for Russian intelligence."

Besides ARTHUR, Sergei would handle a spy in Manhattan known as *AMIGO*. It proved to be a turning point, because Sergei would realize while running the AMIGO case that he was starting to lose his edge.

In 1996, Sergei received a cable from the Center telling him that a Turkish diplomat who had been recruited in Ankara was being sent by his government to the UN. The Center sent along a photograph, a detailed physical description of AMIGO, and instructions about what to say when Sergei identified him.

Sergei began trolling UN briefings looking for a Turkish diplomat who matched the description. After two months, he spotted a likely candidate. Sergei waited until the briefing ended and followed the diplomat down a hallway. He gently tapped him on his shoulder.

"Hello, I bring best regards from Andrei, who used to play tennis with you in Ankara," Sergei said, repeating the "parole" that the Center had told him to say.

For a moment the diplomat simply stared at him, and then his face became pale. "Yes," he stammered, "I played tennis with Andrei."

It was the correct wording to the parole.

"How can I find you?" Sergei asked.

AMIGO jotted his home telephone number on a business card. Sergei noticed the diplomat's hand was trembling. He guessed AMIGO hadn't planned on being contacted by the SVR in New York. He had naively assumed Russian intelligence would leave him alone.

"Okay, my friend," Sergei said, trying to calm him. "I will call you. And please know, we are happy to see you again. Everything will be okay here."

Their meeting had gone exactly as Sergei

hoped. He'd only wanted to make contact, see AMIGO's reaction, and obtain his phone number. In Ankara, AMIGO had provided his SVR handler with cables that described U.S. and NATO operations — or that is what his SVR handler had claimed AMIGO had given him. "It's human nature for an intelligence officer to make his source appear more important than he is," Sergei said later. "I know of incidents when an SVR officer was ordered by the Center to contact another officer's source, only to discover the trusted contact didn't even know he was a spy. When our man repeated a parole, the source would say: 'What are you talking about? Are you insane? Do I know you?' When this happens, you under-stand that one of your comrades has made a source look better than he is, and you have to make a choice. There is no policy here, but most officers decide not to spit in the well because someday you may need to drink from it. This is especially true if someone gets a decoration or an award for recruiting a trusted contact. If you expose them as a fraud, make fun of them, embar-rass them, then when your back needs to be scratched, there will be no one there to do it. Whenever I ran into situations where someone had lied or exaggerated, I always chose to tell the Center the source was nervous and said he was not willing to spy inside the U.S. because the FBI might catch him. I did not spit in the well."

A few days after contacting AMIGO, Sergei left his office at the mission and began walking south along Lexington Avenue. He glanced around to see if anyone was following. After a few minutes, he entered a pet shop with tinted front windows. The glass prevented people on the sidewalk from peering in, but permitted customers to observe people on the street. Sergei watched to see if anyone came inside the store after him. He looked out the one-way glass and searched for persons loitering nearby. After several minutes, he exited and continued walking to Bloomingdale's, where he used a public phone to call AMIGO. Sergei suggested they get together for a drink at Jameson's, an Irish pub on Second Avenue in midtown, which was near AMIGO's apartment. They agreed to meet at 8 p.m. on Friday night, which actually meant they would meet at 7 p.m. on Thursday. This was standard operating procedure whenever the SVR scheduled a meeting with a trusted contact. The date and time were always different from what they actually voiced over the telephone or in written notes. In AMIGO's case, the predetermined code called for meetings to be one hour earlier and one day sooner than the spoken date. If they missed each other, they would try again a week later.

On Thursday, Sergei left Riverdale three hours before the meeting. He wanted to make certain he had time to lose any FBI agents who might be following him. But he didn't make sudden U-turns or drive the wrong way on a one-way street as spies often did in movies. Instead, he drove to a men's clothing store and bought a pair of slacks. From there, he went to a department store to buy a tie. If anyone was following, he wanted them to believe he was simply shopping. The only evasive maneuver he made was incredibly simple. Sergei drove only five miles more than the minimum speed limit — or 45 m.p.h. — on a New York expressway. "At that slow speed, other motorists will honk and then shoot past you. If you spot someone slowing down behind you, then you know you are being followed."

Sergei was relying on more than his car's turtle pace. Before leaving the mission that day, he had given a copy of his route to Jameson's and an exact timetable to the SVR officer in the Post Impulse office. The officer was using that detailed schedule to discern if the FBI or any other law enforcement agency had cars in the same vicinity as Sergei, based on their radio traffic. If there were agents clustered around the same intersection as Sergei, then the officer would know Sergei was being tailed.

Sergei was carrying a beeper, because this was before cell phones had become common. If he received a call on his beeper from a telephone number that began with the area code for Manhattan — 212 — that meant the Post Impulse operator had not observed any suspicious radio traffic and he was clean. But if his beeper registered a call from a 718 number — which was the area code for Riverdale — the FBI was watching him and he needed to abort the meeting.

By the time Sergei reached Manhattan, he felt confident no one was tailing him. Even the weather was working in his favor. It was horrible. Sleet had turned into snow and there were fewer cars than usual on the streets. There was an old joke in Russian intelligence that said FBI agents did not work outdoors during inclement weather. They didn't like staying at work past 5 p.m. or conducting surveillance on weekends or holidays, either, because it increased overtime.

Sergei felt so certain that he was okay that

he went to Jameson's before he'd received an all-clear signal from Post Impulse. He selected a table in the back where he could watch the entrance. He'd just ordered a beer when his beeper buzzed and he glanced down expecting to see 212. Instead, the screen showed a mishmash — 7*1*A*G*S*#*3*4*@. He silently swore and shook the beeper, trying to clear the screen, but the same nonsensical numbers re-appeared. The first two digits — 7 and 1 — were closer to 718 than they were to 212 and that made him nervous.

"The first rule is to not endanger your source. You are expected to pay the consequences if you are identified, but you should never put your contact at risk, so my first reaction was to get out of the pub as quickly as possible before AMIGO arrived."

Tossing a $20 bill on the table to pay for his beer, he stood and began worming through the crowd congregated at the bar. Sergei suddenly felt an odd sensation. "I had been watching these people and had not seen anything suspicious until after my beeper buzzed. But now I noticed several of them were very athletic and they looked professional — like FBI agents — and as I walked through them, I convinced myself that they were, in fact, all FBI agents and I was about to be arrested. It is how the mind works. I felt a strong sense of fear, but I knew I had to fight it. You can't be afraid, otherwise you are guaranteed to make mistakes."

In a flash of seconds, Sergei considered options. If the FBI surrounded him, he would become indignant and explain that he was simply meeting a friend for a drink. He had not done anything incriminating. Still, there was another possibility. What if AMIGO had set a trap? The Turk might have tipped off the FBI to get rid of Sergei. As he reached for the pub's door, AMIGO pulled it open. Sergei hesitated and then stuck out his hand and smiled. AMIGO shook it. Nothing extraordinary happened. No FBI agents sprung forward.

Sergei led AMIGO to the table in the back. A waiter brought them drinks. Like ordinary strangers, Sergei asked about their mutual friend Andrei, which was the real name of an SVR officer in Ankara.

"I know him from Moscow," Sergei volunteered.

"Yes, he's a very nice guy," AMIGO replied.

Sergei spent several more minutes chit-chatting, learning what he could about AMIGO. He did not hurry the conversation, nor did he ask any questions that would have seemed suspicious if either of them was being secretly recorded. Sergei would later explain: "You can't ask a contact to immediately do something for you when you first meet him. You must properly lubricate a source."

After several minutes, Sergei suggested they get together again in a couple of days to have a more substantial discussion. Then he asked AMIGO to leave the pub first. He was still unsure why he'd gotten a garbled Post Impulse signal and he didn't want to risk the two of them walking out together in case the FBI was circling the area. After AMIGO was gone, Sergei ordered another beer and drank it slowly. Finally, he sauntered outside. Nothing happened, but he didn't relax until he was in his car driving to Riverdale. By the time he reached the apartment compound, he was furious. He went directly to the Post Impulse office on the nineteenth floor. Bursting inside, he grabbed the front of his officer's shirt and pulled him close as if he were going to butt him in the forehead.

"What's wrong!" the officer shrieked. "I sent a message! No one was watching you!"

Sergei released the officer and held up the beeper, which still contained the jumbled message.

"I swear, I called from the mission and left the correct area code," the Post Impulse clerk replied. "I swear it."

The officer retraced that night's events. He had kept track of Sergei's schedule and determined there were no FBI agents tracking him. Shortly before 7 p.m., he'd sent Sergei the all-clear — 212 — code.

"What phone did you use?" Sergei asked.

A sheepish look swept across the officer's face. He was supposed to go outside the mission and use a pay phone a few blocks away. But because the weather had turned nasty, he had placed the call from a ground-floor office. He'd then driven to Riverdale to eat dinner with his family before going upstairs to the Post Impulse office on the nineteenth floor to continue monitoring radio traffic.

The next morning, Sergei examined the telephone that the officer had used in the ground-floor office at the mission, and discovered it was an outdated model with rotary dial technology. He decided this was the cause for the jumbled signal.

Sergei met AMIGO several more times during the coming months and the Turkish diplomat agreed to give him cables from the Turkish Mission. But Sergei didn't exploit him.

"He was a young man, very nice and a decent man, and I didn't want to ruin his life by turning him into more of a spy. I was subtly trying to shield him and those feelings made me realize that I had lost my passion for stealing secrets. I was putting my concern for my contact above my professionalism. I asked myself, 'Why do you feel this way?' and the answer seemed obvious. Why should I ruin his life for a bunch of crooks? I had lost my faith in Yeltsin. I had lost it in the Center."

■ ■ ■ ■

Part Four:
The Escape

■ ■ ■ ■

That whenever any Form of Government
becomes destructive of these Ends, it is
the Right of the People to alter or to
abolish it, and to institute new
Government.
— *Declaration of Independence*

All of us, in truth, detest a traitor, no
matter how he sugarcoats his treason or
justifies his betrayal.
— *Aldrich Hazen Ames,*
former CIA employee
convicted of spying for KGB/SVR

THIRTY

Sergei and Helen loved Manhattan with its museums, galleries, Broadway plays, boutiques, and melting-pot richness. Much to his surprise, Sergei became a rabid fan of *Seinfeld, Frasier,* and *Friends,* recording each television episode so he could watch it with Helen late at night after work. The two of them felt relaxed in New York in ways neither had ever experienced, even when they had been vacationing at their beloved dachas.

Over time, the discussion that had begun in Ottawa — about leaving Russia — had continued. Both worried about Ksenia's future now that she was a teenager and in a few short years would be attending college. Neither wanted her to return to Moscow, where, they feared, she would fall in love and marry a Russian, unwittingly becoming condemned to live in a nation they now both believed was morally unsalvageable.

Many of the obstacles that had seemed so monumental in Ottawa — leaving behind their Moscow apartment and dachas — were mere bumps now. It was Revmira, Sergei's mother, who remained the chain on their ankles. They could not leave as long as she was alive and living there.

Sergei did nothing at work that hinted about the thoughts of desertion that he was harboring. Nor did he ease up on his officers despite his own personal misgivings about serving a corrupt Kremlin. He was determined to remain "a total professional."

Russian intelligence saw itself as an exclusive men's club and there was no reason for any of its members to look elsewhere for friendship or socializing. It was an attitude reinforced by SVR terminology. In official communications, SVR officers referred to themselves as "Comrade Colonel," and when Sergei was being introduced to a stranger and the title "Comrade" was used, he knew this was a fellow SVR officer.

At least once each month there was a birthday party or some other get-together at the mission. Most were alcohol-fueled. The SVR had its own formula: a bottle of whiskey per person at a party, plus an extra bottle. The "comrades" joked that their goal at these functions was to replace all the blood in their systems with alcohol. In that raucous spirit, Sergei introduced his own drink — called the 007. It was equal parts orange juice, orange vodka, and 7UP. As deputy *rezident,* Sergei was expected to offer a toast after the *rezident* made his. He never missed a party. But privately, he preferred the quieter, weekly sauna parties that he personally hosted at Riverdale on Tuesday nights. He would invite five of his officers to join him at nine o'clock to eat sandwiches and drink beer inside the building's sauna until midnight. It was during these smaller sessions that Sergei felt a genuine sense of camaraderie. Often, the men poked fun at one another. Their barbs were generally aimed at Lieutenant Colonel Vadim Lobin, code name Comrade *Lorens.*

A graduate of the KGB's paratrooper academy, Lobin had started his career as a Vympel officer before being assigned to Line PR and dispatched to Manhattan. At first, Sergei had been skeptical. Later, he explained why. "I worked in political intelligence. I didn't need a trained killer, I needed intellectuals. Comrade Lobin had absolutely no skills when he arrived." Sergei's first comment to Lobin had been "go buy a decent suit."

Despite that cold reception, Lobin was

determined to prove himself. After several false starts, he announced one morning that he had found a potential target — a Portuguese diplomat who had invited him to dinner. Sergei gave Lobin a bottle of whiskey to offer his host. The next morning, Lobin came directly to Sergei's office. Sergei required his men to tell him every detail whenever they met with a potential source because he wanted to correct any mistakes they may have made.

It had been raining when Lobin arrived at the diplomat's Manhattan apartment. Rather than going to a restaurant, the diplomat invited Lobin inside to dry off. Because he was shivering, his host urged him to take a hot shower while he dried Lobin's clothes. Lobin found a robe next to the shower. When he emerged from the bathroom, the diplomat offered him a glass of wine, and Lobin noticed there was music on and the lights had been lowered. The two men had eaten dinner and then Lobin left.

Sergei began laughing, but Lobin didn't understand why.

"He's a homosexual. He was trying to seduce you," Sergei explained.

Lobin was visibly shaken. He had never knowingly met a homosexual. At Vympel, anyone suspected of being gay would have been savagely beaten by other soldiers.

Sergei's rendition of Lobin's encounter became a sauna party favorite, and after each telling, Lobin would boldly declare that he would have killed the diplomat if he had made a sexual advance.

Lobin's misadventures had continued. One day he arrived at work with a badly bruised face from an obvious fistfight. When Sergei asked for details, Lobin sheepishly explained that he had taken his family to an amusement park where there were several monkeys. A chimp had tried to snatch some fast food from Lobin's hand, and when the Russian jerked the treat out of reach, the monkey slapped him. Lobin instinctively smacked the animal back and the monkey had broken free from its trainer and attacked the Russian's head. Lobin and the monkey had gotten into a melee that ended when angry park officials showed Lobin an exit.

"A monkey beat you!" Sergei laughed. "Imagine the headline: 'Russian Spy Defeated by Chimp.' "

While the main purpose of the Tuesday-night sauna parties was relaxation, Sergei used them to keep abreast of gossip and office politics, which seemed epidemic and especially nasty inside the SVR. In 1997, Sergei got word that someone had written a memo criticizing his management as deputy *rezident*. Through friends, he obtained a copy of the report and was surprised that it had been written and inserted into his personnel file at the Center by the then head of Department A, General Sergei Labur, code name Comrade *Klim*. Sergei had always had a good relationship with Labur, so he contacted him and asked why he'd written such a blistering critique.

"I didn't," Labur declared. He promised to investigate, and a short time later told Sergei in a private letter that someone in the Center had written the memo and forged his signature on it.

Sergei quickly deduced the forgery had been produced by one of Labur's top aides, Peter Solomatin, since he would have been the only SVR official with access to Labur's personal stationery who could have forged his boss's signature and inserted the report in Sergei's personnel folder without attracting attention. A bit more digging revealed that Solomatin was after Sergei's deputy *rezident* job in New York.

Sergei told Labur, but the general shrugged. "Don't pay any attention to his bullshit," Labur advised. "I will always defend you against his plots."

While grateful, Sergei remained irked. He was considering his options when fate intervened. One Saturday morning, Sergei was reading a newspaper in his office at the mission when Lieutenant Colonel Yuri Desyatov, a Line VKR officer, stopped to see him. A few seconds later, they were joined by a code clerk who had just returned from a weeklong vacation in the Crimea. The clerk was single and he started to brag about his sexual exploits at the SVR-operated resort. His first had been an older woman who had come to the hotel without her husband. "She was a volcano. She sexually exhausted me."

The woman was so demanding and controlling that after two days, the clerk had stopped seeing her and had taken up with a younger SVR secretary who worked in the Center. His new girlfriend had noticed the clerk earlier in the week with the older woman and she warned him that he had made a dangerous enemy by dumping her. "She's the wife of a very important person!" the girlfriend explained, but she refused to elaborate. After the clerk returned to New York, he began to stew.

"Tell me, Sergei," the clerk asked, "what do you know about a Comrade Peter Solomatin at the Center?"

Sergei was brutally honest. "Comrade Solomatin is trying to replace me as the next deputy *rezident* here."

An immediate look of horror washed across the code clerk's face. "My career is over! My career is finished!" he moaned.

If Solomatin became the next deputy, the clerk said, his wife would find a way to get the clerk transferred because she would not want her adultery exposed. Or she might chase after him for sex and her husband would find out and ruin his career. Either option wasn't good.

Sergei didn't offer any suggestions and the clerk left distraught. At that point, Sergei and Desyatov continued discussing the escapade. Part of a VKR officer's job was to tell the Center about the private lives of SVR officers stationed abroad, especially if something happened that might make them vulnerable to being recruited by a rival intelligence service. Desyatov left Sergei's office that morning convinced that the code clerk's actions needed to be reported — a point of view that Sergei had not challenged. Sergei had simply sat back and let the VKR officer make his own conclusion.

As soon as Desyatov's memo hit the Center, Solomatin's chances of replacing

Sergei were dashed. An officer whose wife was promiscuous could not be sent overseas, because the VKR considered the couple a security threat since the woman could be seduced by a foreign service. But there was more to it. In the machismo world of the SVR, Sergei knew an officer who couldn't control or sexually satisfy his wife would be castigated. "If he can't run his own house, then he wasn't capable of running a *rezidentura*."

Labur sent word to Sergei. Solomatin had withdrawn his name temporarily from being considered for any overseas post, including New York, while he worked on repairing his crippled reputation.

The Solomatin scandal reinforced what Sergei and Helen both already knew. The forced comradeship, constant socializing, paper-thin walls at Riverdale, and never-ending gossip inside the closed world of the SVR left little room for privacy and no room for mistakes. If they chose at some point to act on their plan, which they were now referring to as the "escape," they would have to be constantly aware of their every word and action. The slightest slipup could spell disaster not only for Sergei, but for the entire family.

THIRTY-ONE

While walking through the first floor of the mission one morning, Sergei noticed a locked door and realized he didn't have any idea what was behind it. He called a security officer to open it. The door led to a suite. The first room was furnished with a bed, table, and chairs. There was bottled water and refreshments in a refrigerator. The second room was stuffed with racks of clothing and shoes in different sizes, along with wigs, hats, and heavy coats. Video cameras were mounted on the walls and there was a private bathroom. Sergei knew instantly why the suite was there. It was a secret room maintained by Line VKR for walk-in volunteers. The most famous in recent times had been John Walker, who, in December 1967 had walked through the front door of the Soviet embassy in Washington, D.C., and volunteered to spy. He had shown the KGB a top-secret document to prove he had access. Walker had been given a long coat and broad-brimmed hat to wear. He'd then been surrounded by beefy operatives who formed a human shield and hustled him out the embassy's back door to a waiting car. He'd been dropped off a half-hour later at a corner with instructions never to return to the embassy because it was watched by the FBI.

Sergei knew that most walk-ins were a waste of time. Many had mental problems. Others were dangles sent by the FBI to trick Russian intelligence. But the chance of having another Walker appear easily justified the secret suite.

Of all the SVR officers at the mission, Sergei was the most frustrated with the Line VKR counterintelligence operatives who worked for him. The Center was partly to blame because it had created a catch-22 situation. The main job of a Line VKR officer was to recruit and turn FBI and CIA agents into spies. Foreign diplomats and other targets were the responsibility of Sergei's Line PR officers. But the SVR had adopted a strict rule that prohibited anyone from having any contact with any known FBI or CIA agents. The moment an SVR officer realized he was speaking to someone in U.S. intelligence, he was required to stop the conversation and back off. This included Line VKR officers. "It meant Line VKR officers were prohibited from performing their primary duty," Sergei said later.

The better ones at the *rezidentura* found ways to follow the rule but still collect useful information about their U.S. rivals. They determined which FBI agents were assigned to foreign counterintelligence work and which were responsible for more traditional chores, such as investigating bank robberies. They compiled a list of the license plates on FBI cars. Sergei was impressed by these officers. If he gave them the name of an FBI agent, they could provide him with a thick dossier of biographical information.

However, these Line VKR officers were rare. Most spent their time in the *rezidentura* trying to find embarrassing information about their coworkers. "They would tell the Center they were keeping a close watch on a clean diplomat, claiming he had been observed acting strangely, when, in fact, the case against him was entirely inside their own imaginations and they were simply trying to justify their existence by making a spy where there was none."

When Sergei had first arrived in Manhattan, he had developed a good working relationship with the Line VKR head, Yuri

Yermolayev, because the two of them had been immediately thrown into handling the Stepashin scandal and the alleged sale of a counterintelligence manual to the U.S. Sergei had respected Yermolayev's willingness to stick his neck out by sending a TA cable directly to Director Primakov. But after Sergei got settled, he decided Yermolayev was too timid. Whenever he pushed Yermolayev to try something inventive, his colleague would find an excuse not to do it.

Once, Yermolayev told the Center that the FBI had as many as fifty cars following his officers whenever they stepped outside the mission. Sergei didn't believe it and told him that even the FBI could not afford that sort of manpower. A year later, the Center released an analytical report about the threats that SVR officers faced worldwide. When Yermolayev received his copy, he hurried into Sergei's office, waving it in the air. The study stated that the FBI in Manhattan routinely used fifty cars to track SVR officers.

"See! See!" Yermolayev proclaimed. "This is why it is so dangerous for my officers here! This study confirms exactly what I've told you. The FBI are everywhere!"

Sergei later found the scene laughable. "The Center had pulled the fifty-cars statistic out of Yermolayev's original cable," he recalled, "and this moron was scaring himself with his own false statistics, much like a dog chasing his tail."

Helen didn't respect Yermolayev, either. Nor did she like his wife. The Line VKR head had his wife invite her for afternoon tea at Riverdale. "This woman kept telling me how she was suffocating in the U.S.," Helen said later. "She complained there was no culture in New York. She kept talking about how she missed her beloved Russia. It was what you would expect someone to say when the Communists were in power. Then she told me, 'Helen, you should organize tea parties for the wives of our officers and diplomats. It would be a wise thing to do because you could monitor their moods and see if they are saying anything disloyal. Then we can report them.' "

In Sergei's opinion, Line VKR officers were less educated and not as sophisticated as their Line PR coworkers. Colonel Vladimir Gryaznov was an example. In addition to its other duties, Line VKR was in charge of internal security inside the mission, the consulate, and at Riverdale. Gryaznov arrived in the mid-1990s and immediately decided to impose a curfew on teenagers living in Riverdale. Anyone under age twenty-one was required to have written permission from their parents if they wanted to leave the compound alone after 10 p.m. The curfew caused a teenage rebellion. Several began sneaking out a gap in the chain-link fence that had not been repaired after lightning struck a tree, causing it to fall on the barrier.

Gryaznov complained to Sergei. "These teenagers aren't listening to me!"

"And why do we need this curfew?" Sergei asked. "This is a safe area. Nothing bad happens here."

"You're wrong! Drugs are being openly sold in the neighborhood. There's even a sign advertising them."

Sergei asked Gryaznov to describe the sign, and his description proved dumbfounding. Gryaznov had mistaken a neon sign hanging outside a neighborhood pharmacy as an advertisement for illegal drugs because it said DRUGSTORE. Sergei later explained: "This fellow was unsophisticated and had never traveled abroad before, but even when I explained the situation to him, he was still suspicious and believed teenagers could buy narcotics in U.S. pharmacies." At Sergei's suggestion, Gryaznov ended the curfew.

Because of such antics, Sergei did not

think highly of Line VKR officers, and when he received a cable in 1996 from Moscow about an American "walk-in," he elected to have his Line PR officers handle the case.

The cable from the Center said that a U.S. resident had contacted Russian intelligence officials while visiting Moscow. The cable identified the American as a Russian immigrant who had settled in California but still had relatives in Russia. He had been visiting his mother when he decided to walk into Lubyanka and offer to spy.

According to the cable, the volunteer did not have access to U.S. political or military information. However, he worked for a California company that stored medical reports and other scientific studies that he claimed could be helpful to Russia. The cable told Sergei how to contact the American and sent photographs of him along with biographical information that he had provided in Moscow. The Center called the case OPERATION BULL.

Not long after that cable arrived, Sergei was told that BULL was on a flight from his home in California to Newark, New Jersey. On the morning of their scheduled meeting, Sergei's officer drove his wife and children to a shopping mall in Westchester, New York. While the family was shopping, the officer slipped away from the mall and caught a commuter train into Manhattan. He switched to another train bound for New Jersey. Meanwhile, BULL had been instructed to loiter outside a chain restaurant at a Newark shopping mall. He had been instructed to hide his first batch of reports in a Macy's shopping bag and to look for a man carrying a copy of *The New York Times.*

Sergei's officer had seen BULL's photograph, so as soon as he spotted BULL in front of the restaurant, the officer walked up and introduced himself. The exchange had gone smoothly until the officer attempted to pay BULL. He refused, but eventually agreed to accept enough cash to cover the cost of his flight. When Sergei's officer asked him to sign a cash receipt, BULL wrote, "Paid to a Patriot."

The sample delivery of documents delighted the Center. They were medical research paid for by the U.S. government. Most described cutting-edge experiments performed by scientists searching for cures for diseases, such as cancer and AIDS. The studies were not released to the general public because many of them contained proprietary information based on medical patents held by U.S. companies. "The reports were extremely technical, and I noticed each had a dollar amount in the index that described exactly how much the U.S. government had spent to pay for this research. Most cost in excess of several million dollars."

The Center ordered Sergei to get as many reports as possible from BULL. OPERATION BULL eventually led to Moscow receiving thirty bound volumes of copied scientific studies — several thousand pages of documents. "We received a congratulatory cable from the Center. In it, General Labur [head of Department A] bragged the SVR had managed to obtain scientific research that cost the U.S. government forty million dollars for the price of eight hundred dollars in airplane tickets!"

After BULL exhausted his supply, his Line PR handler told him how he could contact the SVR in the future by posting an innocent-appearing message on an Internet message board. They then parted company.

"Cases like this happen, but most are not nearly as productive as OPERATION BULL," Sergei later explained. "A genuine walk-in volunteers. They help us with what they can, and then they disappear and we never hear from them again."

THIRTY-TWO

The *rezidentura* attracted not only walk-ins but generals. Officially, they came each winter to inspect SVR operations. But their real purpose was to escape the frigid Russian weather and to reward themselves.

"They were a constant headache," Sergei recalled. "Each general expected to be treated as a king — treated to expensive dinners, given endless drinks and tons of gifts — and I had to pay the bills."

Money for entertaining generals was not part of the SVR's budget, so Sergei padded his officers' expense reports to come up with the extra cash. It became an inside joke. Each winter, the SVR's sources in Manhattan suddenly developed a thirst for $200 bottles of Cristal champagne whenever they met their handlers in a restaurant.

After visiting Manhattan, the generals continued their "inspections" in Washington, D.C., where they expected similar recognition. But no matter how hard the *rezident* there tried to please them, the generals always complained about their accommodations. Their gripes would eventually be used by the SVR to help cover up a covert operation, and although it would be based in Washington, Sergei and his *rezidentura* would be drawn into it.

The visiting generals were housed an hour outside the capital at a resort that the Russians called their "Washington dacha." Located five miles west of Centreville, in scenic Queen Anne County, the forty-acre retreat featured two Georgian-style mansions, six smaller guest cottages, an outdoor swimming pool, soccer field, two tennis courts, and a stretch of sandy beach. The property was situated at the confluence of the Corsica and Chester rivers, which emptied into the Chesapeake Bay. The tract had originally been part of a 1,600-acre estate known as Pioneer Point Farm, created in the 1920s by John J. Raskob, a New York financier and builder of the Empire State Building. Raskob renovated the original mansion and added the second one after he became chairman of the Democratic Party and needed a place for his large family to live while he attended meetings in Washington. After Raskob died in 1950,

Pioneer Point changed hands several times before it was bought in 1969 by a Pennsylvania developer for $2.5 million. He hoped to subdivide it into exclusive parcels, but local residents stymied him through a zoning board. He took revenge by quietly selling the two mansions and best riverfront parcel in 1972 to the Soviet Union for $1.1 million. At first, the new owners alarmed their neighbors by erecting a seven-foot-tall chain-link fence around the tract. But the Soviets soon won the community's support by inviting local residents to afternoon tea parties hosted by the ambassador.

While the visiting generals enjoyed the retreat's amenities, they constantly complained because the SVR didn't own a boat. One of the most popular attractions in New York was cruising around Manhattan on a famed Circle Line sightseeing boat, and when the generals got to the Washington dacha, they wanted to go sightseeing on the Chester River, too. There was a cabin cruiser docked at the property, but it was only for the ambassador and was off-limits to them — a point that further irked the generals.

Several SVR officials in Washington had tried to come up with a reason to justify buying a speedboat. But none could. And then one day, an SVR officer assigned to Line RP (*interception of radio and satellite communications*) thought of a reason. The officer explained that the SVR urgently needed to purchase a boat for Pioneer Point — not because the generals wanted one but because Line RP needed a way to get rid of useless spy garbage.

Over the years, the Washington station had accumulated tons of broken and outdated equipment that its officers no longer used. There were a few exotic, one-of-a-kind James Bond devices, but most was routine junk — bulky code machines, reel-to-reel tape recorders, outdated computers, monitors, printers, telephones, even the huge satellite dishes mounted on the embassy's roof.

The purchase and the disposal of these items had to be done according to exacting rules not only in Washington but at every SVR station. For instance, if Sergei needed to buy a handheld tape recorder, he could walk into any Manhattan electronics store and purchase one. But he couldn't use that recorder. Instead, the SVR required him to send it in a diplomatic pouch to the Center, where it would be exchanged for a tape recorder that had been bought in another country — for example, France. Sergei would then be sent the tape recorder from France and the one that he had bought in Manhattan would be given to another SVR outpost — say, in Spain. This protected the SVR in case the CIA or FBI had managed to install a monitoring device inside the Manhattan-purchased recorder.

The SVR had equally strict rules about disposing of its property. Every item was assigned a serial number. From that moment on, it was carefully tracked. When a piece of equipment broke or became obsolete, the rules required that it be smashed into pieces until its parts could not be recognized. These broken bits were then supposed to be shipped back in a diplomatic pouch to Moscow for disposal. They couldn't be tossed into a trash can behind the SVR *rezidentura* because the FBI was known to dig through trash receptacles and reconstruct discarded items.

On paper, the SVR disposal plan seemed smart, but the SVR *rezidents* in both Washington and New York balked because of the costs involved. Each *rezidentura* had a limited budget when it came to sending materials to the Center. There was an extra charge of $2.50 per pound if an SVR station exceeded 330 pounds in each month's diplomatic container that was flown by

Aeroflot Airlines to Russia. The Washington and New York *rezidenturas* always exceeded their limits, so the *rezidents* there were constantly searching for ways to reduce the weight. Sending smashed transistors and shredded sheet metal back to Moscow was a low priority, so the unwanted spy junk got stuck in basement storerooms to be dealt with at some later date. After several decades, the storerooms became full. There was so much garbage in Washington and New York that both were facing millions of dollars in surcharges to fly the trash home.

And this is where the Line RP officer's ingenious solution came into play. He suggested that the unwanted spy garbage be taken from the Washington embassy basement to the retreat at Pioneer Point and loaded onto a speedboat. Under the cover of darkness, the boat could be driven onto the Chester River and the junk thrown overboard. The Center authorized the secret dumping operation.

During Sergei's tenure, the SVR used the boat to dispose of several tons of smashed metal. All of it was tossed overboard illegally into the Chester and Corsica rivers. (The Russians could not take it into Chesapeake Bay, because they were restricted from boating there under rules adopted when the

Soviet Union and the U.S. both limited travel by foreign diplomats. American personnel at the U.S. consulate in Saint Petersburg were restricted as to where they could boat at a U.S. retreat on the Gulf of Finland.)

"Everyone assumed the boat was bought to appease the visiting generals — even the ambassador and the generals assumed this — because of all of the grumbling. But that boat really was bought as a garbage truck for us. The generals' complaints served as a cover story."

Because there were so many tons of debris to be dumped and the Russians didn't want to attract attention, the Line RP officers made several trips each week and carried only a few hundred pounds at a time. The Center kept the operation secret from everyone except the Line RP officers, who did the actual work, and the SVR *rezidents* and their deputies in Washington and New York. Moscow was concerned that U.S. residents would be outraged if they learned that chunks of busted metal were being thrown overboard into the rivers.

Sergei learned about the dumping when the Center ordered him to begin hauling unwanted spy junk out of the New York *rezidentura's* basement in the mid-1990s. "That boat cost us thirty thousand dollars, but it saved us *not* a million, but millions and millions of dollars in airline fees we would have had to pay to fly the junk back to Moscow," he recalled. The illegal dumping operation had been going on for five years and was still being done when he defected. "I know that many of the generals who enjoy the boat have no idea why it was actually purchased and how it is being used each night while they sleep."

There was one general from Moscow whose visits had nothing to do with boat rides or vacations. When General Trubnikov announced that he was coming to Manhattan, Sergei knew it was a legitimate inspection and warned his men. Trubnikov had toured the Ottawa *rezidentura* when Sergei had been there, and the general had refused the obligatory gifts that other visiting generals demanded from their subordinates. Instead, Trubnikov had spent his entire day working in Ottawa and had only reluctantly taken a one-day break to see Niagara Falls. When his entourage was returning from the tourist attraction, General Trubnikov stopped at a McDonald's restaurant for dinner rather than wasting time and money elsewhere.

Two events during Trubnikov's visit to

Manhattan made a lasting impression on Sergei. The first happened when Russia's permanent UN representative Sergei Lavrov hosted a private dinner at the mission for Trubnikov. Before the main course was served, one of the generals accompanying Trubnikov began complaining about President Yeltsin and the so-called new Democrats running the government. Trubnikov kicked the general under the table because Ambassador Lavrov was one of the new Democrats. That kick was followed by some uncomfortable, silent moments before Lavrov excused himself, claiming that he had a bad cold. He left before the full-course meal was served.

Later that same week, Sergei drove Trubnikov and his cohorts to the Tatiana Café, a Russian eatery in Brooklyn's Brighton Beach neighborhood, which was popular with visiting SVR generals. At one point, Sergei and General Trubnikov were walking ahead of the others.

"I never hid my contempt for Yeltsin," Sergei said later. "I was always complaining that he was a crook, that he was stealing as much as he could. I said to General Trubnikov, 'How can we continue working for someone such as this drunk Yeltsin?' And he said to me, 'Stop, we can't discuss this.'

Then he added, 'Sergei, you must understand that we are servicemen. We serve the state. That is our duty. To obey, not question. And as long as we work for the government, we must be loyal to the president.' I remember thinking at the time — he is right. If you didn't like the president or his administration, you should leave government. You are either part of a team or you leave."

Trubnikov's words stayed in Sergei's mind after the general returned to Moscow. It was clear that Trubnikov and his peers did not believe in the democratic reforms under way in Russia, nor did they respect Yeltsin. Trubnikov's rationale had seemed logical when Sergei had been walking with him to the café. After all, Trubnikov and Sergei were military soldiers, and soldiers did as ordered. It had been enough to satisfy the general's conscience. But it was no longer enough to appease Sergei's.

THIRTY-THREE

Sergei telephoned his mother at the family's Moscow apartment on December 31, 1996, to wish her a Happy New Year. But Revmira didn't sound like her normal exuberant self. When he asked why, she complained that she was tired. A tradition held that a Russian household needed to be in order when a new year began, and Revmira, then age seventy-three, had spent the entire day cleaning the apartment. Sergei noticed her speech was slurred and when he pressed her, she explained that she might have suffered a minor stroke. Sergei telephoned friends in Moscow, who went to check on her. Revmira was getting ready to go to a party, but they drove her instead to a hospital, where she was admitted for observation. Helen flew to Moscow to be with her. Revmira was in good spirits, but doctors confirmed that she had suffered a stroke and they were nervous about possible damage to the left side of her brain. Ten days after she was admitted, Revmira died. A distraught Sergei flew home to bury her.

"My mother was my whole world," he later explained. "All of my achievements, my career, everything I had done, in my mind, I did for her, to make her proud of her son. When she died, I lost this drive."

The laws that govern the CIA's resettlement program prohibit defectors from revealing information about the mechanics of their defections. This includes discussing when and how they first contacted U.S. officials. Because of this restriction, Sergei cannot recount during interviews any conversations that he might have had with U.S. intelligence before or after his October 2000 defection. The reason for this ironclad restriction should be obvious. Neither the FBI nor the CIA wants a rival intelligence service to learn the procedures that were used after a defector got in touch with them. In Sergei's case, there are other matters at stake. Discovering when Sergei initially contacted U.S. officials could help the Russians assess how much damage he has done to the SVR. Did he contact the FBI before he defected or did he seek asylum on October 2000 after he and his family disappeared from their Riverdale apartment? Did he ever spy for U.S. intelligence and, if so, for how long? Did he volunteer in Ottawa, Moscow, or New York?

Although U.S. intelligence officials have steadfastly refused to answer these questions publicly, two did speak privately about Sergei's case during interviews for this book after they were promised anonymity. It had been six years since Sergei defected and they argued that the few tidbits they were willing to expose about his case would be information that the SVR already had deduced while performing a damage assessment. While both officials were evasive about pinpointing an exact date, they acknowledged that Sergei had, indeed, spied for the U.S. before he defected. They also confirmed that he worked for U.S. intelligence while he was still deputy *rezident* in New York, adding that he did it for a "lengthy period," which meant "more than a couple of years."

Revmira died in January 1997. She had been the only connection that was keeping Sergei tied to Russia. Early in his career, Sergei had seen firsthand how the KGB dealt with traitors. Nearly all had been executed and their families stripped of their personal belongings, shunned, and turned out into the streets. Given the closeness of his relationship with Revmira, logic suggests that he would never have put her into such a risky position. After she died, however, he and Helen would be free to act on their whispered conversations.

Based on his expertise as a veteran SVR intelligence officer, Sergei would have known how to contact the FBI in New York in early 1997 without arousing suspicion inside his own mission from Line VKR counterintelligence officers. He also would have understood another rudimentary fact. If an SVR officer decided to switch allegiances, the welcome that he would receive from the U.S. would be much warmer and much more financially rewarding if he worked for the FBI as a mole burrowed inside Russian intelligence *first,* before he came knocking on its door.

During interviews, Sergei would not speculate even in general terms about the dangers that an SVR officer would face in New York if he contacted the FBI and became a U.S. spy inside the Russian Mission. Nor would he discuss how such a spy would successfully keep from being caught while working for the U.S. under the noses of his Russian colleagues. When pressed, Sergei said: "During my whole professional career, I was training myself not to be afraid of anything. Fear, in this context, is the main enemy, and it must be replaced by fact-based analysis, deep professional knowledge, and intuition. Every decision must be taken exceptionally thoroughly, everything must be precalculated. Yes, risk is inevitable, but without taking precalculated risk one would never be able to make a successful career and will always drink water instead of champagne, especially in my specific profession. My whole family tried to live according to these principles, and the fact that we got through a lot of obstacles and situations proves that we used these principles correctly."

THIRTY-FOUR

The instructions in the cable from the Center were explicit.

A delegation from the Russian Ministry of Finance would soon be arriving in Manhattan. Sergei was told to make certain the official in charge, a finance minister identified as Deputy Y. Volkov, received special treatment. A short time later, the head of the SVR's financial department, Major General V. Lysenkov, made a special trip to New York to reiterate the importance of Deputy Volkov's visit and to make certain everything was in order.

"What's so special about this guy?" Sergei asked.

General Lysenkov's answer came in a hushed voice. Deputy Volkov had access to the SVR's so-called invisible budget.

Sergei had heard tales about hidden monies, but this was the first time anyone had acknowledged they existed. General Lysenkov filled in the gaps.

When it became clear the old Soviet system was about to end, the leaders of the Communist Party began to fret about what would happen to the party's vast wealth. They decided to protect it by transferring billions of dollars out of the country, but because of the restrictive Soviet financial system that they had helped create, there was no way for them to send money easily from the Central Bank of Moscow to foreign banks. They turned to then KGB head Vladimir Kryuchkov for help, and he signed a secret decree in 1991 that authorized the KGB to create private businesses in Moscow for the "purpose of protecting state security," even though private ownership was still illegal at that time. Money from the Communist Party's coffers was moved into these shell companies and secreted through them out of the Soviet Union. This systematic looting of the Communist Party's funds was documented in a KGB memo titled "Emergency Measures to Organize Commercial and Foreign Economic Activity for the Party." It was written by the Communist Party's administrative director, Nikolai Kruchinin, to explain why the party's leaders were taking such a drastic step. According to the memo, the money was to be saved until it could be used to finance a return to Communism in Russia. The memo was supposed to be kept secret, but it was found and disclosed after Kryuchkov's failed August 1991 coup attempt against Gorbachev.

The new Democrats, who had rallied behind Gorbachev and Yeltsin, were outraged and demanded the cash be returned. However, when Gorbachev sent investigators to interview Communist Party director Kruchinin, they found him and his top aide both dead. Medical examiners concluded the deaths were "suspicious suicides," which sparked rumors that they had been murdered by the KGB to keep them from revealing where the party's wealth had been hidden.

In 1992, the members of the Supreme Soviet voted to investigate the whereabouts of the missing loot. Legislators put Lev Ponomarev, a Moscow politician, in charge of finding it. Ponomarev would later estimate that between $15 billion and $50 billion had been shuffled out of the country by Kryuchkov. The party's missing assets reportedly included sixty metric tons of gold and eight metric tons of platinum.

Ponomarev and his auditors went to work,

but when the paper trail led them to the SVR's Center, they hit a wall. By this time, the KGB had been dismantled and SVR officials, with the backing of the new Russian Federation Ministry of Finance, refused to reveal any information about the transferred billions. The generals at the Center said it would be irresponsible to turn over information to Ponomarev because if they did, they would be revealing how Russian foreign intelligence secretly moved cash around the world to fund its operations. A determined Ponomarev asked President Yeltsin to intervene, but he refused. Instead of ordering the Center to hand over its records, Yeltsin suggested Ponomarev find some other way to locate the money. He gave Ponomarev permission to hire an American firm, Kroll and Associates, to help. The U.S. firm joined Ponomarev's search, but after several wheel-spinning months, they turned up nothing. The SVR, meanwhile, began exerting pressure on the leader of the new Russian Parliament, Ruslan Khasbulatov. Not long after that, Khasbulatov pulled the plug and Ponomarev was told to stop hunting.

"As members of the Communist Party, Helen and I both had a percentage of our wages automatically deducted each month to pay our party dues," Sergei later said, "and this was done to every party member all across the entire Soviet Union — so everyone knew the Communist Party had billions in its treasury before the Soviet Union ended."

General Lysenkov did not tell Sergei the exact role that Deputy Volkov played in the missing-billions mystery, only that he had access to some of the party funds and the Center was intent on keeping Volkov happy. The general warned Sergei that Volkov would be traveling with an assistant named Svetlana, who had a reputation for being pushy, arrogant, and difficult to please. Even though Volkov was married, he and Svetlana were having a sexual affair, and because they were lovers, she could easily influence his opinion. Keeping her content was just as important as making certain Volkov had a good time.

There was another complication, General Lysenkov explained. Officially, Volkov and Svetlana were coming to New York to conduct a routine inspection of the Russian consulate. But they were actually coming to investigate complaints about Ivan Kuznetsov, the Russian consul general, who was one of the highest-ranking Russian diplomats in Manhattan. The Russian Ministry of Finance suspected Kuznetsov of embezzling funds.

Sergei wasn't surprised. He had already concluded that the diplomat was a thief. As consul general, Kuznetsov sat on top of a gold mine. The consulate routinely collected as much as $5 million in cash per month from visa application fees and other charges levied against persons who wanted to conduct business in Russia. That cash changed hands several times inside the consulate before it was eventually deposited in a diplomatic pouch and sent to Moscow. The accounting system in the consulate was not computerized and most clerks were the wives of other mission employees. They had little or no training in bookkeeping. Even experienced consulate officials had trouble keeping track of the income, making the system vulnerable to errors and theft.

Sergei had quietly conducted his own probe of the consul general after Kuznetsov took charge of a multimillion-dollar building renovation project under way at the consulate. Sergei found evidence of kickbacks. "These crooks would purchase the least expensive materials possible — the cheapest wooden door, for instance, that cost less than a hundred bucks — but when they submitted a bill, it would be for an expensive, thick solid oak door that cost several hundreds of dollars. Kuznetsov would approve it and they would kick back money to him."

In one instance, the Ministry of Foreign Affairs had been charged $180,000 for a new front door. "The front entrance door was made from bulletproof, armored glass and obviously was not cheap, but that price had been exaggerated at least ten times by the time it was sent to Moscow." Because the ornate consulate building was often used to host diplomatic events, Kuznetsov convinced his bosses at the MFA to cover the walls of the building's reception area with 24-karat gold. After the first layer was installed, Kuznetsov claimed the job hadn't been done properly. He had the gold plating replaced with a new layer. That second one proved to be ten times more costly to install than the first, Sergei discovered, and the first gold covering simply vanished after it was removed.

Sergei had shown his detective work to the SVR *rezident,* but he refused to act. He told Sergei that Kuznetsov would use his political connections in Moscow to destroy them both if they exposed him.

"The price of the renovations in New York became famous inside the SVR," Sergei said later. "The project went millions and millions over its budget, but Kuznetsov was never criticized, not once."

Not surprisingly, Deputy Volkov and Svetlana started their inspection at the consulate after they got settled in town. But they soon found themselves as confused as everyone else when they tried to follow the circuitous route that cash went through inside the consulate. After several frustrating hours, a clearly irritated Volkov demanded to speak to someone who could unravel the cumbersome procedure. Officials hustled Helen into the room to explain the system to Volkov and Svetlana. Helen had worked at the consulate for nearly four years by this point. Neither of them knew that she was married to Sergei.

Helen succeeded in guiding Volkov and Svetlana through the system. She also pointed out flaws where funds could easily go missing. "You are the only expert here who knows what she is doing," Svetlana gushed after Helen's presentation.

That night, the ambassador at the mission hosted a private dinner party for Volkov and Svetlana at Windows on the World, the exclusive restaurant on the 106th and 107th floors of the North Tower of the World Trade Center. Only clean diplomats were invited, but Sergei learned later that Svetlana had complained bitterly during the entire meal. She was especially irritated because of the liquor. She considered herself a connoisseur when it came to Hennessy cognac, and she insisted the cognac that she was served was not authentic.

"She said it was fake Hennessy because it tasted different from what she drank in Moscow," Sergei recalled. "She was convinced the Americans were cheating her when, in fact, this woman was so provincial she didn't realize the Hennessy that she drank in Moscow was the fake stuff, not the cognac being served at one of Manhattan's best restaurants."

Protocol required that the SVR *rezidentura* also host a dinner, and Sergei took charge of finding an appropriate restaurant. "I decided to take a different tactic from the ambassador's Windows on the World approach. I was absolutely sure I could fool this group of Russian rednecks and I had no interest in wasting my budget taking them somewhere expensive."

Sergei and Helen drove to City Island, an area in the Bronx that had the look and feel of an old seaport. They went from one restaurant to another until Sergei found a manager willing to negotiate a cheap price for a lobster dinner prepared for ten guests.

The owner told Sergei that most lobsters in City Island sold for a minimum of $25 each, but he was willing to sell his for $12 because they were dead, smaller than normal, and kept frozen. However, he insisted his cook could season them so that none of Sergei's guests would be able to tell the difference from lobsters fished from a tank moments before a meal. Although it was illegal, the owner also offered to let Sergei bring liquor from the Russian grocery store at Riverdale with him into the restaurant to further cut costs.

"The seafood restaurant looked okay from the outside, but it was dirty and run-down inside," Sergei said later. "The bathrooms were so filthy, they reeked."

He decided it was perfect.

The night of the dinner, Sergei and Helen rode with Deputy Volkov and Svetlana in one of the mission's limousines to City Island. En route, Sergei explained that he was taking the couple to an extraordinary restaurant that was kept secret by New Yorkers because they didn't want tourists overrunning the place. He said the owner kept the interior shabby to further frighten away tourists.

"When we stepped inside and the woman saw fishing nets hanging on the walls and an aquarium with dead fish floating in the water, she announced, 'Oh, I love this place. It is quaint. Not like the pretentious World Trade Center.' " Sergei began offering toasts with cognac from Riverdale and Svetlana declared that this liquor was the "real Hennessy" and not the fake drink she'd been served at the World Trade Center. By the time the lobsters arrived, everyone was so drunk that Sergei was feeling especially bold. "I had no interest in eating these dead, frozen lobsters, so I told everyone I was allergic to seafood. They actually felt sorry for me!" The lobsters looked like crawfish and what little meat was inside them was still frozen, but that didn't stop Sergei. "I said, 'Listen, everyone, I don't want to show off, but these lobsters are a special breed. They were caught in a deep hole near Maine and they are intentionally small and taste different from big lobsters which live in polluted waters and have metal particles in them.' And this foolish woman took a bite and declared it was delicious. Now these lobsters were so bad they looked barely edible, but everyone began raving about how great they tasted. I had a few more drinks and found myself getting even more carried away. I stood up and declared, 'Okay, if you promise not to tell anyone, I will tell you another secret. This restaurant, it is not only the best seafood restaurant in New York, but also in the entire East Coast.' By the time desserts were served, everyone was so drunk and happy that I told the woman it was not only the best seafood restaurant in the East Coast but also in the entire U.S., and before long, Deputy Volkov and his lover were demanding they have their photographs taken with this famous chef who knew how to prepare this special breed of lobster. He came out to pose with us and we took tons of photos. By the time we were leaving, I told the woman this was not only the best restaurant in the U.S. but in the entire world, and she and Volkov were agreeing with me."

The next day, a bleary-eyed Deputy Volkov met with Sergei to discuss the preliminary results of his inspection. "He told me privately that he had found evidence that Consul General Ivan Kuznetsov was embezzling." Volkov said he would report his findings to the MFA, but he was not optimistic. Kuznetsov was a close friend of Yeltsin's prime minister, Viktor Chernomyrdin, and Volkov predicted that no one in the MFA would be willing to risk irritating the powerful oligarch. "What he was saying was that Kuznetsov was too well connected even for him to challenge."

Later, Sergei met with Svetlana and she again complimented him about their City Island lobster feast. That dinner had cost Sergei a total of $300 for the meal, plus a fifty-dollar tip. The ambassador had spent several thousand dollars entertaining Svetlana and the others at the World Trade Center. Yet she had preferred his restaurant choice.

Shortly after Deputy Volkov and Svetlana returned to Moscow, President Yeltsin fired Chernomyrdin as prime minister. Almost immediately, Consul General Kuznetsov was recalled by the MFA. Two different criminal investigations were launched against him. But he used his political connections with Chernomyrdin's oligarch pals to keep from being imprisoned. The charges against him were eventually dropped, and Kuznetsov was appointed by the Yeltsin administration to a government panel that oversaw the import and export of Russian diamonds.

The SVR's control of secret Communist Party funds, the visit by Volkov and his rude lover, and Kuznetsov's brazen thefts reinforced what Sergei already had decided. "The more corrupt and ignorant you were in Moscow under Yeltsin, the more you were admired. In such an environment, only fools dared to be honest."

THIRTY-FIVE

On August 9, 1999, President Boris Yeltsin fired his prime minister and sacked his entire Cabinet. Yeltsin had become infamous during his two terms for impulsively firing his staff. Polls showed Yeltsin's approval ratings had dipped to an all-time low of 5 percent. In a surprise move, he named Vladimir Putin as his new prime minister, the fifth to serve in that job in less than eighteen months. He also announced that Putin was the candidate who he hoped would succeed him.

Putin was a virtual unknown and initially was not believed to have much of a chance of being elected in the March 2000 presidential elections. The front-runner was former SVR head Yevgeny Primakov. Known for his integrity, Primakov was campaigning on a reform campaign, promising to clean up the corruption that Yeltsin had encouraged. There were rumors in the Moscow media that Primakov would prosecute Yeltsin's money-grubbing oligarch pals if elected.

The political mood in Russia, however, shifted on September 9, 1999, when a bomb exploded in a Moscow apartment building, killing ninety-four people. A second blast ripped through another complex four days later, murdering 119, and three days after that, a third blast in the city of Volgodonsk left seventeen dead. The unprecedented wave of domestic terrorism stunned Russians. Appearing on national television, Putin blamed Chechen terrorists and in a calm demeanor declared that he would pursue the killers no matter where they tried to hide and would — in a phrase that quickly became famous throughout Russia — *"ikh zamochit' v sortire,"* which translates to "waste them in the shithouse." His use of crude criminal slang appealed to viewers, and overnight he became the most popular politician in Russia.

Putin ordered the Russian military to bomb the Chechen capital, and he sent more troops into the war zone. On December 31, 1999, Yeltsin abruptly resigned. In accordance with the Russian Constitution, Putin became acting president. His first presidential action was to sign a decree

457

granting Yeltsin and members of his "Family" absolute immunity from prosecution for any misuse of their power while they were in office and for any violation of laws, including corruption, bribery, or treason. In this case, the "Family" meant not only Yeltsin's blood relatives, such as his daughter Tatyana Dyachenko, whom Yeltsin had appointed to his administration, but also his closest advisers, mostly oligarchs. The new president assured "Family" members that he would not try to recover the billions that they had amassed, nor would he seize any of Yeltsin's personal assets. Records would later show that Yeltsin had become a multimillionaire during his presidency despite his meager salary. Among Yeltsin's reported holdings were two Swiss-manufactured yachts, each valued at a half-million dollars, and a villa in France worth $11 million.

Putin's law-and-order image and surging popularity made him the presidential candidate to beat. To guarantee his election, Yeltsin's oligarchs put their money behind him, launching a fiercely nationalistic public relations campaign. He easily won during the first round of voting.

It was a rags-to-riches story. Putin had begun his career as a rank-and-file KGB internal affairs officer (Line VKR) in Saint

Petersburg (then called Leningrad), where he worked without distinction from 1975 until 1984. The KGB next sent him to Dresden, East Germany, where he also served without any marked attention. During his sixteen-year stint in the KGB, he rose only to the rank of lieutenant colonel. After the Soviet Union collapsed, Putin quit the intelligence service to work for the mayor of Saint Petersburg, Anatoli Sobchak. When Sobchak was voted out of office in 1996, Putin helped Sobchak flee Russia before he could be indicted by his successor for stealing millions in city funds. Several members of Yeltsin's cabinet who had been friends of Sobchak's were impressed by Putin's loyalty. They arranged for him to get a job at the Kremlin. Yeltsin eventually put him in charge of the Federal Security Service, but journalists would later note that Putin had been unpopular with its generals.

"Inside Russian intelligence, Putin was not highly regarded," Sergei recalled, "because he had a nothing career. If anything, he was viewed as being low-class. And then, suddenly, he was the Russian president."

Unlike Sergei and other top intelligence officers at the Center, Putin had not grown up in a privileged KGB family, nor had he attended the Soviet Union's elite schools.

His father had been a factory foreman, and Putin would later recall how he had lived in a rat-infested apartment as a youth and often went to bed hungry.

As president, Putin brought his own pals into the Kremlin. They were soon identified in the media as *siloviki,* from the Russian for "power," because most were former KGB or other military officers. Putin's *siloviki* had no loyalty to the new Democrats, who had followed Gorbachev, or to Yeltsin's oligarchs.

Despite the new faces, Putin did not replace everyone. Aleksandr Voloshin, who was secretly funneling millions from the UN Oil-for-Food Program into the hands of his buddies on the Russian Presidential Council, had no intention of quitting. Called the "Gray Cardinal" because of his clout, Voloshin moved seamlessly as chief of staff from the Yeltsin presidency into that same position for Putin.

During the summer of 2000, the Center informed Sergei that President Putin would be attending the UN Millennium Summit being held September 6 and 7 in New York. Aleksandr Lunkin, the deputy head of the Federal Protection Service (FSO), was being dispatched to Manhattan to help make security arrangements for Putin's trip.

Sergei invited Lunkin to his apartment for

a private dinner when he arrived. The two men had known each other for twenty years. Lunkin had been a member of the Komsomol when Sergei had been in charge of the KGB's foreign intelligence Komsomol committee, and during their dinner Sergei urged Lunkin to tell him about Putin and his top aides.

Lunkin said Putin was especially close to two men. The first was General Yevgeni Alekseyevich Murov, who was a *silovik* — a former KGB counterintelligence officer. He and Putin had become friends in Saint Petersburg and Putin had brought him to Moscow to run the FSO.

The second close pal of Putin's was Colonel Viktor Zolotov — another *silovik*. Putin had put him in charge of the Presidential Security Service, which provided Putin with bodyguards. Zolotov's officers were known as the "Men in Black" because they dressed in all-black suits and wore black sunglasses.

Lunkin said Zolotov was not considered to be very intelligent but he and Putin were inseparable, in part because Putin's hobbies were boxing and judo, and Zolotov was his sparring partner. Born into a working-class family, Zolotov had been a steelworker before he was hired as a bodyguard by the

Saint Petersburg mayor. He had met Putin through that job and they had become close friends. Whenever Putin appeared in public, Zolotov could be spotted walking directly behind him.

During their gossip session, Lunkin warned Sergei to be wary of both Murov and Zolotov. "They are common thugs," he declared. To illustrate, Lunkin said that he had been with both men in Moscow when Aleksandr Voloshin's name had been mentioned. Lunkin claimed that Murov and Zolotov had talked openly about Putin's feelings of jealousy toward Voloshin and the political power he wielded. Putin wanted to fire the "Gray Cardinal," but for political reasons couldn't. Lunkin told Sergei that Murov and Zolotov had suddenly begun discussing ways to murder Voloshin. One idea was to kill him and blame Chechen terrorists. Another was to make his execution appear to be a "hit" by the Russian Mafia, the result of some sordid business deal gone bad.

"They were quite serious," Lunkin assured Sergei. "This was not a joke."

"What happened?"

The longer they talked, the more they agreed that killing Voloshin would not end Putin's political problems. Key members of

Voloshin's staff and other oligarchs would have to be purged, too. They would also have to begin murdering members of the Russian press corps who would be sure to investigate Voloshin's death.

According to Lunkin, General Murov and Zolotov decided to make a list of politicians and other influential Muscovites whom they would need to assassinate to give Putin unchecked power. After the two men finished their list, Zolotov announced, "There are too many. It's too many to kill — even for us."

Lunkin claimed the two men's conversation had made him uneasy, especially since both held high administration positions. As director of the FSO, Murov controlled some twenty thousand troops whose job was to protect the Kremlin. Among other things, the FSO operated underground command bunkers and a special subway system that connected key government facilities. It also kept track of the famed "black box" that followed the Russian president whenever he traveled so he could launch a nuclear attack. Zolotov, meanwhile, oversaw a presidential guard force that under Yeltsin had operated much like an unchecked private police force. At one point, Yeltsin's security head had sent his men to arrest and detain a political rival.

Years later, Sergei would recall his thoughts during his conversation with Lunkin. "These two men's solution was to simply kill everyone who opposed Putin. This was the mentality that Putin had surrounded himself with, and these were the caliber of men whom he was calling his best friends."

A few weeks later, General Murov and Colonel Zolotov arrived in Manhattan for a final security review before Putin's UN visit. Sergei met frequently with both, and one afternoon they asked him to take them to Brighton Beach to eat at the Tatiana Café, which was where he had taken General Trubnikov and other important visitors. Murov, Zolotov, and Sergei were sipping beer and waiting for their meals when Sergei asked Zolotov about the specialized training that his "Men in Black" received. Zolotov boasted that his bodyguards were much better trained than their U.S. Secret Service counterparts. President John F. Kennedy had been assassinated while riding in an open car, he declared. Whenever Putin traveled, his motorcade consisted of seven specially constructed automobiles, none of which was a convertible, making it impossible for a sniper to know in which car the president was riding. Indian prime minister Indira Gandhi was murdered by her own security service in 1984, Zolotov continued. This was why Putin had only his closest friends, such as the two of them, in charge of his security. Gandhi's son was killed when a woman suicide bomber threw herself at him while setting off explosives hidden in a bouquet of flowers. Putin was always ringed by at least twelve of Zolotov's bodyguards whenever he was in public to prevent any such attack. "No one can get through my men and me and attack him," Zolotov proudly declared.

Clearly enjoying himself, Zolotov told Sergei that Putin's "personals" — as his most trusted "Men in Black" were called — carried 9mm "Gyurza" pistols that held eighteen bullets and were powerful enough to penetrate bulletproof vests up to fifty-four yards away. They rode in armor-plated jeeps equipped with AK-74 assault rifles, AKS-74U machine guns, Dragunov sniper rifles, RPK machine guns, grenade cup dischargers, portable "Osa" (wasp) rocket launchers, and other powerful armaments that, Zolotov insisted, would enable them to destroy an "entire battalion" if necessary. In addition to having that weaponry, each "personal" was a martial arts expert, capable of killing an attacker with a single blow.

Without any warning, Zolotov suddenly swung his hand in the air and struck Sergei in his temple. The blow knocked him off his chair and unconscious on the café floor. Moments later, Sergei awoke with Murov and Zolotov standing over him. Murov was furious.

"You could have killed him!" he yelled.

Zolotov began apologizing as he helped Sergei into a chair.

"Lunkin was correct," Sergei said later after meeting Murov and Zolotov. "They were dangerous. I didn't see a difference between Yeltsin's people and these unsophisticates who were the president's closest friends. For me, they all came from under the same rock. They were like rats. When Putin took charge, a new rat replaced an old rat. One wasn't better. He was just a different rat."

Thirty-Six

Sergei and Helen believed they knew their daughter well enough to guess her reaction to their plans. Still, they needed to discuss them with her. Helen decided to tell Ksenia while the two of them were shopping in Manhattan on a Saturday morning. Helen took her daughter's hand as they were walking out of a department store.

"Listen, I have to ask you something, and it is really important," she said. Helen paused to emphasize that this was serious and then continued. "You know your father and I — we never make any important decision without considering your opinion."

Ksenia nodded, signaling yes.

"What would you say if I told you that your parents are not planning to return to Russia?"

Ksenia stopped in the middle of the sidewalk. She was clearly surprised. "But what will happen after Dad's posting in

467

New York ends?" she asked quietly. They were speaking in Russian.

"We'll stay in the United States."

They started walking, but Ksenia didn't speak for several moments. Instead, she stared at the sidewalk. Helen, still holding her teenage daughter's hand, studied Ksenia's face, searching for a clue. Later, Helen would recall her feelings at that moment. "I can't say I was nervous. No, I was sure that my daughter was mature and smart enough to understand and approve of the reasons for our decision, which I was about to explain to her. Yet I realized that neither Sergei nor I could ever force our daughter to do something of this magnitude if she didn't want to do it. For a brief second, I wondered what we would do if she said no."

Ksenia turned to her mother and asked: "Does this mean Dad will betray Russia?"

"No!" Helen replied. "He is not a traitor! You watch Russian news every day [there was a satellite dish on the roof of the Riverdale building that allowed residents to watch Russian TV channels] and you know what is going on. Your father doesn't want to keep serving this corrupt Russian government."

Ksenia squeezed her mother's hand. "I understand," she said.

Helen explained the reasons why they didn't want to return. Ksenia listened without asking a single question. She had complete faith in her parents. She always had.

"I had always known my father was a spy," Ksenia recalled later in an interview. "When I was about seven, we would go on these weekend outings for employees of the KGB. We would ride in a black limousine, and I knew my father was someone important and I knew that everyone at these getaways were KGB and they treated him like he was their boss." By the time she was eight, her father had clued her in. "We would take walks in the woods near our summer house and he would tell me stories about what he did and I began to think of him as a Russian James Bond and I was very, very proud. I was not exposed to any negative stories about the KGB because it was not something children generally discussed."

Ksenia adored her parents and her grandparents. When Ksenia was born, Grandmother Revmira told Helen and Sergei: "Okay, this child is mine. If you want your own, then you should have others." Her parents laughed, but Revmira had only been partly joking. Because Sergei and Helen had demanding jobs in Moscow at the time, Ksenia lived with Revmira and Oleg in their apartment until she was five. When her parents finally took charge, they frequently treated Ksenia more as a contemporary than as a child. "Because of my father's job, there were always secrets in our family," Ksenia recalled, "but these were secrets that we kept from outsiders, not from each other. In the home, we talked openly about everything, and by the time that I was nine my parents didn't have to tell me what I could and couldn't say to others, because I pretty much knew."

Ksenia was not a rebellious child. "My friends used to be shocked because I considered my parents to be my best friends and I shared everything with them. I did not see them as two different people. They each had their own different strengths, but I saw them as one — a team — and together they were a powerful force."

The close family bonds were strengthened in Canada. At first, Ksenia felt out of place. She especially missed her grandmother. (Her grandfather died in 1985.) But when the family returned to Moscow after spending nearly five years in Ottawa, fourteen-year-old Ksenia realized she had become Westernized. "I was happy to see my grandmother and I was able to reconnect with my friends, but it wasn't the same." Ksenia was used to watching U.S. television shows. Her favorites were *Full House, Family Matters,* and *The Fresh Prince of Bel-Air* — programs that portrayed youngsters growing up in U.S. families. "I didn't like Russian programs and television was important to a growing teenager. I looked very Russian. I spoke Russian. But I couldn't understand the slang in Moscow, and even when I learned it, I still didn't get why they were using it. I didn't understand Russian humor. I understood American humor."

There were other differences. In Russia, most young people lived with their parents until they got married. "I wanted to go to college and eventually get my own little place and live by myself before one day starting a family of my own." Ksenia was used to wearing loose-fitting flannel shirts, blue denim jeans, and Doc Martens when she went out with other teenagers. In Moscow, girls dressed in high heels, miniskirts, and fancy blouses. The poverty in Russia and the government's failure to provide for the elderly shocked her. One night she watched a Russian grandmother describing on a nightly news telecast how she divided a single tomato into three parts so she would have a vegetable to eat for three days with her bread.

When her parents announced they were moving to New York City after spending only a year in Moscow, Ksenia was eager to go. "From the moment we landed in Manhattan, I felt at ease. The same television programs were on and I made friends with other Russian teenagers whose parents lived at Riverdale. We would hang out at the swimming pool or in the little gym at Riverdale and we would talk about our futures — going to college and getting careers — and, of course, teenage things, such as movies and crushes. But when I went back to Russia, my girlfriends were talking about getting married and having children."

The Soviet Union had dissolved and the Communist Party's stranglehold on politics had ended by the time Ksenia was attending high school classes in the Russian school at Riverdale. "There wasn't a big emphasis on Communism or on Socialism. I wasn't really interested in politics, but I was aware of the main principles of both, and from my parents I had learned that neither Communism nor Socialism had worked in Soviet society. Meanwhile, I liked what I saw in America. I felt that it was closer to my ideas and my beliefs."

Much of her fondness for Moscow was

472

tied to Revmira. "I couldn't imagine going back and opening our apartment door and not having my grandmother greet us. She was the center of our family, and when she died, I thought: 'What is Russia now without Grandmother?' The idea of returning to the apartment and not seeing her was scary to me."

Ksenia said later that she had no clue her parents were planning to defect. "I was busy. Like most teenagers, I was involved in my own world, but when my mother told me, I was surprised but then I was not really that surprised. I wasn't afraid because I knew they wouldn't do anything without thinking it through all of the way and without knowing the outcome. I knew my dad would never do anything to hurt my mother or me. When I thought about it, I understood why they were taking this step."

Ksenia didn't think of her father as a traitor. "I felt he was making a really good decision. I am a very driven person. I got this from my parents and grandparents and I knew that in the U.S., I could do anything if I worked hard enough. I could get into the right schools and get a good job and become whatever I wanted to be, except the U.S. president. I knew they wanted me to have opportunities, and none of us believed that would have happened in Russia."

The thought of not being able to return to Moscow didn't upset her. "When I used to get homesick — it was for my grandmother. I missed talking to her, sharing things. Even in New York, I missed her because she was such a good friend. But after she died, all I had were memories of my childhood, the summers in the country houses, picking mushrooms with my grandfather and father, and memories about how beautiful Moscow was. Sometimes, I would become teary-eyed, but that world was in my past and the U.S. was my future. I had really spent most of my developmental years in Canada and in the U.S., and I felt more American inside than I did Russian, so when my mother told me, I actually felt relieved that we were not going back. I decided that this was just another thing that I was not supposed to discuss with anyone outside the family. I accepted it and waited for my parents to tell me when we would leave."

THIRTY-SEVEN

Valeri Koval rushed into Sergei's office inside the Russian Mission's "submarine" late one afternoon. The SVR *rezident* had just received a "For Your Eyes Only" cable from the Center.

"We have a traitor!" Koval declared.

"Who?" Sergei asked.

Koval thurst the cable forward. One of Sergei's officers, Colonel Yuri Bokanyov, was about to defect, the alert warned.

"They want us to send him home immediately," Koval announced.

It was standard operating procedure. Whenever the SVR became suspicious of an officer, it looked for an excuse to get him back to Moscow. Sergei later recalled: "Often, we would tell someone he was being promoted or he was going to get a special decoration in Moscow as a ruse to persuade him to get on the airplane without creating a scandal."

The KGB used this tactic famously in November 1985 when it tricked Valeri Martynov, a KGB lieutenant colonel stationed in Washington, D.C., into flying home after it discovered he was an FBI spy. Martynov had been told his KGB bosses had handpicked him to serve on an "honor guard" escorting another KGB official back to the Soviet Union. He walked into the trap and was later executed.

The "For Your Eyes Only" cable said Bokanyov had told a U.S. official less than twenty-four hours earlier that he wanted to defect. Bokanyov had worked for Sergei in New York for five years posing as an official at the Russian Association for International Cooperation (RAMSIR). During Soviet times, RAMSIR had been called the Union of Friendship Societies. It was a governmental organization that promoted cultural exchanges between the Soviet Union and other nations. The intentions of RAMSIR and its predecessor sounded high-minded, but Moscow had riddled both with intelligence operatives. The cable said Bokanyov had approached the U.S. official after a RAMSIR meeting. Bokanyov said he was hoping to "find a job" in New York when his tour ended and he wondered if the American could help him.

"We had officers posing as cultural exchange officials so Bokanyov naturally assumed the American was an FBI agent or someone working for the FBI," Sergei later explained. But the U.S. official wasn't, and instead of alerting the FBI, he telephoned the Russian embassy in Washington, D.C., and complained to Bokanyov's RAMSIR boss. The RAMSIR director was an SVR co-optee, and she alerted the Washington station's SVR *rezident.* Because everything had to go through the Center, the *rezident* sent a cable to Moscow and it, in turn, had sent the "For Your Eyes Only" message to Koval. Not certain what to do, he had hurried into Sergei's office.

"I never liked Bokanyov as a human being, but I decided to do what I could to save him," Sergei said later. "What he had done was stupid, not treason."

In a reply to the Center, Sergei argued that there were "too many clouds" in the accusation to take disciplinary action against Bokanyov. He urged the generals not to judge Bokanyov so quickly. "Why do you trust this American who telephoned Washington? This is probably a provocation by the FBI."

The Center didn't agree. After an exchange of cables, Sergei was ordered to get

Bokanyov back to Moscow on the next available flight. The Center told Sergei to tell Bokanyov that RAMSIR needed him to give a lecture at a cultural exchange conference being held in Moscow. He was to tell Bokanyov that another RAMSIR official who was supposed to make the presentation had become ill.

Sergei did as he was told, but before he put Bokanyov on the flight, he warned him about what was happening. "Bokanyov was terrified, of course. I told him the only way he could survive would be to insist the entire affair was a provocation by the Americans. That was his only hope."

As soon as the flight landed in Moscow, Bokanyov was taken to Lubyanka and interrogated. He did exactly what Sergei had suggested. He insisted the American cultural exchange official had lied to cause trouble and had falsely put him under suspicion. Apparently, Bokanyov was convincing. He was allowed to return to Manhattan to complete his RAMSIR tour. The moment he arrived in New York, he thanked Sergei. When his tour ended a short while later, Bokanyov returned to a job in the Center.

Sergei had taken an unnecessary risk. If interrogators had gotten Bokanyov to admit that he had been trying to defect, there was a good chance he would have told them that Sergei had warned him about their suspicions and advised him to lie. Tipping off Bokanyov had been an instance where Sergei listened to his conscience rather than his instincts. That was dangerous and his actions made him edgy.

The Bokanyov incident supported a theory that Sergei held. On their own, Line VKR officers in Manhattan were so timid and so inept that the chances of their actually identifying a traitor inside the mission or stopping someone from defecting were slight. As long as an officer was smart and didn't make obvious mistakes, there was a good chance that his treason would go undetected. The real threat came from outsiders. Bokanyov had foolishly approached a U.S. official who had reported him. The danger faced by a U.S. mole in the mission was that someone in U.S. intelligence would sell his identity to the SVR — just as Ames had done to his victims. In such a scenario, there would be no advance warning. The mole wouldn't know that he had been identified until it was too late to escape.

Not long after the Bokanyov episode, the New York *rezident* once again hurried into Sergei's office waving a cable. This time, he announced that Major General A. Zarubin, one of the most-feared men in the Center, was going to inspect the *rezidentura*s in New York and Washington, D.C. Zarubin, whose code name was Comrade *Konstantinoff,* was in charge of the SVR's internal security, the equivalent of internal affairs in a police force.

"Sergei, I know this guy," Koval clamored, "and he is a monster. Nothing good comes from meeting with him. He can look right through your eyes and read your mind."

A few days later, General Zarubin began his tour in Washington. Sergei telephoned the acting *rezident* there, who happened to be Vitali Domoratski, his former colleague from Canada.

"He's very tough, very cruel," Domoratski said about Zarubin, "and he is impossible to read."

Based on that fearsome comment, Sergei assumed Zarubin would be an imposing figure. But when the general arrived in Manhattan, he was pencil thin, wearing a worn polyester suit, and was a chain-smoker with badly discolored teeth, stained fingers, and a perpetual cigarette cough. During their four-hour session together, Zarubin grilled Sergei about his performance as deputy *rezident.*

"Do you believe the FBI and CIA have identified who our operatives are inside the mission?" the general asked.

Sergei answered with a question. "General, how long have you worked in our system — thirty, forty years — and you still don't have an answer to this question?"

His impertinence seemed to throw Zarubin off guard.

Sergei explained that for thirty years the KGB and now the SVR had used the same diplomatic cover assignments inside the mission as ruses for intelligence operatives. Nothing could be done because the Russian Ministry of Foreign Affairs refused to vary the covers that the SVR used. "Of course they know who we are," Sergei declared.

Zarubin asked Sergei what he thought of the FBI. "They are very serious enemies and we should never underestimate them," Sergei replied. "We must always respect our enemies."

Zarubin asked: "How can you be certain your sources are not being used by the FBI to send us misinformation or to spy on us?"

"We can't," Sergei answered, "but if I cut off all of the sources who are suspicious, you might decorate me for having excellent security, but we would lose information. It means we must trust our expertise and the expertise of the Center, and we must select our sources with great care."

At the end of their session, Zarubin closed his notebook and announced: "You have given me the correct answer each time I have asked a question." Zarubin then disclosed that in Washington, Domoratski had not done as well. Zarubin said Domoratski had belittled the FBI, calling its agents "morons." He'd claimed that none of the *rezidentura*'s sources in Washington were FBI dangles, adding that it would be impossible for U.S. intelligence to penetrate the SVR's operations because internal security in his station was foolproof.

"Domoratski is a fool," Zarubin declared, "because he underestimates his main enemy. But you, Sergei, respect the Americans."

Zarubin told Sergei that he planned to interview each SVR officer in New York. He would start his rounds the following day. The next morning before Zarubin arrived at the mission, Sergei met with his officers. "I told them exactly what to say — that we 'respected the FBI's ability and took them seriously as our counterparts.' And that is precisely what each of them told Zarubin during their interviews with him."

Sergei would later wonder aloud how

Zarubin had gotten such a fierce reputation. "It was an enigma to me. His ideas were outdated. He told everyone — if any SVR operative befriended a code clerk at the mission, then he should automatically be investigated because he was trying to learn codes to sell to our enemies. It was nonsense. Code clerks did rote work and most retained nothing in their heads. If you kidnapped a code clerk, turned him upside down, and shook him to get information, he wouldn't be able to recall even the codes he'd used earlier in the day."

Completely by chance, the head of Line VKR in Manhattan happened to be visiting the Center when Zarubin returned there and filed his preliminary report. The VKR head told Sergei that Zarubin had given Domoratski and the Washington station low marks. But he had described the permanent mission in Manhattan as one of the "most secure and most loyal" in the entire world. He wrote that Sergei and his men understood their enemies and were diligent about protecting the SVR from being penetrated.

It would prove to be an ironic statement — given that the general had unknowingly been sitting directly across the table in New York from an FBI mole, who was only a few weeks away from defecting.

THIRTY-EIGHT

Sergei had had enough.

He'd caught a cold and stayed in the apartment in Riverdale on Monday and Tuesday. He told his officers that he would return to work in the submarine at the mission on Thursday. But when Sergei woke up on Wednesday, October 11, 2000, he decided it wasn't only a cold that was causing his malaise. He called Helen and Ksenia into the living room where he was lying on the pull-out sofa. Helen had recently quit her job at the consulate and Ksenia was home because she had graduated from high school and was taking a night course in computer programming.

"Girls," he announced, "today is the day."

Sergei wanted everyone to get dressed so that they could leave immediately. But Helen insisted that she needed at least four hours. She wanted to return several books to the neighborhood library and mail checks to pay their bills. She also wanted to get some cash from their bank account. Helen left the apartment on foot because Russian women whose husbands worked at the mission were not permitted to drive. Ksenia began packing two small bags. The family couldn't take much, otherwise it would be obvious they were going somewhere unexpectedly.

Sergei felt confident that no one suspected they were about to defect. He was such a high-ranking officer that the Center would have taken immediate action if they suspected him. At a minimum, it would have assigned operatives to watch him around the clock until it could figure out a ruse to get him back to Moscow. There had been no hints. If anything, the Center seemed genuinely pleased with his work. Sergei's tour had been recently extended to six years, a record for a deputy *rezident* stationed in New York. He'd also been promised that when he returned to Moscow, he would be promoted to the rank of general.

While Helen was running errands, Sergei began to write a note to leave behind. He had thought about what he wanted to write a thousand times. It was his chance to explain, complain, criticize, and condemn. He and Helen were about to sever all ties with their past. For a moment, Sergei thought about what that meant, emotionally and financially. He and Helen would be shunned by their Russian friends and acquaintances. No one in the SVR would want to have any contact with them ever again. They would not be able to visit the graves of their parents and grandparents in Russia. They would never be able to return to Moscow to visit the familiar sites from their childhoods or relive memories there. Sergei would go from being a highly admired SVR officer to being called a traitor. He would be stripped of his Russian citizenship. There would be a financial loss, as well. The family's five-room apartment in Moscow was easily worth a million dollars in the red-hot market being fueled by Russia's nouveau riche. Sergei had more than three thousand books, many of them antique, in his personal library there. Over the years, his family had collected rare tapestries, oil paintings, a collection of fine china, and Russian icons. Then there were the two dachas that he and Helen had inherited. The value of their apartment, its furnishings, and the dachas easily topped two million dollars. Sergei would be giving up his military career, too. He was only forty-four and he was only one year away from becoming a general. The perks that came with that rank were legendary. It would be his turn to conduct "inspections" in New York and Washington and receive the expensive meals and unlimited drinks and gifts from subordinates. After eleven more years in the SVR, he could retire, collect a pension, and go to work in a private-sector job, like many of his predecessors. There were other options. Given his training, rank, and experience, he might be able to transfer into the Russian Ministry of Foreign Affairs and become an ambassador.

Sergei began writing on the sheet in front of him, but he paused mid-line. Why was he helping the counterintelligence officers who would be assigned to investigate his disappearance? Why should he make their job easier? Still, he wanted to leave a clue — something that would confuse them, something that would make them think.

Sergei slipped off his wristwatch. He had paid $1,000 for it. He decided to leave it behind. He would tell Helen to leave a mink coat, too. It also had been an expensive purchase. Would the counterintelligence officers understand? He wasn't certain, but he understood and that was good enough. The wristwatch and the mink would provide investigators with everything they needed to deduce his motives. The watch and mink were possessions, just like the Moscow apartment and family dachas. It was as simple as that.

Sergei jotted a note: "Helen has found a good job. I don't feel good physically. We have decided to stay in this country." He put down the pen, folded the paper.

By the time Helen returned, it was almost one o'clock. Most of the security guards at Riverdale had just begun their lunch breaks. Many ate with their wives in their apartments. Ksenia had already carried their bags to the trunk of the car in the underground garage. Before leaving their cramped, tenth-floor apartment, Sergei and Helen took a final glance. Helen had insisted that he destroy any documents, letters, photos, or other personal items that they could not take with them. She was a private person and the thought of SVR investigators pawing through their papers or examining their photographs made her uneasy.

Sergei said, "Let's go."

The three of them walked down the hallway to an elevator. All of them had wondered how they would feel at this moment. Sergei was characteristically calm. To him, the afternoon seemed no different from any other. Helen was fearful, uncertain. Ksenia was excited. Helen was carrying a bag with their snow-white Persian cat, Matilda, inside. She would defect with them. When they reached the basement, they got into the car and Sergei drove up the ramp into the afternoon sun. He stopped at the compound's gate, where he spoke into a speaker. "Tretyakov," he said, knowing the guard stationed inside Riverdale would routinely mark down the time that he was leaving and who was with him in the car.

Years later, Helen's eyes would fill with tears when she remembered that Wednesday afternoon waiting for the gate to open. The scene came to her with the crystal clarity that is etched forever in one's mind during a life-changing moment. "We had only a bare minimum of belongings — yes — because we didn't want to call attention to us going, but also because we didn't want to take anything with us from that previous life except our good memories of our relatives, friends, and our parents. We were making a totally fresh start, beginning a new beginning in a new society that was really free and really democratic. But what was most important was that it was a new beginning for our daughter. I kept thinking about what Sergei's mother had told us in Ottawa about how she hated thinking her only granddaughter would have to grow up in this new, corrupt Russia. We were giving her a future, and that was worth more than mink coats and wristwatches."

When the gate swung open, Sergei edged the car forward and then stopped. This was an SVR rule. Anyone leaving Riverdale in a car was required to wait on the sidewalk until the gate behind them had fully closed and locked. This prevented another car from speeding through the gap while the electric gate shut.

It was the last SVR rule that Sergei would obey.

THIRTY-NINE

Trying to evaluate Sergei Tretyakov's value as a U.S. spy was much like assembling a jigsaw puzzle with dozens of pieces missing. His case was simply too fresh.

A spokesman for Russian foreign intelligence in Moscow declined to discuss Sergei's defection. The relocation agreement that Sergei signed barred him from disclosing any information about his relationship with the FBI and CIA. Despite repeated requests, U.S. intelligence officials refused to comment publicly.

However, a high-ranking U.S. intelligence official agreed to answer some general questions for this book after being promised anonymity. He was directly involved in Sergei's defection and he described the Russian as "one of the most productive" spies in recent memory.

Sergei delivered more than *five thousand* top-secret SVR cables to the FBI in New

York, according to the official. He supplied his handlers with more than a *hundred* classified SVR intelligence reports. The U.S. used them to prepare more than *four hundred* classified intelligence reports for U.S. intelligence services and, in many cases, the State Department and the White House. That number of reports coming from a single spy was unprecedented in recent times. Presidents Clinton and Bush were provided with analytical papers produced from Sergei's materials. "The scope of this case is breathtaking," the official said. "It is one of our biggest success stories."

The SVR cables and intelligence reports that Sergei provided contained information about Russian political and military activities in Iran, Iraq, North Korea, the Middle East, and the former Yugoslavia. He turned over Russian intelligence about Islamic groups operating in former Soviet republics, active measures being conducted in former Soviet republics to disrupt relations with the West, and SVR intelligence operations in European countries.

Sergei gave the FBI the names of the SVR's agents and trusted contacts in Canada and in Manhattan, including the alleged spies identified in this book. He told the FBI which Russian diplomats and journalists in New York, Washington, D.C., and San Francisco were SVR officers. He provided the bureau with the SVR code names used by its operatives. This was important because it enabled U.S. intelligence to track SVR officers in cables that it had collected from other sources. Sergei's directory helped the FBI and CIA identify which SVR officers were involved in previous covert operations and which were conducting more current ones. Because of Sergei, it is likely that the SVR was forced to change the code names of its officers, a costly and cumbersome process.

"Without going into detail, I can tell you that this man saved American lives," the official said. "It would not be an exaggeration to write that his actions played a significant role in influencing our nation's overall foreign policy, especially our ongoing relationship with Russia."

An FBI agent who worked with Sergei before retiring was blunter: "He was a hell of a spy. It will be a long time before we get another as good and we may never get one as productive."

In addition to the political and military information that Sergei provided, he also told the FBI how the SVR operated in New York. His description of the Post Impulse surveillance system resulted in the FBI changing how its agents communicate with one another when they track SVR officers.

In spite of the U.S. government's reluctance to officially comment, interviews with several intelligence sources in Washington and New York for this book have revealed other bits and pieces about Sergei and his spying.

- In 1997, the White House pushed NATO to admit three former members of the Warsaw Pact — Poland, the Czech Republic, and Hungary — into the European alliance. The Clinton administration said admitting them would promote democracy and a respect for human rights. It also would protect against a possible resurgence of Russia in the region. The White House's actions unnerved Yeltsin and threatened a rift in relations between the U.S. and Russia. Sergei gave the FBI diplomatic cables and intelligence reports that enabled the Clinton administration to determine what was happening during this period in the Kremlin. The cables about NATO helped U.S. officials determine when Yeltsin was serious and when he was blustering.

- Sergei provided the FBI with cables and SVR intelligence reports about NATO's military campaign in Kosovo. Yeltsin threatened several times to withdraw from international diplomatic talks because he vehemently opposed NATO's bombing campaign. Once again, Sergei's spying gave U.S. intelligence officials an insider look at Yeltsin's intentions.
- On the basis of a warning from Sergei, U.S. intelligence persuaded the State Department to cancel a visit to a foreign capital by then Secretary of State Madeleine Albright. The SVR had planned an active measure that would have badly embarrassed her if she had gone to the capital.
- While Sergei was deputy *rezident*, the FBI asked him to prepare detailed biographies of more than a dozen Moscow officials, including Presidents Yeltsin and Putin. Since his defection, U.S. intelligence has continued to call on Sergei to identify and provide background information about top Kremlin officials.
- In December 1999, the FBI revealed that it had found a listening device hid-

den inside a U.S. Department of State conference room in Washington, D.C. The device was discovered after State Department security officers noticed a Russian diplomat, later identified as Stanislav Borisovich Gusev, loitering outside the building late one night. U.S. officials found electronic equipment inside Gusev's vehicle that could be used to download information from a transmitter. This led to them undertaking an extensive search and the discovery of the bug. The FBI described the device to Sergei and asked him about it. It didn't know how it had been put there, how long it had been in place, if there were others, and how much damage it had caused. At the time, Sergei's longtime colleague Vitali Domoratski was acting SVR *rezident* in Washington, and Sergei reportedly questioned him about the bug without Domoratski realizing that he was speaking to a U.S. mole. While Sergei was not able to learn from Domoratski the identity of the person who planted the device, he did discover that it was installed in 1997 — nearly two years before it was discovered. He warned U.S. officials that the device had caused much more damage to the U.S. than what was being disclosed in the American media. Sergei told U.S. intelligence that the SVR used information that it collected from the bug to prepare more than a hundred intelligence reports, including dozens that were read by President Yeltsin. He told U.S. officials that Russian intelligence considered the bug a direct pipeline into then Secretary of State Albright's office. The SVR bugging operation was considered such a monumental success that General Trubnikov was awarded Russia's highest military honor — Hero of the Russian Federation — for overseeing the operation. Sergei further told the FBI that the device's miniature battery was being recharged with a laser beam, a unique process that CIA's technical experts had not reportedly perfected at the time.

- After Sergei told U.S. intelligence officials that Deputy Secretary of State Strobe Talbott had been identified by the SVR as a SPECIAL UNOFFICIAL CONTACT, the FBI asked Secretary Albright not to share information with him about the government's ongoing probe in 1999 into how a Russian bug was planted inside the State Department. Jaime Dettmer, a reporter with the news website Insight on the News, revealed the FBI's unusual request to keep Talbott out of the loop in a story published January 10, 2000. In it she quoted an unnamed CIA source saying, "Talbott has long been widely seen at Langley as being too close to the Russians — a sort of trusted friend, you might say."

- In an incredibly bold move, FBI agents met secretly with Sergei in Las Vegas, Nevada, while he was still working as the SVR's deputy *rezident* in Manhattan. Sergei flew there under the pretense of going on a family vacation. FBI agents spent several days at a Strip hotel debriefing him.

- The FBI urged Sergei to defect at least ten months before he did. It was worried about his safety because it had discovered there was a Russian mole in Washington. The FBI suspected the mole was a CIA officer, but it turned out to be Special Agent Robert Hanssen. The FBI investigated to see if he had known about Sergei. He hadn't. When Hanssen was arrested in February 2001, *The Washington Post* and other news organizations speculated that Sergei had tipped off the FBI about Hanssen. The newspapers made this erroneous assumption because Sergei's defection had been made public on January 30, 2001, and Hanssen had been arrested less than three weeks later. However, Sergei had nothing to do with identifying Hanssen and did not know about his spying for Moscow.

- In the past two years, U.S. intelligence officials have begun sharing Sergei with other nations. Traveling at government expense with armed escorts provided by U.S. intelligence, Sergei has been taken to Britain, Israel, and Canada to brief allied services there about SVR operations in their respective countries.

- Within hours after Sergei defected in New York, he and his family were whisked to a safe house in New Jersey. Later, they were moved under guard to a secret location. In the months that followed, U.S. officials offered Sergei and his family a relocation package that was more lucrative than any previous resettlement package awarded to a

Russian defector. The cash equivalent was determined, in part, based on the length of Sergei's spying, the risks that he and his family had taken, and the value of the information that he had provided the U.S. government. Although the total dollar amount remained classified, officials said it was higher than the previous record of two million dollars.

"The fact we accepted a Russian defector after the Cold War ended says a lot," an FBI official explained. "The fact that this defector was given a financial package significantly higher than what any other previous Russian spy has ever received is a strong indication of how valuable he has been to us and how much the U.S. appreciates what he did."

Today, Sergei and his family own a house valued at more than $600,000. Helen drives a Porsche Boxster. Sergei drives a Lexus SUV. Both have retired and are living off their investments. Ksenia recently received a master's degree from an Ivy League university.

EPILOGUE

The words of Sergei Tretyakov:

In Moscow, lies are being spread about my disappearance and why I escaped. I would like to address these rumors. No one recruited me. No one pitched me. No one convinced me to do what I did. I was never approached by a foreign intelligence service. I was never targeted by U.S. intelligence, I believe, because of my image. I was not perceived as a new Russian democrat, and although I was young, I had a reputation for thinking like the old-style KGB officer. I was considered a tough, untouchable Russian. It is important for me to explain that I was neither seduced nor blackmailed nor bribed. The decision that I made was mine without any outside influence.

It is important for me to explain that I never suffered any unfair attitude inside the SVR. I had a skyrocketing career, promotions, decorations, respect, and a very promising future. I did not have any financial concerns or any need for money.

I've been told some of my former colleagues in the SVR believe I am now living under a bridge, in total poverty and so unhappy that I would immediately return to Russia if only the United States were not holding me hostage. This is nonsense. It is true that I forfeited my professional future, and with the publishing of this book, I am confident the Russian government will now feel legally justified to seize all of our family property and real estate and private possessions in Moscow and our dachas. But neither Helen nor I have had to work a day since we escaped. We are living comfortably and none of us has ever regretted — even for a moment — our decision. Even our beloved cat Matilda seems happier!

I want it known that I never asked even for a penny from the U.S. government. When I decided to begin helping the U.S., money was never mentioned by me. What has been given to me — this has all been done by the U.S. government by its own choosing. It was not something I demanded or negotiated. I did not present a bill for services or even once discuss any financial remuneration.

What was done financially, I believe, was done because of genuine appreciation and respect for the risks that I took. I knew nearly all of the Russians who were exposed by Aldrich Ames and Robert Hanssen, and knew they were executed because they were helping the U.S. This means that I was — better than anyone else — fully aware of the dangers that I was taking and the danger that my family was placed in as a result of my actions. Because of my high rank and position, which were uncomparably higher than those of the KGB officers who were executed, there is no doubt in my mind that I would have shared their fates if I had been arrested.

Why, then, did I choose to do what I did — given that I had a promising career and money was not my motivation? Why would I put my life and the lives of Helen and our daughter in jeopardy? There were two reasons. I have tried to express both in this book. But I will repeat them now, for they explain everything.

The first was my growing disgust and contempt for what has happened and is happening in Russia. These feelings of revulsion first surfaced in Ottawa when I saw a new breed of bureaucrat who was taking power. Neither I nor Helen was naive, nor did we idealize the Soviet system, its immorality, cruelty, repression, and ineffectiveness. Yet it was our motherland, which, like your parents, you cannot choose. I was trying to serve my country the best possible way and was always ready to sacrifice myself defending its national interests. I became extremely enthusiastic and optimistic when Gorbachev came into power and started his famous *perestroika* and *glasnost*. Even though he often sounded as if he were an uneducated Russian peasant, I believed that Gorbachev would start a new era of democratization in the Soviet Union. But instead, the Soviet Union ceased to exist, civil war started in different parts of Russia and in the Soviet republics. The economy collapsed, and people became desperate and miserable. Since then Russia has been repeatedly raped and looted by its leadership. I call this process GENOCIDE of the Russian people performed by a group of immoral criminals.

Yeltsin may be best remembered in the West for his impassioned speech outside a besieged White House in Moscow while standing on a tank. But as a president, he was an alcoholic with a deranged mind who surrounded himself with gluttons who stole and robbed and cheated our nation in order to become billionaires. His successor, President Putin, is not a drunk, thankfully. But he was created and chosen by Yeltsin's clan, and for years his presidency was controlled and supervised by the former head of Yeltsin's administration, Aleksandr Voloshin, who remained in his position as chief of staff. In what normal country does a president inherit the administration of the previous president and for years is helpless to appoint his own?

For fifteen years I have waited for any positive changes in the "new" Russia. Working in intelligence for a long time in a high position, I had access to the real information about what was going on in Russian politics. I saw firsthand what kind of people were and are running the country. I came to an ultimate conclusion that it became immoral to serve them, and I didn't want to be associated with them in any way. I developed a strong allergy toward every new wave of Russian leaders. My friends often ask me if I ever met Putin during my years in the KGB/SVR. I explain that of course I did not. Not only because we worked in different regions of the world, but first of all because I was a successful officer working in the Center and Putin was never successful in intelligence and never had a chance to work in the headquarters. He was always kept in a provincial KGB station in a low and unimportant position.

I realized that it didn't matter what intelligence information I delivered to the Center, it didn't in any way affect the Russian people or make their lives better, but only was used to contribute to the totally corrupt political system that didn't show any signs of improvement.

Ironically, I started thinking that I could do something good for my people working not for the corrupt Russian bureaucrats, but instead helping the world democratic leader — the United States of America — to better understand who it was dealing with.

The second reason I decided to escape was my daughter. She deserved a better future — in a nation that has a future.

Those are my two reasons.

Now there is something else I wish to address — why I have chosen to tell my story. I want my new compatriots to know who and what I am, and why I am now in this country. Speaking out enables me to give my qualifications, and after giving them, I can sound an alarm.

After the collapse of the Soviet Union, the United States and Russia entered into what was supposed to be a new era of cooperation. The Cold War was behind us. We could become friends. Many in the U.S. believe today the old Spy-versus-Spy days are finished. The September 11 terrorist attacks shifted the American public's attention away from Russia toward international terrorism, especially Islamic fanaticism. Russia was suddenly, and is today viewed as, an ally, even a friend of the U.S.

In speaking out, I hope to expose how naive this is. During the Cold War, in the Soviet military doctrine there was the definition of the MAIN ENEMY, which was also used by intelligence as a basic guiding principle. It was the United States, followed by NATO and China. What is the official guiding line for the modern SVR today? The terms have changed. It is now called the MAIN TARGET. But it is exactly the same: the United States, followed by NATO and China. Nothing has changed. Russia is doing everything it can today to embarrass the U.S. Let me repeat this. Russia is doing everything it can today to undermine and embarrass the U.S. The SVR *rezidenturas* in the U.S. are not less, but in some aspects even more active today than during the Cold War. What should that tell you?

This year, Helen, Ksenia, and I became U.S. citizens. We went through the same process as everyone else. The day that we became citizens was one of the very best in our lives. Ironically, as new citizens we have found ourselves easily being offended when we see how natural-born Americans take their liberties for granted. Sometimes I believe only someone who has lived in a corrupt society can truly understand the importance of America's liberties. I find this frustrating.

As a professional intelligence officer who

specialized in North American matters, I was studying U.S. history all the time and I could probably lecture as a part-time university professor about it. Yet it was a totally different feeling and meaning for me when I was refreshing my memory reading the Declaration of Independence before taking the citizenship test. I found its words of special importance.

When in the Course of human events, it becomes necessary for one people to dissolve the political bands which have connected them with another, and to assume among the powers of the earth, the separate and equal station to which the Laws of Nature and of Nature's God entitle them, a decent respect to the opinions of mankind requires that they should declare the causes which impel them to the separation.

I have tried to explain in this book the "causes" that made me separate myself from Russia. The Declaration continues:

. . . Whenever any Form of Government becomes destructive . . . it is the Right of the People to alter or to abolish it. . . . It is their right, it is their duty, to throw off such Government . . .

My wants and my desires were not much different from those early colonists'. In the end, I came to believe I was not betraying Russia. I felt its leaders had betrayed Russia and me.

If I attempted to return to Russia, I would be immediately arrested, sentenced to death, and executed. But I really don't care what they think about me in Russia, especially in the SVR. I am now an American, and I consider myself — not a traitor nor a spy, but a new patriot.

A COMMENT ABOUT SOURCES

The skeleton of this book is based on extensive interviews with Sergei Tretyakov. I tape-recorded 126 hours of face-to-face conversations with him. Because he was prohibited by the U.S. government from discussing or even acknowledging his relationship with U.S. intelligence, Sergei could not answer questions about the details of his defection. While he faithfully adhered to these legal restrictions, he answered questions about his career in Russian intelligence and his personal thoughts and emotions without hesitation.

The FBI and CIA initially introduced me to Sergei, so I assumed both would be willing to disclose the role that U.S. intelligence played in his defection and also substantiate his charges. There were precedents. The FBI had cooperated with nonfiction authors in the past who were writing about notorious cases. While I was researching my book about Aldrich Ames, the CIA gave me access to the mole-hunting team that had helped identify him as a traitor. During preliminary conversations with U.S. intelligence officials, I remained optimistic. But the attitude at the CIA changed after Porter Goss took charge in late 2004. A former Republican congressman from Florida and onetime head of the House Intelligence Committee, Goss opposed having the CIA cooperate with journalists. The agency's stance became "no books." Access dried up and I was asked by one nervous official if I would delete any information in this book that revealed the CIA had been involved in helping Sergei meet me. I also was asked if I would provide an advance copy of the finished manuscript to the FBI and CIA. I declined.

After Goss became director, getting CIA and FBI officials to speak on the record became difficult. No one in the CIA wanted to risk being prosecuted and losing their career, and the CIA's mum attitude soon was adopted by the FBI. I was able, however, to get several intelligence officials to speak to me privately after I assured them of anonymity. Reporters prefer to identify their sources, especially when writing about intelligence, but the CIA director's policy, regrettably, made this impossible.

When I investigated the Ames spy case, I traveled to Moscow and interviewed former KGB officers who had handled him. However, my trips there were made shortly after the end of the Soviet Union and during a period when U.S. and Russian relations, even among the rival intelligence operations, were friendly. I was strongly advised by Russian journalists and other contacts in Moscow not to risk traveling to Russia to dig into Sergei's past or talk to SVR officials about his defection. An author who had information about the whereabouts and the secrets that a former SVR deputy *rezident* had disclosed to U.S. intelligence would be putting himself at risk in the current political climate, I was told. Consequently, I contacted Russian intelligence through faxed letters, and the result was much as I had expected. The SVR had no official comment. I was, however, able to substantiate information from Sergei about the Red Banner Institute, the Center, and several KGB officials by talking to ex–KGB officers who defected to the U.S.

I reviewed hundreds of pages of documents, newspaper clippings, magazine stories, and other published material while researching this book. Many were investigations into the UN's Oil-for-Food Program. Others had to do with biographical information about UN diplomats whom Sergei identified as Russian spies.

One of the questions readers are bound to ask is whether or not Sergei told me the truth. I am convinced that he has. Sergei wants his opinions and criticisms of Moscow to be taken seriously, and he knows his critics would use any exaggeration or mistake that he might make to attack his credibility. During our interviews, I found Sergei adamant about making certain that I understood exactly what he was explaining because he was intent on not having any factual errors in my writing. Whenever it was possible, I sought to verify Sergei's statements, and in those instances, I found that his accounts were accurate. As an experienced SVR intelligence officer, Sergei had an unusually keen memory. He loathed using tape recorders as an officer and instead when talking to SVR sources he would memorize conversations that he later re-created in his cables to the Center. He took great pride in his ability to remember long passages of dialogue, and I found that his memory was accurate when I was able to compare his renditions to published accounts.

Obviously, many of the stories and much of the dialogue in these pages is based solely on Sergei's recall. This is because the other participants are still Russian intelligence officers or are persons whom Sergei has identified as Russian spies. It is not in their best interests to acknowledge his version. I have been told by FBI officials that during debriefings Sergei buttressed his stories and charges with SVR cables and intelligence reports. However, I have not seen copies of these classified Russian documents. Consequently, readers should be aware that much of what has been written here remains *his* version. Given the nature of his revelations, this should not be surprising.

Because the FBI and CIA introduced Sergei to me, readers also may wonder if U.S. intelligence officials are using him for propaganda purposes. The simple answer is yes and no. There is no doubt that Sergei intends to damage the SVR and embarrass Russia's political leaders by making disclosures. Much like a recent born-again Christian, he is fervent in his newfound love for the U.S. He has become a vocal cheerleader for democracy. I do not doubt that he recalled every possible critical story about Russian intelligence that he knew while his comments about U.S. intelligence were gushing. These prejudices do not mean, however, that he changed facts, invented scenarios, or fabricated claims.

When it comes to understanding the role that the CIA and FBI played in this book, what might seem sinister to some readers strikes me as being predictable in Washington based on my twenty-eight years as a reporter in our nation's capital. Initially, the CIA and FBI agents who handled Sergei were eager for him to tell his story. Mostly, I suspect, they were proud of the role they played in successfully and safely handling him while he was a Russian intelligence officer in New York. As this book documents, Sergei was the first major Russian intelligence officer to defect since Russia became independent, giving him historical importance. The FBI and CIA officers involved in his spying clearly outwitted their SVR rivals and, no doubt, wanted credit. It's cases such as his that lead to promotions. Another factor was at play here. Since the September 11 terrorist attacks, the CIA and FBI agents assigned to intelligence and counterintelligence operations against Russia have found themselves pushed to a back burner. The hunt for Osama bin Laden and the war on terrorism became a top priority. Sergei's case was a timely reminder that the U.S.

was still vulnerable to attack from its older enemies. When Goss became CIA director, the officers involved with Sergei's case were reeled in. The idea that the CIA and FBI may have plotted this scenario in advance and are using Sergei as a shill in some intelligence game would make a good plot in a novel, but seems far-fetched, given the interagency cooperation that such an operation would require and the disappointment and frustration that I observed when I spoke to those who genuinely wanted to tout Sergei's case and the role that they played in handling him.

ACKNOWLEDGMENTS

I would like to thank Sergei, Helen, and Ksenia Tretyakov for having the courage to tell their story. The bizarre poisoning death in November 2006 of former KGB officer Alexander Litvinenko in London occurred while I was completing my final interviews with them. On his deathbed, Litvinenko blamed President Putin and Russian intelligence for planning his death. A vociferous Putin critic, Litvinenko accused the Russian president of having "no respect for life, liberty, or any civilized value." Litvinenko's murder happened only weeks after another Putin critic, internationally known journalist Anna Politkovskaya, was gunned down outside her Moscow apartment.

Although Sergei found both assassinations troubling, neither made him change his mind about revealing secrets about Russian intelligence, corruption inside the Yeltsin and Putin administrations, and in describing his firsthand encounters with such top Putin *siloviki* as General Yevgeni Murov and the president's personal sparring partner, Viktor Zolotov.

The murders of Litvinenko and Politkovskaya are reminders of how dangerous it can be for a defector from the Russian intelligence or a vocal critic of Russian leaders to speak out publicly. Sergei is both.

I would like to thank several U.S. intelligence officials who spoke to me off the record. For reasons already mentioned, I cannot name them, but I am grateful. I wish to publicly thank several journalists in Moscow who helped me with research but whose names I am reluctant to reveal. Forty-four journalists have been murdered in Russia since 1992, according to the Committee to Protect Journalists. With each passing day, my Russian friends' efforts to write objectively about events in their nation become more difficult.

This book could not have been written had it not been for Neil Nyren, my editor at Putnam. He recognizes good stories and knows how to get his authors to tell them.

I wish to thank John Silbersack, my literary agent at Trident Media Group, for finding this book a publisher.

As always, I am grateful to my wife, Patti,

and my children, Steve, Kevin, Tony, Kathy, Kyle, Evan, and Traci. Other family members whom I'd like to acknowledge include: my parents, Elmer and Jean Earley; Gloria Brown, James Brown, LeRue and Ellen Brown; Phillip and Joanne Corn; Donnie Davis; George and Linda Earley; Michelle Earley; William and Rosemary Luzi; Charlie and Donna Stackhouse; and Jay and Elise Strine. In addition, I want to thank Nelson DeMille, William Donnell, Philip Gerard, Walt and Keran Harrington, Marie Heffelfinger, Don and Susan Infeld, Reis Kash, Richard and Joan Miles, Jay and Barbara Myerson, Mike Sager, Lynn and LouAnn Smith, and Kendall and Lynn Starkweather. My sister-in-law, Dana Davis, succumbed to cancer while I was writing this book. She was a wonderful friend and is deeply missed by all of us who loved her.

I invite readers to post comments about this book on my website: www.peteearley .com. While I may not be able to respond to every message, I read all of them.

The employees of Thorndike Press hope you have enjoyed this Large Print book. All our Thorndike and Wheeler Large Print titles are designed for easy reading, and all our books are made to last. Other Thorndike Press Large Print books are available at your library, through selected bookstores, or directly from us.

For information about titles, please call:
  (800) 223-1244

or visit our Web site at:
  http://gale.cengage.com/thorndike

To share your comments, please write:
  Publisher
  Thorndike Press
  295 Kennedy Memorial Drive
  Waterville, ME 04901